CONVERSATIONS ON ETHICAL LEADERSHIP

Lessons Learned from University Governance

Edited by Ingrid Leman Stefanovic

T0281789

Highlighting ethical leadership strategies, *Conversations on Ethical Leadership* explores what makes for strong, well-informed, morally sound decision-making at all levels of an organization. In addressing a range of challenges faced by universities and applying those lessons to the broader community of the public and private sectors, Ingrid Leman Stefanovic and her contributors tackle a host of issues related to advancing ethics, diversity, inclusiveness, and the art of moral leadership.

Each chapter, written by an author with roots in the academy, includes a subsequent commentary by a community leader who highlights the broader takeaways that emerge for society from the university experience. In this way, the book becomes a conversation between the academic and non-academic worlds about issues that affect any prominent organization. It offers a unique range of novel and timely topics, from responsibility-centred budgeting to post-pandemic planning, responsiveness to climate change, Indigenous leadership, free speech, academic integrity, and much more. In doing so, *Conversations on Ethical Leadership* ultimately reveals how we can build and preserve an ethically responsible sense of purpose at our post-secondary learning institutions and beyond.

(UTP Insights)

INGRID LEMAN STEFANOVIC is a professor emerita in the Department of Philosophy at the University of Toronto and a professor and dean emeritus in the Faculty of Environment at Simon Fraser University.

ⓘ UTP insights

UTP Insights is an innovative collection of brief books offering
accessible introductions to the ideas that shape our world. Each
volume in the series focuses on a contemporary issue, offering
a fresh perspective anchored in scholarship. Spanning a broad
range of disciplines in the social sciences and humanities, the
books in the UTP Insights series contribute to public discourse
and debate and provide a valuable resource for instructors and
students.

For a list of the books published in this series, see page 345.

CONVERSATIONS ON ETHICAL LEADERSHIP

Lessons Learned from University Governance

Edited by Ingrid Leman Stefanovic

UNIVERSITY OF TORONTO PRESS
Toronto Buffalo London

© University of Toronto Press 2023
Toronto Buffalo London
utorontopress.com
Printed in Canada

ISBN 978-1-4875-0907-1 (cloth)   ISBN 978-1-4875-3966-5 (EPUB)
ISBN 978-1-4875-5249-7 (paper)   ISBN 978-1-4875-3965-8 (PDF)

Library and Archives Canada Cataloguing in Publication

Title: Conversations on ethical leadership : lessons learned from university
    governance / edited by Ingrid Leman Stefanovic.
Names: Leman Stefanovic, Ingrid, editor.
Description: Includes bibliographical references and index.
Identifiers: Canadiana (print) 2023043942X | Canadiana (ebook) 20230439446 |
    ISBN 9781487552497 (paper) | ISBN 9781487509071 (cloth) |
    ISBN 9781487539658 (PDF) | ISBN 9781487539665 (EPUB)
Subjects: LCSH: Universities and colleges – Administration. |
    LCSH: Educational leadership – Moral and ethical aspects. |
    LCSH: Decision making – Moral and ethical aspects.
Classification: LCC LB2341 .C67 2023 | DDC 378.1/01 – dc23

Cover design: Hannah Gaskamp
Cover image: art4all/Shutterstock.com

We wish to acknowledge the land on which the University of Toronto Press operates.
This land is the traditional territory of the Wendat, the Anishnaabeg, the Haudenosaunee,
the Métis, and the Mississaugas of the Credit First Nation.

University of Toronto Press acknowledges the financial support of the Government of
Canada, the Canada Council for the Arts, and the Ontario Arts Council, an agency of the
Government of Ontario, for its publishing activities.

Canada Council   Conseil des Arts
for the Arts   du Canada

ONTARIO ARTS COUNCIL
CONSEIL DES ARTS DE L'ONTARIO

an Ontario government agency
un organisme du gouvernement de l'Ontario

Funded by the   Financé par le
Government   gouvernement
of Canada   du Canada

Canadä

MIX
Paper from
responsible sources
FSC® C016245

Contents

Illustrations and Tables

Illustrations

Tables

Acknowledgments

I begin by thanking each chapter and commentary contributor, whose insights ensured that the conversations in this volume are meaningful to members of the academy, as well as the broader community. It has been exciting to work with such thoughtful friends and colleagues, each of whom agreed to share experiences and to ensure that the discussions in this volume are rich, diverse, and inspiring in the journey towards ethical leadership.

I thank the anonymous reviewers, who have taken the time to provide their useful feedback to improve the overall quality of the finished product.

Jodi Lewchuk, acquisitions editor at the University of Toronto Press, provided continuing support of this project, from start to finish. I am, as always, truly grateful to her for her advice and kindness.

A brief word of thanks to the copy editor, Ian MacKenzie, whose fine editing eye and final oversight of key chapters ensured quality control.

And certainly, there are many people who have inspired me with their visions and operationalization of ethical university leadership. However, four colleagues particularly stand out for me.

Wayne Sumner, one of our chapter contributors, hired me into the Department of Philosophy many decades ago, when he was chair. Now he holds the highest rank of university professor, and his reputation as a brilliant ethicist, diligent mediator, and talented manager is widely recognized not only within the department but across the institution. Without realizing it, he taught me a great deal about honest and high integrity leadership.

Pekka Sinervo served as dean of the Faculty of Arts and Science at the University of Toronto when I was director of the Centre for Environment (now renamed a "School.") What I loved about working with him was his transparency, openness, and willingness to listen. I recall how, one day, we finished a meeting without resolving an issue, just as he was scheduled to head to the provost's office. "Walk with me," he said, as he headed out to the five-minute walk. "Finish what you were saying." The respect that Pekka showed his chairs and directors was immense and is remembered and appreciated to this day.

I will thank two more colleagues, this time from Simon Fraser University, where I served as dean of the Faculty of Environment. The provost who hired me was Jon Driver, an archaeologist by training. Here is another example of an administrator who always showed respect, knew how to listen and to guide, and gave exemplary advice. Jon is a true gentleman, in the best sense of the word. He is gracious, professional, and expert in the duties of university vice-president, academic. One reason that I decided to uproot my family and move across the country, after a quarter of a century of a rewarding and happy career at the University of Toronto, was the inspiration provided by Jon Driver. I knew that I could work with him, learn from him, and be respected for my own commitment to environmental teaching and research. I knew that he supported the idea of a new Faculty of Environment and that he would stand by me in my efforts to build the institution and make it unique.

The final person I wish to thank is Andrew Petter, who served as president of Simon Fraser University before and during my tenure as dean. Andrew was, to my mind, always fair, courageous, and equitable. His warmth and collegiality, despite his high position, was infectious and inspirational. And watching him navigate university politics with grace and unwavering determination to do the right thing, no matter how difficult the choices, taught me some important lessons about the meaning of ethical leadership. He was deeply committed to the good of his institution, even at some personal stress and cost. He was an exemplary university president, one who understood not only the meaning of academic excellence but of genuine, impactful community engagement.

Finally, I thank my family and particularly my husband, who, for almost four decades, has stood by me as cheerleader and my one true love. The times he propped me up through my most challenging moments as an administrator are too many to count. He helped keep life in perspective for me, as he always focused on the bright side of university challenges. Without him, I would not be me. And I certainly would have never had the courage to embark on administrative leadership roles that, in the end, also brought me my most cherished memories at universities across the country.

Ingrid Leman Stefanovic

CONVERSATIONS ON ETHICAL LEADERSHIP

Opening the Conversation

INGRID LEMAN STEFANOVIC

> In addition to being more numerous, today's universities are larger by multiples and more complex than their predecessors, with bureaucratic capacity to match.... And they have more social responsibilities.
>
> – Peter MacKinnon, president emeritus, University of Saskatchewan

At a recent garden party, a friend made a remark that I have heard more than once before: "Why people choose to involve themselves in university administration is beyond me. I made it a point to avoid such invitations throughout my academic career." He continued by pointing out that, as a tenured faculty member, he would never sacrifice his research for the pointless stress of administration. In fact, he proudly emphasized that he had intentionally let it be seen that he was disorganized and regularly late in meeting course deadlines, just to guarantee that he would never be asked by his department chair to serve.

I have often been probed in such conversations about why I not only accepted such invitations but seemed to welcome them. "I loved enabling the creation of new programs and units," I would explain. "And," I would add, "it was a privilege to have an opportunity to impact the next generation of students in ways other than teaching."

For me, there was a special responsibility, pride, and passion associated with enacting positive institutional change. Some of my happiest moments as a teen and a woman in my early 20s happened at university. I loved the joy of learning, of reading, of sharing ideas in student seminars, of exploring the impact of historical traditions upon our present ways of understanding the world. As a professor, I hoped to share that passion with my students: where else could the joy of discovery be celebrated as earnestly and meaningfully as at a university? Being a program director, associate chair, or dean meant I could channel that passion into the evolution of new structures to support student learning, teaching, and research.

President MacKinnon (2018, pp. 90–1) was right to point out that universities are ever changing, and their responsibilities are increasing. In some cases, like in California, Iowa, and Maryland, post-secondary institutions are the largest state employers (Hartocollis, 2020). In the United States alone, roughly 4,000 public and private colleges and universities educate around 20 million students annually (Hartocollis, 2020). Canada, with a population of almost 38 million, 80% of whom reside in urban centres, supports 163 public and private universities, as well as 183 public colleges and institutes (Council of Ministers of Education, 2017). More than half of Canadians aged 25 to 64 hold university degrees, as Canada continues to rank first among OECD countries in proportion of college and university graduates (Statistics Canada, 2017).

Globally, higher education continues to grow, with 150 million students across the world and expectations of over 260 million by 2025 (Maslen, 2012). Two and a half million students were internationally mobile prior to the COVID-19 pandemic (Mulgan et al., 2016). How that figure will change once traditional in-class course delivery resumes is open to speculation at the time of this writing, although some express growing concern that those numbers will continue to fall, introducing new challenges for universities worldwide (Mutton, 2020).

Still, across the globe, engagement in and impact of post-secondary education on the general population is significant. This book is being assembled as the COVID-19 vaccine rollout continues across the world, and the pandemic endures in the face of new variants on the global stage. There is considerable speculation about how universities will emerge in 2023 and beyond (Hubler, 2020; Jones, 2020; Lopis, 2020; Williams, 2020). In worst-case scenarios, some universities are being forced to file for credit protection (CBC News, 2021a). Some suggest that such a scenario has emerged directly as a consequence of the failure of government to provide stable public funding, both throughout the pandemic and in the longer term (CBC News, 2021b).

Less drastically, universities with which I regularly engage are already planning to retain some staff to work from home – a proposition that, pre-pandemic, was discouraged. Hybrid models of course delivery are now more common, as questions whirl around tuition fees, budgets, and the strategic significance of future faculty hires.

The authors in this book address these and similar issues as part of a larger project to explore significant governance and management challenges that university leaders face today. Many of the authors explore what kind of ethical hurdles emerge at these institutions. As project management research reveals, "responsible leadership requires a focus on leadership ethics" (Clarke et al., 2018, p. 12). Having spent almost half of my academic career in administrative positions at universities, it has become clear to me that leaders regularly confront uniquely important moral dilemmas. The authors in this volume describe some of those quandaries and point towards resolving them in an ethically defensible manner.

Whether it is a question of determining morally sound, responsibility-based budget models, defining the meaning of academic freedom, or considering how to lower the carbon impact of institutional investments in an era of global climate change, university deans, vice-presidents, presidents, and program directors must deal with problems that are complex and often confounding. Yet one would hope that these leaders will make decisions that are driven by compelling, ethically defensible reasoning. This volume presents case studies and critical analysis to inform such reasoning.

The motivation for this book comes from my growing sense that decision making at universities needs to be driven by a renewed system of values that include a vision of civility, virtue, and collaboration. There is much truth to the proposition that "[r]esponsible leaders are like weavers whose strength lies in the ties that bind stakeholders together. This also means that they will lead from the centre, focusing on relationship building rather than power development" (Clarke et al., 2018, p. 13). Values such as territoriality, lack of transparency, or lack of cooperation lead, in my view, only to a divisive, unproductive culture at post-secondary institutions. Helping to ensure that a strong, well-informed moral vision drives decision making at all levels – through teaching, research, service, and administration – is the goal of this book.

While focusing on university examples, the volume explicitly aims to address moral challenges that might also be faced by communities outside of academia. We wonder whether lessons learned could apply equally to other private and public settings that rely upon ethical leadership as a guide to responsible management and decision making.

For this reason, each chapter includes a short set of remarks presented by community leaders who link some of the lessons of university administrators to broader, non-academic venues. In some cases, commentators recognize parallel issues of leadership that emerge within their own sectors. In other cases, the comments take lessons learned from each chapter and enlarge upon those messages within the context of their own community's concerns. In all cases, a brief dialogue ensues to enrich the conversation on the significance of systems of sound university governance. While not necessarily an in-depth or lengthy exchange, the commentaries are meant to point to overlapping interests and new insights informed by each chapter, so that the reader might reflect upon these broader community concerns as well.

Someone asked me recently, "How did you choose these community representatives? What were the criteria for including them in the book?" My response was that they had to be potentially already grappling, in their own fields, with some aspect of the chapter assigned to them. In each case, they were known to me as reputable leaders in their own right. And they needed to be able to understand the importance of the chapter at hand and to write non-specialized, insightful, and creative responses that were comprehensible to a variety of audiences.

Like others in the wider community, university leaders certainly encounter management and decision-making challenges daily. That said, universities are also unique institutions where members such as tenured professors are hired for life and where students – our primary "stakeholders" – take their first steps towards career paths that will shape their lives. For this reason, there are distinctive lessons to be learned from universities, even as some of those lessons continue to be informed by society at large as well.

The other day, I was chatting with a friend from the corporate sector. "Universities can learn a lot about management from the business sector," she mused, "but I can't imagine that the corporate sector could learn much from universities about these matters." I would argue that there are iterative co-learning opportunities on both sides. This volume illustrates how not only corporate leaders, but also the public sector and broader communities, can learn much from a better understanding of some of the experiences that define universities today, just as universities can learn from the input that they receive from those outside the academy.

A colleague recently told me a story about her grandson who had asked his mother whether he could have a piece of candy. "Not before dinner," she replied. The little boy then went into the next room and asked his grandmother for the same thing. Not aware of the mother's response, my colleague happily opened a candy wrapper and handed it to her grandson.

Kids can be wily when they want something. So can department chairs. Years ago, a chair requested funding from her dean for a new position. The request was rejected, because a research chair in the same area had already been approved but also because budgetary restrictions made another position impossible.

However, just like my colleague's grandson, the chair then went around her dean and approached the provost – who unwittingly approved the position, no doubt having been pressured because the position was presented as part of a politically sensitive EDI (equity, diversity, inclusiveness) strategy.

One might chuckle at the wiliness of both the grandson and the department chair, but at universities – and in any institution that relies upon protocols for good reason – unethical, manipulative behaviour and disrespect of reporting levels of authority lead to a breakdown of order and fairness. As our paramount educational organizations, universities have a leading responsibility in society to put ethics front and centre in their guiding visions, as well as in everyday decision making.

That said, except for those educated in business faculties, university administrators receive next to no training in either management or leadership ethics. So much is simply learned on the job, as diverse challenges present themselves day after day. Perhaps that explains why books like this one are all the more helpful to assist university officials and others in the broader community to navigate their way forward, in the absence of such formal training.

Circumventing levels of authority is only one example of morally questionable management practices that I have personally witnessed at universities. Sometimes, there have been legally objectionable actions – such as when a department chair requested that I be back at work three weeks after giving birth to my daughter if I wanted to keep my job. (The chair's assistant hastily educated him about the law, shortly after I left that meeting!)

University lawyers ensure that legal transgressions are addressed in a timely manner. But moral issues can often be more nuanced, and they invite sometimes controversial judgment calls.

Take the example of a dean who (wisely) started his term by convening a strategic planning committee. Month after month, he reported to chairs and directors that the committee was moving ahead, but any interim progress report was impossible, since all deliberations were "behind closed doors."

I remember sharing the story with my husband – a project management executive – at dinner. "Why?," he asked me. "Why are deliberations being held in secret?" I stared at him. "That's a good question. I actually don't know," I answered.

When the committee eventually came out publicly with its recommendations that included many dramatic cost-cutting measures, three days of national media coverage reported the vitriolic reactions from the university community. As plans were amended in the face of such widespread criticism, one could not help but wonder whether more transparent consultations, more wide-spread, meaningful information gathering, and interim sharing of the committee's leanings might have prevented the public embar-rassment as well as simply been more ethical and representative of the broader university community's concerns.

Honesty, collaboration, and collegiality are important values that need to be privileged at universities. When a provost pub-licly revealed little interest in interdisciplinary education at a time when new interdisciplinary schools and programs were seeking final approval after years of broad, consultative planning, it was no surprise that support for such programs was held back. And yet, one has to wonder whether ethical leadership demands that the provost make what could be perceived as a difficult, but neces-sary decision to deny approval of a new program, or whether she should have consulted more broadly to become better informed than she was about the value of interdisciplinarity – and the impor-tance of long-term, broad community support for such programs.

Time and again, university leaders are tasked with making deci-sions that significantly affect students, faculty, and staff. Judgment calls are made, while biases, attitudes, values, and world views are revealed. It is vital that critical analysis accompany decision mak-ing when complex challenges, from pandemic planning to climate change, affect the nature of the educational experience. This book contributes to such analysis through conversations with academ-ics and others in the broader community.

Universities today face a growing array of challenges, an impor-tant sampling of which is explored in this book. As a guide for the reader, we have divided the volume into four parts.

"Part One: The Sustainable University" explores a key moral and practical challenge not only for universities but for the planet: how to address climate change and move towards a healthier global environment. Any healthy society depends on a healthy planet. Ingrid Leman Stefanovic and Simone Hausgnecht provide in Chapter 1 a Canadian perspective on the state of university pro-gramming in this area, suggesting that more remains to be done to appropriate the environmental challenges meaningfully and substantively throughout all levels of post-secondary learning, research, operations, and governance. The commentary by Todd Latham, president of Actual Media Inc., shows how corporations have a parallel, pressing duty to continue to inform social and economic investment decisions through the framework of environmental impacts.

In Chapter 2, John Robinson and his colleagues similarly acknowledge environment and climate change as defining issues of our generation. Noting how institutions have a moral responsibility to reduce their greenhouse gas emissions, they present a case study from the University of Toronto, exploring challenges in assessing how to factor air travel emissions into an institution's sustainability initiatives. The authors would likely agree with Emily Thomas, author of *The Meaning of Travel*, that "lots of business travel just isn't necessary" (quoted in CBC News, 2021d, para. 9). Reducing unnecessary flying "seems like a really easy way of cutting down our carbon footprint in a way that doesn't actually damage anyone" (quoted in CBC News, 2021d, para. 9). Interestingly, even proposals to amend national policies are being proposed, such as in France, where lawmakers have voted to support a bill to ban short-haul flights where the same trip could be made in less than two and a half hours by train (BBC News, 2021). In his commentary, Kevin Nilsen, president and CEO of ECO Canada, recommends that universities and corporate institutions should work closely with the aviation industry to advance research and innovation that will minimize Scope 3 emissions globally.

Chapters 1 and 2 illustrate how university leaders are morally obliged to situate their missions within the context of significant global environmental pressures. But leaders are equally obliged to attend to local issues raised in "Part Two: Pursuing Excellence and Integrity." In Chapter 3, Gord Myers discusses how to equitably resource academic excellence at universities. Increasingly, post-secondary institutions are adopting responsibility centre budgets, disrupting historical incremental models of financial allocation. In her commentary, Esther Bergman, a consultant with Benchmark Performance Inc. and World Class Productivity Inc., draws parallels with similar decentralized models of accountability for work performance that define the corporate sector. She argues, however, in favour of a continuing need for centralized resources to support strategic outcomes.

In Chapter 4, Emma Thacker makes the case for a "holistic" institutional approach – in place of reactive punitive practices – to protect academic integrity. In her commentary on this chapter, Sue McGeachie, head of the Bank of Montreal Climate Institute, argues that the same kind of holistic systems approach should inform the integrity of a large-scale transition to a low carbon economy among governments, business, finance sectors, and civil society at large.

Sarah King presents in Chapter 5 a "relational approach to student-centred leadership" (p. 121). She highlights the importance of privileging student voices and inviting meaningful partnerships to shape universities. Presenting a case study from Grand Valley State University, she illustrates how providing students with leadership opportunities results in extraordinary and unique projects that are not merely pedagogically useful but also implement impactful change within communities. Lois Lindsay, from Evergreen Foundation, then responds in her commentary, reiterating the importance of "relational leadership" and listening to and deciphering essential community needs in relation to the work of NGOs.

Further building on the importance of community relations, "Part Three: Community Engagement and Diversity" reflects the fact that universities are morally obligated to be more than isolated ivory towers and instead must be informed by and inform a variety of voices beyond the academy. In Chapter 6, Anne Giardini, a former chancellor herself, discusses how such a role provides unique opportunities to communicate, internally and to the external world, a vision of the institution's principal values and what each university stands for. Alex Leman, co-founder of Vitruvian Group, notes that, despite the differences between universities and corporate boards, both benefit from acknowledging taken-for-granted moral viewpoints and seeking an alignment among plural perceptions, attitudes, and value systems.

Trish Glazebrook then addresses in Chapter 7 ethical issues of growing importance to universities and societies at large, relating to equity, diversity, and inclusiveness (EDI) – how to close the gaps and open minds. Commentator Margie Zeidler, president of Urban-Space Property Group in Toronto, shows how EDI must similarly find expression in the most successful city design projects as well.

How ethics is manifest in professional education is discussed in Chapter 8, where Thomas Barrie addresses issues arising in the field of architecture. He shows how professional programs specifically have a moral duty to engage pressing societal needs that are more than simply material but are also ecological and even spiritual. Architect and project manager Sabrina Leman builds on these insights, emphasizing the need to approach the architectural profession itself, less in terms of *what* is done than *how* it is done – a synthesizing process that, she agrees with Barrie, must include a better understanding of social, cultural, historical, environmental, and spiritual contexts. Leman would certainly concur with Deepa Prahalad, CEO of Anuvaa LLC, that "we're today looking to leaders to become kind of creators of common ground, the ones who synthesize all of these different tensions" (The New Leadership Dynamics, 2021, The Great Synthesizers section).

Deborah McGregor, Lorrilee McGregor, Cindy Peltier, and Susan Manitowabi close Part 3 by addressing the moral demands of Indigenous leadership and governance at universities as they relate to reconciliation. Commentators Anne Koven, honorary registered professional forester, and PhD student Stephanie Seymour respond by extending the lessons and drawing parallels to the forestry industry. Noting how in Canada, forested lands are mostly Crown lands, they constitute the places for deconstruction of colonial relationships between Indigenous peoples and the state.

From acknowledging the importance of equity, diverse voices, inclusiveness, and community engagement, we move to "Part Four: The Ethics of Expression." Former university president Harry Fernhout discusses in Chapter 10 how a faith-based university aimed to guide creativity and controversy while opening its arms to welcome Omar Khadr, an alleged terrorist, as a student. Commentator Nada Conić, a consultant in spiritual counselling, enlarges the conversation by suggesting that this measure of openness, forgiveness, and tolerance should extend to attitudes within the larger community as well.

Wayne Sumner similarly argues in Chapter 11 that universities have a moral obligation to protect and support a broad range of free speech and dialogue, on the condition that it proceeds safely and within the limits of the law. In his commentary, Chris Ollson, environmental health scientist and risk assessor, describes how similar obligations to hear opposing views arise in controversial infrastructure projects, such as oil sands developments or initiatives in renewable energy. In such cases, as emotions run high, opposing groups are free to express their views, no matter how distasteful – but, as Sumner notes, always within the constraints of the law.

As university leaders seek to navigate such moral hazards, it becomes increasingly clear, as noted in "Part Five: The Art of Leadership," that decision making is much more than a technical skill or set of procedures to be followed from a handbook. Leadership happens within the holistic context of space and place. So, in Chapter 12, Bruce Janz asks us to consider the possibility that virtue is to be understood more than in simply individualist terms. Instead, he invites us to "rethink the space of the university as a space of possible virtue" (p. 271), wherein specific ethical ideals and leadership initiatives are enacted. Indira Samaresekera, senior advisor and corporate director at the legal firm of Bennett Jones, agrees in her commentary that addressing issues of virtue requires more than "extolling its value"; it involves the complex task described by Janz of "creating the space" for virtuous actions through governance and administrative structures, at universities as well as in corporations, governments, and society at large.

Bob Mugerauer then shows us how leadership is less a technical skill than "the art of having the right thing happen" (p. 291). David Miller, former mayor of Toronto and managing director of the C40 Centre for Urban Climate Policy and Economy, enlarges the conversation by bringing his own lessons learned from his political experience to the table. He agrees with Mugerauer that the art of genuine listening is of primary importance for leaders across the board, who must ensure that they "represent and protect that sense of common purpose at all times" (p. 307).

The book concludes with a discussion by the editor of how leaders must ultimately help to build a university's strong moral sense of place – a task that again requires more than a how-to manual but invites the deciphering of, and sensibility towards, sometimes nebulous though central elements of an institution's identity. That universities, at the time of this writing, are enduring the most significant *displacement* as a consequence of the COVID-19 pandemic, helps to situate these concluding remarks around the importance of sense of place.

Although this book covers a broad and significant range of topics, no single volume captures the myriad challenges faced by universities today. Immediately, additional issues come to mind that university leaders confront daily:

- *The continuing decline of state funding:* In the United States alone, government funding of higher education declined between 1995 and 2019 as the student share of total revenue has grown, reportedly reaching 46% of total university revenues (SHEF, 2019). Similarly, in Canada, public funding fell from 81% of operating revenues in 1985 to 50% by 2015 (Broadbent Institute, 2019). How much state funding ought universities legitimately expect?[1]
- *University autonomy:* Ironically, decreased funding does not necessarily lead to less government oversight. While there are diverse levels of autonomy and external governance systems across Canadian universities, six universities surveyed from 2012 to 2015 "were experiencing increased provincial regulation. A great deal of decision-making authority formerly exercised by university bodies had been assumed by governments" (Eastman, 2018, para. 4). The trend has apparently continued, with provinces now regulating matters ranging from executive compensation and procurement management to sexualized violence and occupational health and safety. "The shrinking of the decision-making jurisdiction of universities in Canada in recent years appears to be part of a global phenomenon," raising questions about the moral legitimacy of such accountability and responsibility (Eastman, 2018, para. 5).

- *Advancement and donor ethics:* Some argue that decreased government funding opens the door to increased "corporatization" of universities as they increasingly depend upon wealthy donors. In Canada, only 2% of operating revenues came from neither public money nor user fees in 1985, quadrupling to almost 10% by 2015 (Broadbent Institute, 2019). What role ought donors play at universities, and how can universities ensure that the donations do not, implicitly or explicitly, drive research agendas?
- *Equitable tuition rates:* A variety of questions arise about tuition rates. The COVID-19 pandemic has caused some to ask whether students should be paying the same fees if their courses are now, and perhaps in the future will be, delivered online. Andreas Schleicher, director for Education and Skills at the OECD and a highly influential voice on higher education policy, believes that tuition should be cut, given that physical contact restrictions have compromised the rationale for attending university (Matthews, 2020). Alternatively, during pandemic planning, Australia has taken a somewhat controversial step of overhauling its tuition system that will more than double the cost of humanities degrees while halving the cost of agriculture and math courses. In this way, it plans to accommodate increasing demands for certain career-oriented programs (Ross, 2020). What should tuition rates be, and how do we justify raising or cutting them?
- *The integrity of university rankings:* According to mathematics professor Michael Thaddeus, university rankings place financial priorities ahead of education as institutions such as Columbia manipulate statistics to advance their status amongst students and the academic community. The ethics of apparently unjustified growth of administrative and "secretive" bureaucratic services are also at issue. Challenging the reports of class sizes and faculty degrees, Thaddeus found that the statistics for Columbia were "inaccurate, dubious or highly misleading" (McGreal, 2022, para. 6). An external investigation of these claims led to the university dropping from 2nd to 18th place in the United States. Thaddeus may not

be alone to state that he has "long believed that all university rankings are essentially worthless. They're based on data that have very little to do with the academic merit of an institution and the data might not be accurate in the first place" (see McGreal, 2022, para. 14). Ensuring integrity amongst such reporting reflects on the honour of the institution overall, so it is vital that we get it right.

- *The changing role of the humanities:* Despite the story from Australia, according to the National Association of Colleges and Employers' annual Job Outlook survey, employers continue to seek skills that are central to humanities programs, from interpersonal skills to advancing critical thinking skills (Martin, 2021). Many believe that the humanities help to advance awareness of the importance of evidence as a condition of rational arguments – skills that are increasingly essential and in short supply in an age of social media disinformation. Yet, some studies have shown that "over the course of the twentieth century, the humanities diminished in relative prominence" (Frank & Gabler, 2006, p. 82). Universities Canada reports a "serious decline" in liberal arts enrolment in recent years, driven by an increasing emphasis on vocational training (see Universities Canada, 2016). As humanities enrolments fluctuate, reputable groups continue to ask themselves, "Will the humanities be extinct by 2024?"[2]

- *The challenge of retaining strong leaders:* A recent study shows that university presidents and sector leaders are not remaining within their posts as long as they used to. Reasons for decreased longevity include the fact that private search firms are biased towards recruiting presidents from other institutions; an atmosphere of secrecy around the search process that precludes faculty and others on campus from providing input to the process; the paucity of academic experts within most search firms; and low incentives to dig deep into candidates' backgrounds.[3] The result is increased disruption and lack of consistency in leadership, management, and decision-making strategies.

The list could go on and on. How should universities respond as student expectations rise within an increasingly competitive job market? Will students legitimately turn to less expensive, quicker avenues to vocational competence rather than standard university degrees? With so much dependency on technology in education, how secure are digital platforms? How will what some call "the grand distance learning experiment" extend into a post–COVID-19 era (Bennett, 2020)? Should universities reposition themselves as change agents in society and if so, in what manner?[4] And how shall universities seek to "future proof" themselves in increasingly unstable times (Falkenberg & Cannon, 2021)?

Finally, as we move through the greatest global disruption since the Second World War, how radically should universities be willing to reform their identities? The Minerva Project, founded in 2012, is a venture-backed Silicon Valley start-up that aims to revolutionize higher education, with all teaching performed online in interdisciplinary subjects, such as "multi-modal communications," "complex systems," and "empirical analyses." With no physical campus, is Minerva a legitimate response to the need to develop new pedagogical strategies while attending to what some see as the problematic use of physical facilities (Vedder, 2021)? In 2020, the university received 25,000 applications from 180 countries to undergraduate programs: it admitted only 2%, "making it the most selective degree programme in the developed world" (Clarke, 2020, para. 2). Founder and businessman Ben Nelson maintains that he realized early on that "colleges were fundamentally failing in their promise to educate. A liberal arts education is supposed to teach students to think freely, critically, and logically. But our elite universities no longer do that at all" (Clarke, 2020, para. 3). Does Minerva's success story say something about the directions that universities today ought to follow in future or, as one editorial asks, is this "just hype" (Clarke, 2020)?

Ultimately, these conversations about university structures and governance are necessarily ongoing. There is certainly only growing urgency to address these and similar questions about the future of our post-secondary educational institutions. This book is a step along the way, though more remains to be done. I invite our readers to engage with the ideas raised by our contributors and to enlarge upon them by taking their own initiative to help to ensure that universities and our places of higher learning get the support they require and deserve.

The president of Simon Fraser University, Joy Johnson (2020), notes that, in response to the difficult times endured through COVID-19, what has also emerged are "seeds of a more humane, just, and sustainable future" (para. 2). In that regard, her view is that the role of universities is to "carve out that path forward" (para. 2). After all, as Michelle Obama put it to the graduating class at City College of New York during her last commencement speech as first lady, public education "is our greatest pathway to opportunity. So, we need to invest in and strengthen our public universities today, and for generations to come" (Sebastian, 2016, para. 36).

NOTES

1 This issue is particularly important for Laurentian University, in northern Ontario. On 12 April 2021 approximately 100 faculty members lost their jobs as the university moved through an insolvency process. Many people, including faculty associations, called for the Province of Ontario to step in and save the university through a unique fusion of funding. As of the date of this writing, no intervention has been approved. See CBC News (2021c).
2 See information about a panel discussion at The Aspen Institute (2014).
3 For more, see the report about the George Mason University study (Basken, 2021).
4 For some ideas, see 14 change agent roles identified by a Canadian group of university presidents (McConnell Foundation, 2021).

REFERENCES

The Aspen Institute. (2014, 2 July). *Humanities enrollment by the numbers*. Internet Archive. https://archive.org/details/Humanities_Enrollment_by_the_Numbers

Basken, P. (2021, 23 November). *Executive search firms blamed for shrinking presidential tenures*. Times Higher Education. https://

www.timeshighereducation.com/news/executive-search-firms-blamed
-shrinking-presidential-tenures
BBC News. (2021, 12 April). *France moves to ban short-haul domestic flights.*
https://www.bbc.com/news/world-europe-56716708
Bennett, P.W. (2020, 11 May). *This grand distance-learning experiment's lessons
go well beyond what the students are learning.* CBC News. https://
www.cbc.ca/news/opinion/opinion-distance-learning-education
-covid-1.5547062
Broadbent Institute. (2019, 31 January). Canada's universities and
colleges are being taken over by big corporations and wealthy donors.
PressProgress. https://pressprogress.ca/canadas-universities-and
-colleges-are-being-taken-over-by-big-corporations-and-wealthy-donors/
CBC News. (2021a, 1 February). *Laurentian University files for creditor
protection.* https://www.cbc.ca/news/canada/sudbury/laurentian
-university-creditor-protection-1.5896522
CBC News. (2021b, 12 April). *Laurentian University Cuts 100 professors, dozens
of programs.* https://www.cbc.ca/news/canada/sudbury/laurentian
-negotiations-insolvency-terminations-restructuring-1.5982114
CBC News. (2021c, 13 April). *"An ugly stain for years to come": Laurentian
University students, staff reeling from cuts.* https://www.cbc.ca/news
/canada/sudbury/laurentian-university-job-program-cuts-reaction
-1.5984577
CBC News. (2021d, 19 March). *What does "ethical travel" mean?* https://
www.cbc.ca/news/technology/what-on-earth-ethical-travel-1.5954998
Clarke, B. (2020, 30 July). The future of education or just hype? The rise of
Minerva, the world's most selective university. *The Guardian.* https://
www.theguardian.com/education/2020/jul/30/the-future-of-education
-or-just-hype-the-rise-of-minerva-the-worlds-most-selective-university
Clarke, N., D'Amato, A., Higgs, M., & Vahidi, R. (2018). *Responsible leadership
in projects: Insights into ethical decision making.* Project Management
Institute.
Council of Ministers of Education, Canada. (2017). *Responsibility for education.*
https://cmec.ca/299/Education-in-Canada-An-Overview/index.html
Eastman, J. (2018, 24 July). *University autonomy in Canada: It's time for a
check-up.* University Affairs. https://www.elle.com/culture/career
-politics/news/a36849/michelle-obama-ccny-commencement-speech/
Falkenberg, L., & Cannon, M.E. (2021, 14 April). To "future proof"
universities, leaders have to engage faculty to make tough decision. *The
Conversation.* https://theconversation.com/to-future-proof-universities
-leaders-have-to-engage-faculty-to-make-tough-decisions-155285

Frank, D.J., & Gabler, J. (2006). *Reconstructing the university: Worldwide shifts in academia in the 20th century.* Stanford University Press.

Hartocollis, A. (2020, 15 April). After coronavirus, colleges worry: Will students come back? *New York Times.* https://www.nytimes.com/2020/04/15/us/coronavirus-colleges-universities-admissions.html

Hubler, S. (2020, 14 May). Campus life in the fall? A test with no clear answer. *New York Times.* https://www.nytimes.com/2020/05/14/us/college-coronavirus-fall.html

Johnson, J. (2022, 28 February). *A world of difference: How universities must evolve in a post-COVID world.* LinkedIn. https://www.linkedin.com/pulse/world-difference-how-universities-must-evolve-joy-johnson/

Jones, S. (2020, 31 March). Covid-19 is our best chance to change universities for good. *The Guardian.* https://www.theguardian.com/education/2020/mar/31/covid-19-is-our-best-chance-to-change-universities-for-good

Lopis, G. (2020, 17 October). Post-pandemic: How must colleges and universities re-invent themselves? *Forbes.* https://www.forbes.com/sites/glennllopis/2020/10/17/post-pandemic-how-must-colleges-and-universities-reinvent-themselves/?sh=f6f11a03e88c

MacKinnon, P. (2018). *University commons divided: Exploring debate and dissent on campus.* University of Toronto Press.

Martin, A. (2021, 18 February). *The role of higher education and the humanities.* Office of the Chancellor, Washington University in St. Louis. https://andrewdmartin.wustl.edu/the-role-of-higher-education-and-the-humanities

Maslen, G. (2012, 19 February). *Worldwide student numbers forecast to double by 2025.* University World News. https://www.universityworldnews.com/post.php?story=20120216105739999

Matthews, David. (2020, 22 June). *OECD education head: pandemic disruption should mean lower fees.* Times Higher Education. https://www.timeshighereducation.com/news/oecd-education-head-pandemic-disruption-should-mean-lower-fees

McConnell Foundation. (2021). *How we developed this narrative on the role of Canadian universities in society.* https://re-code.ca/wp-content/uploads/2021/10/Role-of-Canadian-Universities-in-Society.pdf

McGreal, C. (2022, 16 September). Columbia whistleblower on exposing university rankings: "They are worthless." *The Guardian.* https://www.theguardian.com/us-news/2022/sep/16/columbia-whistleblower-us-news-rankings-michael-thaddeus

Mulgan, G., Townsley, O., & Price, A. (2016, March). *The challenge-driven university: How real-life problems can fuel learning.* Nesta. https://media.nesta.org.uk/documents/the_challenge-driven_university.pdf

Mutton, A. (2020, 2 December). *Opportunities for international recruitment post-pandemic*. University World News. https://www.universityworldnews.com/post.php?story=20201202134456579

The new leadership dynamics: Organizations are emerging from the pandemic with reshaped expectations and opportunities – and a radical vision for change. (2021). *PM Network, 35*(2), 18–47. https://www.pmi.org/learning/library/post-pandemic-organizations-reshaped-expectations-opportunities-12924

Ross, John. (2020, 19 June). *Doubts emerge over effects of Australia's sweeping fee changes*. Times Higher Education. https://www.timeshighereducation.com/news/doubts-emerge-over-effects-australias-sweeping-fee-changes

Sebastian, M. (2016, 3 June). *Michelle Obama rips Donald Trump in moving speech about the power of diversity*. Elle. https://www.elle.com/culture/career-politics/news/a36849/michelle-obama-ccny-commencement-speech/

State Higher Education Finance (SHEF). (2019). *State Higher Education Finance (SHEF) report*. https://shef.sheeo.org/report/

Statistics Canada. (2017, 29 November). Education in Canada: Key results from the 2016 census. *The Daily*. https://www150.statcan.gc.ca/n1/daily-quotidien/171129/dq171129a-eng.htm

Universities Canada. (2016, 17 September). *The future of the liberal arts: A global conversation*. https://www.univcan.ca/the-future-of-the-liberal-arts-report/

Vedder, R. (2017, 29 August). Seven challenges facing higher education. *Forbes*. https://www.forbes.com/sites/ccap/2017/08/29/seven-challenges-facing-higher-education/?sh=4b1fd9b93180

Williams, K. (2020, 22 July). Universities are vital to the post-pandemic future of Wales. We must protect them. *The Guardian*. https://www.theguardian.com/education/2020/jul/22/universities-are-vital-to-the-post-pandemic-future-of-wales-we-must-protect-them

PART ONE

The Sustainable University

chapter one

Universities and the Ethics of Environment

INGRID LEMAN STEFANOVIC AND SIMONE HAUSKNECHT

We're going to have clean coal, really clean coal.

– Donald J. Trump

We live in unprecedented times of environmental change that threaten our livelihoods and social stability. Climate student activist Greta Thunberg famously puts it this way: "People are suffering. People are dying. Entire ecosystems are collapsing. We are in the beginning of a mass extinction. And all you can talk about is money and fairy tales of eternal economic growth. How dare you!" (Thunberg, 2019, para. 3).

We begin this book by asking, What role are universities obliged to assume under such pressing circumstances?

Certainly, there are those who continue to question the magnitude of the environmental problems that we face: witness how almost 150 federal climate *deregulation* initiatives were reportedly undertaken during US President Trump's term of office (Sabin Center for Climate Change Law, 2020). But the reality remains that global challenges continue to emerge around biodiversity and natural resource depletion, migration pressures, food and water security, human and ecological health, and economic resilience.

Even the debilitating COVID-19 pandemic is being directly linked by experts to the imbalances that permeate our relations with animals and the natural world (Weston, 2020). As journalist Katherine Viner (2020) concludes, "The global climate crisis is the emergency of our times. Amid all the fear and sadness of 2020, it remains the overwhelming long-term threat to our planet and to everyone's health and security" (para. 1).

To an important extent, universities are starting to step up to the plate. Leaders, for instance, are being encouraged to commit to carbon neutrality (Hart et al., 2015). Many are proposing to allocate more resources to research and skills creation through initiatives such as the Declaration of Climate Emergency and 3-point Action Plan, to which almost 250 higher education institutions have already committed.[1] In the authors' home country, the University of Toronto and over a dozen Canadian universities have signed the "Investing to Address Climate Change" charter in 2020, acknowledging that "[c]limate change is one of the most urgent challenges facing our world" (Vitello, 2020, para. 4). As of September 2021, 520 educational signatories globally had signed on to the Talloires Declaration, acknowledging and committing to prioritize environmental sustainability (UULSF 2020).

That said, the moral commitment must extend beyond signatures.

This chapter suggests that, while universities have rapidly expanded their commitment to address climate change and environmental sustainability over the last several decades, more needs to be done. At the time of this writing, the COVID-19 pandemic has pushed universities into a crisis mode, as they confront challenges of wholescale displacement, compromised enrolments, hiring freezes, budgetary deficits, and even threats of bankruptcy. Global climate change presents similar, related, long-term dangers to the health and well-being of our universities. How will our post-secondary institutions better prepare for both the crises and opportunities that future planetary changes present to university leaders? How will we take appropriate action to address what some refer to as the significant "climate stress" and anxiety about the future that our own students are regularly experiencing (McKie et al., 2020)?

We begin by presenting an overview of where we stand today in universities' environmental programming and commitments to sustainability. We report on some findings that emerged through a study on the nature and evolution of interdisciplinary environmental programming in universities across Canada.

On the basis of critical reflection on these findings, we then propose strategies that university leaders might follow to continue to identify useful pathways to a more environmentally sustainable world. We suggest that a far-reaching, moral paradigm shift, embracing a culture of positivity and deep, collaborative, evidence-based environmental awareness, led by top executives and implemented across all institutional levels, must define the core vision of universities if leaders are to respond to planetary environmental changes in a responsible, ethically defensible manner. We need to ensure that all graduates emerge from their studies well versed in the scientific and policy implications of a warming climate and associated environmental impacts and well prepared to enact productive change. And we need to communicate, to our students but also beyond the university boundaries, that a positive, hopeful vision of the future will provide the inspiration for genuine change.

The strongest, most influential university will be defined at its core by its positive, optimistic commitment to advancing global, environmental sustainability.

I. Environmental Education: The Canadian Universities Context

At the UN Climate Change Summit in 2014, US President Barack Obama made it clear that "there's one issue that will define the contours of this century more dramatically than any other, and that is the urgent threat of a changing climate" (para. 2). While the recent pandemic has suddenly rocked the planet in a more dramatic way than any other single event since the Second World War, the related social and economic threats of climate change promise to pose longer-term challenges of the same or larger order of magnitude. In the words of Dr. Margaret Chan, executive director of the World Health Organization, "[A] healthy planet and healthy people are two sides of the same coin" (quoted in Lee, 2016, para. 3).

Christiana Figueres, secretary of the United Nations Framework Convention on Climate Change, adds that "climate change increasingly poses one of the biggest, long-term threats to investments" on a range of socio-economic levels (Volcovici, 2014, para. 4).

It is becoming increasingly clear that now is the time to act if we are to address these challenges in a meaningful way. Universities have a particularly vital role to play, as they prepare students to deal with an uncertain future (Adomssent & Michelsen, 2006; Cortese, 2003; Curren, 2009; Escrigas, 2016; Henderson et al., 2017; Orr, 2004). Graduates will move on to careers in science, education, law, policymaking, engineering, and management, and "hence need to be conscious of the impact their professions have both on the environment as a whole and on the climate in particular" (Leal Filho, 2010, p. 2).

The history of environmental education stretches back multiple decades. In the late 1960s, Canadian universities began to develop major faculties, schools, centres, departments and institutes of environmental studies, just as classic, monumental works such as Rachel Carlson's *Silent Spring* and the Club of Rome's *Limits to Growth* raised alarms about large-scale pollution, wasteful overconsumption, and a planet out of balance (Carlson, 1962; Meadows et al., 1972). In 1972, at the UN Conference on the Human Environment in Stockholm, an International Environmental Education program was proposed, resulting in an Intergovernmental Conference on Environmental Education five years later. Today, the United Nations Environment Programme (UNEP) continues to work with over 800 universities worldwide "to inspire the next generation of leaders."[2] Over the decades, programs in environmental sustainability have exploded worldwide: by 2020, there are reportedly more than 2,800 sustainability-related programs running across 27 countries worldwide, including all American states and territories and nine Canadian provinces (AASHE, 2020).

Some argue convincingly that the "first wave" of efforts to integrate environmental concerns into higher education occurred during the 1970s and 1980s. With the publication of *Our Common Future* and the popularization of the concept of sustainability, a "second wave" focused on greening campus operations (WCED,

1987). What is described as a "third wave" argues against compartmentalizing these activities, focusing instead on integrating teaching and learning with sustainable operational priorities across the institutions as a whole (Henderson et al., 2017, p. 5; Lozano et al., 2013; Vincent & Mulkey, 2015).

Certainly, many of us sense that much has changed in post-secondary institutions over the decades. Yet, critics argue that there has been too little study of how university programming in the broad area of environment and sustainability has evolved and where it should be focused in the future (Vaughter et al., 2013, 2016). Joseph Henderson and his colleagues (2017) have a point when they note that "[t]here is a need for more systematic and comparative research on sustainability education policy and practice, including in relation to the Canadian educational system" (p. 4).

In an effort to address this need, and as part of a federally funded study, our team conducted surveys and interviews with leaders of many Canadian environmental programs to investigate how university environmental curriculums evolved over the decades, and where those programs are now headed.[3] A survey was sent to leading environmental administrators – directors of schools and centres, and department chairs – at universities across Canada. Approximately 100 faculty members and program leaders were invited to complete the survey, with a response rate of 38 across 30 universities from coast to coast. The sample covered every province, except New Brunswick and Prince Edward Island, where no responses were returned. Most respondents came from Quebec (21%), Ontario (34%), and British Columbia (29%). About half of the respondents worked in the sciences and the other half in social sciences, with only two in the humanities.

In addition, one-on-one, qualitative, semi-structured interviews were conducted with six faculty deans, eight school directors, and seven department or institute heads. Finally, to identify emergent trends in environmental programming, we undertook archival research, analysing changing language patterns in course and program descriptions collected from the end of each decade at eight representative universities across Canada (Stefanovic et al., 2016). Identifying universities coast to coast where significant quality programming reached back into the 1970s, we aimed to ensure that the selection of institutions' programming reflected both official languages and was geographically representative. Courses were identified through websites and/or hard copy program brochures, and then coded for word frequency, revealing the top 100 words used within each decade. In-depth, comparative analysis of word patterns helped to reveal changing environmental priorities through historical modifications in curriculum content and design. This archival, hermeneutic research was inspired by a similar methodology utilized by UN researchers to investigate paradigm shifts through changing language patterns of water discourse in international environmental treaties (Bielak & Mount, 2011).

Collectively, this multi-year research program produced a range of findings, including rich, personal narratives relating to perceptions of changing trends in environmental post-secondary education in Canada. There was a consensus amongst survey respondents and interviewees, corroborated by the archival research, that the quantity, scope, diversity, and complexity of issues addressed in academic programming has considerably expanded over the decades, with environmental and sustainability issues becoming more mainstream at universities since the 1980s. While originally focused in the early 1970s upon more narrowly biophysical issues, the environmental field was seen to have broadened in the present to include anthropogenic issues of social justice, gender, policy, planning, governance, sustainability, and traditional, Indigenous, non-Western perspectives, to name just a few examples.

Our archival research of university programs confirmed that the quantity, richness, and depth of environmental curriculums expanded exponentially over the decades. To draw from just one salient example, while courses in environmental planning were offered in the early years at one Ontario university, later course titles increased in number, range, and complexity, covering more nuanced themes such as Landscape Ecology in Planning; Recreation and Tourism: Planning and Management; Community Planning and Housing; Land Use Planning and Law; Politics and Planning; and GIS Applications in Planning and Resource Management. New course titles began to appear through offerings in environmental ethics, sustainable development, political ecology, conservation science, impact assessment, and global climate change. In short, the "environmental" curriculum was exploding across disciplines, not only within the sciences but the social sciences and humanities as well.

Interestingly, through our surveys, some respondents felt that, over the years, ecosystems themselves came to be differently framed. In the 1970s, they were perceived as largely stable and predictable and, in the words of one such respondent, the perception was that "it was possible to engineer the environment to meet human needs." Over the decades, however, a "paradigm shift has resulted in recognition of complex systems that are unpredictable and hence more challenging to understand and manage." Notions of sustainability came to be seen as embedded in and infusing many fields, rather than constituting a "specialized disciplinary area." In the words of one respondent, the field of environmental studies itself has, over the years, developed a "sustainability and systems-science focus."

Another change noted in surveys was a perceived movement away from "micro" elements, "such as particulate studies of acid rain, dioxin effects, etc.," to macro issues such as climate change, biodiversity, sustainability, planetary scale changes, and a growing interest in broad relationships between human nature, policy, and science. Problems related to fisheries, for instance, have moved from being defined exclusively through a specific, natural science framework on stock assessments for single species, to consideration of larger social issues of fisheries management, including economic and human behavioural implications that demand a broader "ecosystem approach" to problem solving and policymaking.

One of the deans interviewed noted that internal research reflected that "the Faculty of Environment doesn't define itself in terms of *what* they study; instead, it's *how*.... We want solutions to real world problems.... The idea is to focus on the practicality of what we do as scholars." The importance of praxis to environmental teaching was emphasized across other interviews, surveys, and the archival research as well – echoing similar findings in the literature that emphasize the significance of problem- and project-based (PPBL) learning (Menon & Suresh, 2020). Not a single survey respondent, for instance, felt that co-op or internship opportunities were "not important" to undergraduates. Virtually everyone who expressed an opinion felt that experiential learning, co-op, and internships were anywhere from "somewhat" to "extremely important" for undergraduate students. At the graduate level, over 80% judged such programs to be of major significance. Overall, most survey respondents felt that "some kind of 'real world' learning" is important and "should be promoted or mandatory" at the university level.

Given the growing importance of praxis, it is no wonder, then, that there is growing pressure to integrate environmental teaching more closely with systematic sustainability efforts in campus operations and institutional priorities overall. "Environmental education" has become intimately tied to institutional change and sustainability initiatives, and there is growing pressure to deliberately value community-engaged teaching and research within academia (Frondizi et al., 2019; Henderson et al., 2017).

A final point that was noted particularly by survey respondents was the growing role of the internet and the "availability of digital data." Technological innovations, such as GIS and virtual reality simulations, were identified as ground-breaking, holding the promise of new directions for environmental teaching and research. The COVID-19 pandemic hit some time after the completion of the surveys; both positive and negative environmental effects have been noted, though the repercussions on universities of distance education and Zoom meetings have been felt in a more dramatic way than any of our survey respondents might have imagined (Zambrano-Monserrate et al., 2020). Certainly, the overlap between "environment" and "health" has been long recognized within university programming but it has only become more visible and timely, particularly in recent years.

Both this research as well as the broader literature recognize the bourgeoning role and increased significance over the decades of environmental teaching and research at universities. Whether programming is focused on climate change or broad concerns about sustainability, it is increasingly clear that there is not only a need to educate students about environmental issues but also to take a leading role in the community to both provide degree-based and lifelong learning opportunities, and to "walk the walk" on institutional management decisions and university identity (Henderson et al., 2017). "It is at universities and colleges that students of all ages can explore the complexity of the world" (Krogman, 2022, p. xix). And, realistically, while climate change education is important to education at all levels, "it is in the higher education sector that the need to tackle it in a systematic way is particularly acute "(Leal Filho 2010, p. 1).

II. Reflections and Next Steps

A recent article pointedly asks, "Could universities be doing more to address climate change?" (Segaren, 2019). Certainly, as our research indicates, the breadth, depth, and quantity of environmental programming at universities have increased over the years. That said, it is still safe to say that "while there are some who are leading the way... many are lagging behind" (Segaren, 2019, para. 4). Too few are managing to integrate environmental sustainability priorities across the entire spectrum of institutional needs (Lozano et al., 2013).

The fact is that if universities are to lead on issues such as climate change or sustainable development, then certain obstacles need to be addressed.

For instance, some of our own survey respondents pointed out that universities' budgets and governance models still are primarily rooted in old compartmentalized, discipline-based structures. One respondent pointed out that "the obstacles often concern access to resources or to the sharing of those resources." The overriding perception is that budget models allocate funding primarily to discipline-based departments. As a result, according to this survey respondent, "interdisciplinary programs ... require external or supplemental funding to be offered in addition to disciplinary programs."

Discussion on resources did not simply relate to funding but also extended to challenges in staffing. In many interdisciplinary environmental programs, faculty members hold joint appointments with discipline-based departments. Those departments perceive a loss of teaching and research capacity when they are asked to "share" their faculty with interdisciplinary units. Moreover, as one respondent commented, many interdisciplinary programs often rely upon "the voluntary participation of professors from diverse discipline-based departments" and do not have any ability to hire new professors. In the words of another respondent, the "rhetoric for support of the program is strong, but actual resource allocation to support and grow programs is weak."

Several of our survey respondents felt that universities still lacked a commitment to "true interdisciplinarity," that is, "science and social science integrated." Given that QS and other global rankings rarely measure success rates in interdisciplinary programs where faculty members are cross appointed, one respondent felt that, consequently, there was little incentive to commit to those programs in a serious way.

Faculty members themselves are rarely rewarded for interdisciplinary work when they are assessed within discipline-based departments. In the words of one respondent, "Assessment and reward are tied to old departmental structures," and since "research tends to be strongly anchored within the disciplines," it is often "evaluated and rewarded as such both internally (e.g., tenure review) and externally (e.g., by funding agencies)."

Many respondents commented on the tension between the old and the new, with university executives reportedly often being resistant to change and innovation. Beyond the challenges of shifting historical allocations of discipline-based resources, there was a growing tension felt between traditional "specialists" and interdisciplinary "generalists." Often, standard, "old" institutional practices and structures were seen to be favoured, through a "'structural determinism' imposed by institutional resource allocation models which explicitly favour full-major students in entrenched disciplinary programs."

Some respondents felt that territoriality and traditional silos in departments hindered interdisciplinary collaboration. Competition for students as well as resources means that "colleagues from disciplinary backgrounds are suspicious of the value of interdisciplinary programs." Moreover, one respondent noted that "interdisciplinary programs are seen to 'take away' from attendance in regular classes." In fact, there is a "fear ... that environmental studies replaces demand for traditional disciplines."

A related challenge emerged on the nature of governance of an interdisciplinary program. As one respondent pointed out, there are "no appropriate faculty and administrative structures for managing interdisciplinary programs." Overall, many respondents felt that it was still "difficult to work between academic units because of reporting structures ... and institutional frameworks." Furthermore, others felt that collaboration of faculty from different departments could be difficult to manage since interdisciplinary projects are "often run off the side of faculty desks ... outside their home departments." In the end, respondents seemed to agree with Julie Thompson Klein (2000) that disciplinary loyalties ultimately "undermine interdisciplinary work" (p. 17).

Clearly, there is a need to identify new budget models and institutional structures that will more readily enable interdisciplinary environmental programming at universities. For example, by utilizing responsibility-centre budget models and allocating funding according to course, rather than program enrolments, departments who offer discipline-based courses that contribute to interdisciplinary programs may be financially rewarded through higher student enrolments.

Other strategies include creating central seed funding and incentive grants, interdepartmental research centres and institutes, and developing policies and practices to encourage recruitment of faculty with interdisciplinary strengths (Creso, 2008, pp. 542ff). The creation of sustainability offices that integrate facilities and services operations with student teaching and research becomes critical. More and more universities are investing in such initiatives and looking for ways in which to both measure and report on their overall institutional sustainability initiatives (see STARS, n.d.).

Some believe that every student graduating from university must be introduced to basic scientific and ethical principles around climate change and environmental sustainability. Providing a required course is sometimes proposed, although, as one dean pointed out to us during our research interviews, new funding for such initiatives must be identified from the start. Others feel that improved environmental awareness is best enabled when the sustainability message infuses the campus, through concrete initiatives such as banning bottled water or through community-based marketing prompts that encourage sustainable behaviour (McKenzie-Mohr, 2011). Certainly, whatever the measures, presidents, provosts, and deans have a responsibility to ensure that each and every student leaves the university with a better understanding about society's most pressing problems around environmental sustainability and climate change.

In addition to attending to *internal* governance structures, however, university leaders have a responsibility to look outward as well. Environmental issues affect everyone and therefore, both teaching and research require genuine community engagement. Embedding the importance of community engagement within the core vision of the institution is vital to advancing environmental sustainability in a meaningful way.[4]

Committing to the environment is also financial in nature. Many universities – more than half in the United Kingdom, for instance – have begun to divest from the fossil fuels industry (Ibrahim, 2020). In 2020, the University of California became the largest school in the United States to sell more than $1 billion in fossil fuel assets from its pension, endowment, and working capital pools and invest in clean energy projects (Asmelash, 2020). In Canada, the Université du Québec à Montréal claims to be the first university foundation in the country to have fully withdrawn all its investments in fossil fuels (Ferraris, 2020). In the words of spokesperson for UdeM sans pétrole, the fact that educational institutions in Quebec adopted declarations of a climate emergency is "great, but now it's time to put those words into practice. The climate crisis won't be resolved with signatures; it will require concrete action" (Ferraris, 2020, para. 9).

To be sure, divestment is certainly not uncontroversial: in Canada, philosophy professor Gregory Mikkelson resigned from his position at McGill University in protest when the board of governors refused to divest from the fossil fuels industry (Lowrie, 2020). University presidents and boards call for more time to resolve complex investment portfolio issues while maximizing returns. Other universities, such as the University of Toronto at Mississauga, have instituted a variety of new policies, committing to reducing the carbon footprint of their pension and endowment investment portfolios by 40% or more by the end of 2030, reportedly resulting in three times as much carbon reduction as divestment (UTAMC, 2019).

As university leaders contemplate their own universities' financial pathways, it is important to recognize the scale of society's growing demands for investment in innovative, energy-efficient technologies. Ernst & Young report that more than 80% of millennials believe that environmental, social, and governance (ESG) criteria must drive future investments. Considering that millennials "account for $1 trillion in consumer spending, it's clearly worth listening to their demands" (Eckerman, 2020). Reportedly, Google, Apple, and Amazon are "leading a $30 trillion assault on Wall Street companies" (Eckerman, 2020, para. 93). Goldman Sachs is starting a $1.5 billion ESG fund, while Jeff Bezos has launched a $10 billion Global Earth Fund. New products, "from pens to planters," are being designed to capture carbon, as others engage in a "skyward surge" in environmentally sustainable investments (Bakx, 2021; Eckerman, 2020).

Investors like Storebrand – a major asset manager with US$91 billion in investments – have chosen to make the extraordinary move of divesting from companies like ExxonMobil and Chevron, who are reputedly lobbying against climate regulations and the Paris agreement. Institutions such as DeutscheBank and HSBC have announced similar exclusions as they reduce their exposure to fossil fuel impacts (Stewart, 2020). Major international companies, from Ikea to Henkel, are pledging to become climate positive in the near future (Noble, 2020).

Within this corporate context only, it seems reasonable to expect that responsible university leadership will ensure that their institutions are not left behind when developing their own sustainable, ethical investment portfolios.

One final issue to raise here relates to challenges and opportunities that arise for universities post-COVID-19. The pandemic has introduced disruption and loss of life in communities across the globe. On the environmental front, food supplies have been threatened, conservation efforts funded by tourism receipts are at risk, and there has been increased competition for scarce resources overall (Crawford, 2020). At the same time, the decreased air pollution while students and many employees have remained at home has, according to some, been one important consequence of limited travel. The pandemic itself is credited for having helped to slow human consumption of earth's resources in the short term, resulting in a smaller ecological footprint (McNalty, 2020).

Some – such as the former president of the United Nations General Assembly – have argued that that "greatest opportunity for action against the climate crisis" comes from the pandemic, offering opportunities for "building societies that are greener, sustainable and more resilient, rather than redoubling on the fragile models of the past" (Espinosa, 2020, para. 6). The outgoing head of the Organization for Economic Cooperation and Development, Ángel Gurría, similarly suggests that while the most pressing priority in 2021 is to combat COVID-19, "the single most important intergenerational responsibility is to protect the planet," attaching significant environmental conditions, such as "a big fat price on carbon," to any economic bailouts (Harvey, 2021, para. 3).

Others agree that "Covid-19 is our best chance to change universities for good" (Jones, 2020). According to one author,

> Opportunities are everywhere. With no school-based exams this year, university admissions could finally take place in ways that allow fairer access. The move to online teaching could accelerate the decolonization of curriculums. The shift away from on-campus research could open doors for more collaborative scholarship. Unfettered by physical location, and the compulsion to erect ever-shinier buildings, universities suddenly find themselves free to regain their place in society. (Jones, 2020, para. 8)

How radically universities change following the forced rethinking demanded by this pandemic is yet to be seen. We suspect that just as society will likely not wholly "return to normal" in the sense of how it looked pre-COVID-19, the same is true of universities. New opportunities have arisen for distance learning, although the social, in-person interaction of education has also come to be valued in a new way as well. Still, many argue that campuses can be expected to look and function differently, in both subtle and obvious ways, long after the pandemic is behind us. With increasingly tight budgets and the broader adoption of online work and learning, universities will likely continue to reassess how their places work and how much in-person engagement is efficient or necessary (Diep, 2021).

III. Concluding Remarks

There are clear lessons here for university leaders. In an era of the most severe global environmental challenges that we have ever faced, universities have a responsibility to lead the way in education, research, and community engagement. Internally, they need to commit to advancing environmental sustainability, not simply through occasional course offerings but as a core element of their very mission, one that weaves its way through every facet of the organization (Martin et al., 2012; Sterling et al., 2013; Vincent & Mulkey, 2015). They need to ensure that they walk the walk through sustainable physical operations, just as much as they need to ensure that every student, faculty, and staff member is fully aware of the environmental challenges that need to be addressed by the world as a whole. University leaders need to step up to address structural, budgetary, and governance barriers to interdisciplinary collaboration. They must acknowledge that universities have already expressed a growing commitment over the recent decades to teach our students about a range of complex problems from environmental science to environmental ethics. That momentum must be preserved and enhanced as the world continues to face a variety of social, economic, cultural, and existential challenges relating to a warming climate.

And they must acknowledge that none of this can happen successfully in isolation from the communities of which universities are a part. Community engagement needs to be more than a tag line. It must define research, education, and service that both contribute to and learn from praxis.

Finally, perhaps the most significant contribution that universities can make is to inspire hope. We live in difficult times. Environmental challenges often appear daunting as they threaten our health, our well-being, and our very existence. But without hope and a positive vision of the future, we lack inspiration. In the words of Graham Saul, executive director of Nature Canada,

> [E]nvironmentalists don't do hope very well. If we are honest with ourselves, we peddle mainly in fear. There are good reasons to be deeply worried about the state of the world, but at the same time, we also need to find ways to provide a message that is hopeful and moves and motivates and inspires people to take action. (Neal, 2018, para. 5)

The Norwegian psychologist and economist Per Espen Stoknes (2015) puts it so well when he reminds us that "whatever we do should be inspiring, be engaging, and stimulate community. A solution works so much better when people want it, like it, love it rather than when they implement it by duty, guilt, rule, or fear of punishment" (p. 90). If university leaders embrace the environmental mission as core to their institutions, and if they do so in a hopeful manner, then perhaps we will have the conditions in place for meaningful, positive, global societal change.

NOTES

1 See Global Climate Letter (n.d.).
2 For more, see UN Environment Programme (n.d.).
3 The study was funded by the Social Sciences and Humanities Research Council (SSHRC) in Canada, and the Dean's Research Grant, Simon Fraser University. Research assistants, over the course of the six-year project,

included Simone Hausknecht, Kristina Welch, and Stefan Crampton of Simon Fraser University, and Zachary Shefman, Eric Mathison, and Charles Dalrymple-Fraser at the University of Toronto Department of Philosophy.

4 See, for example, Simon Fraser University. Its strategic vision is to be Canada's engaged university, "defined by its dynamic integration of innovative education, cutting-edge research, and far-reaching community engagement" (SFU, n.d., para. 2).

REFERENCES

AASHE (Association for the Advancement of Sustainability in Higher Education). (2020). *Academic programs.* Campus Sustainability Hub. https://hub.aashe.org/browse/types/academicprogram/

Adomssent, M., & Michelsen, G. (2006). German academia heading for sustainability? Reflections on policy and practice in teaching, research and institutional innovations. *Environmental Education Research, 12*(1), 85–99. https://doi.org/10.1080/13504620500527758

Asmelash, L. (2020, 20 May). *The University of California has fully divested from fossil fuels. It's the largest school in the US to do it.* CNN. https://www.cnn.com/2020/05/20/us/university-of-california-divest-fossil-fuels-trnd/index.html

Bakx, K. (2021, 2 March). *From pens to planters, this online store only sells items made partly from captured C02.* CBC News. https://www.cbc.ca/news/business/bakx-ccs-ccus-carbon-expedition-air-1.5932550

Bielak, A., & Mount, D. (2011). *Liquid language: A global water discourse.* United Nations University. http://unu.edu/publications/articles/liquid-language-the-deepening-and-shallowing-of-global-water-discourse.html#info

Carlson, R. (1962). *Silent spring.* Houghton Mifflin.

Cortese, A.D. (2003). The critical role of higher education in creating a sustainable future. *Planning for Higher Education, 31*(3), 15–22.

Crawford, A. (2020, 9 June). *The environmental consequences of COVID-19 in fragile states.* International Institute for Sustainable Development. https://www.iisd.org/blog/impact-covid-fragile-states

Creso, S. (2008, May). Interdisciplinary strategies in American research universities. *Higher Education, 55*(5), 537–52. https://doi.org/10.1007/s10734-007-9073-5

Curren, R. (2009). *Education for sustainable development: A philosophical assessment.* Philosophy of Education Society of Great Britain.

Diep, F. (2021). *Rethinking campus spaces*. The Chronicle of Higher Education.

Eckerman, J. (2020, 27 July). *Google, Apple and Amazon are leading a $30 trillion assault on Wall Street companies*. The Market Oracle. http://www.marketoracle.co.uk/Article67449.html

Escrigas, C. (2016). *A higher calling for higher education*. Great Transition Initiative: Toward a Transformative Vision and Praxis. http://www.greattransition.org/publication/a-higher-calling-for-higher-education

Espinosa, M.F. (2020, 10 December). The climate crisis should be at the heart of the global Covid recovery. *The Guardian*. https://www.theguardian.com/commentisfree/2020/dec/10/the-climate-crisis-should-be-at-the-heart-of-the-global-covid-recovery

Ferraris, F.S.G. (2020, 20 January). *Some universities are shifting their endowments to more low-carbon investments*. University Affairs. https://www.universityaffairs.ca/news/news-article/some-universities-are-shifting-their-endowments-to-more-low-carbon-investments/

Frondizi, R., Fantauzzi, C., Colasanti, N., & Fiorani, G. (2019). The evaluation of universities' third mission and intellectual capital: Theoretical analysis and application to Italy. *Sustainability*, *11*(12), 3455. https://doi.org/10.3390/SU11123455

Global Climate Letter. (n.d.). Declaration of climate emergency and 3-point action plan: Petition to Canadian University Presidents and Universities Canada. https://docs.google.com/forms/d/e/1FAIpQLSe_QZI5FfJqY5ONSOyVJNpZTmC1meEG3D3FPojPdv508L_0PA/viewform

Hart, D.D., Bell, K.P., Lindenfeld, L.A., Jain, S., Johnson, T.R., Ranco, D., & McGill, B. (2015). Strengthening the role of universities in addressing sustainability challenges: The Mitchell Center for Sustainability Solutions as an institutional experiment. *Ecology and Society*, *20*(2), art. 2. https://doi.org/10.5751/ES-07283-200204

Harvey, F. (2021, 17 February). "Put a big fat price on carbon": OECD chief bows out with climate rally cry. *The Guardian*. https://www.theguardian.com/business/2021/feb/17/oecd-chief-angel-gurria-environment-covid-price-carbon

Henderson, J., Bieler, A., & McKenzie, M. (2017). Climate change and the Canadian higher education system: An institutional policy analysis. *Canadian Journal of Higher Education*, *47*(1), 1–26. https://doi.org/10.47678/cjhe.v47i1.187451

Ibrahim, Z. (2020, 13 January). Universities divesting from fossil fuels have made history, but the fight isn't over. *The Guardian*. https://www.theguardian.com/education/2020/jan/13/universities-divesting-from-fossil-fuels-have-made-history-but-the-fight-isnt-over

Jones, S. (2020, 31 March). Covid-19 is our best chance to change universities
for good. *The Guardian*. https://www.theguardian.com/education/2020
/mar/31/covid-19-is-our-best-chance-to-change-universities-for-good

Klein, J.T. (2000). A conceptual vocabulary of interdisciplinary science. In
P. Weingart & N. Stehr (Eds.), *Practising Interdisciplinarity* (pp. 3–25).
University of Toronto Press.

Krogman, N., & Bergstrom, A. *The future of sustainability education at North
American universities*. Edmonton: University of Alberta Press, 2022.

Leal Filho, W. (2010). Climate change at universities: Results of a world
survey. In W. Leal Filho (Ed.), *Universities and climate change* (pp. 1–19).
Berlin: Springer-Verlag.

Lee, J. (2016, 6 July). Climate, energy and environment. *United Nations
Foundation*. https://unfoundation.org/blog/post/7-quotes-on-climate
-change-and-health/

Lowrie, M. (2020, 20 January). *McGill University principal defends decision
not to divest from fossil fuels after professor quits*. Global News. https://
globalnews.ca/news/6435536/mcgill-university-principal-prof
-resignation-divest/

Lozano, R., Lukman, R., Lazano, F.J., Huisingh, D., & Lambrechts, W. (2013).
Declarations for sustainability in higher education: Becoming better
leaders through addressing the university system. *Journal of Cleaner
Production*, *48*(June), 10–19. https://doi.org/10.1016/j.jclepro.2011.10
.006

Martin, J., J.E. Samels & Associates. (2012). *The sustainable university:
Green goals and new challenges for higher education leaders*. Johns Hopkins
University Press.

McKenzie-Mohr, D. (2011). *Fostering sustainable behavior: An introduction to
community-based social marketing*. New Society Publishers.

McKie, D., Keogh, D., Buckley, C., & Cribb, R. (2020, 2 December). Across
North America, climate change is disrupting a generation's mental
health. *Canada's National Observer*. https://www.nationalobserver.
com/2020/12/02/eco-anxiety-youth-mental-health-climate-change

McNalty, S. (2020, 27 August). *The pandemic has slowed consumption of earth's
resources – for now*. CBC News. https://www.cbc.ca/news/technology
/what-on-earth-overshoot-day-1.5702578

Meadows, D.H., Meadows, D., Randers, L.J., & Behrens III, W.W. (1972). *The
limits to growth: A report for the Club of Rome's Project on the Predicament of
Mankind*. Universe Books.

Menon, S., & Suresh, M. (2020). Synergizing education research, campus
operations, and community engagements towards sustainability in higher

education: A literature review. *International Journal of Sustainability in Higher Education, 21*(5), 1015–51. https://doi.org/10.1108/IJSHE-03-2020-0089

Neal, A. (2018, 20 November). *Environmental movement needs hope to survive, activist says.* CBC News. https://www.cbc.ca/news/canada/ottawa/hope-can-save-planet-environmentalist-says-1.4912334

Noble, S. (2020, 4 December). As consumers we all have tremendous impact": Why becoming climate positive is the business world's greatest challenge. *The Guardian.* https://www.newsbreak.com/news/2372528655162-as-consumers-we-all-have-tremendous-impact-why-becoming-climate-positive-is-the-business-world-s-greatest-challenge

Obama, B. (2014, 23 September). *Remarks by the president at U.N. Climate Change Summit.* https://obamawhitehouse.archives.gov/the-press-office/2014/09/23/remarks-president-un-climate-change-summit

Orr, D.W. (2004). *Earth in mind: On education, environment, and the human prospect.* 10th Anniversary edition. Island Press.

Sabin Center for Climate Change Law. (2020). *Climate deregulation tracker.* Columbia Law School. https://climate.law.columbia.edu/climate-deregulation-tracker

Segaren, S. (2019, 17 September). *Could universities be doing more to address climate change?* Study International. https://www.studyinternational.com/news/universities-more-climate-change/

SFU. (n.d.). *SFU Engage.* http://www.sfu.ca/engage.html

STARS. (n.d.). *The Sustainability Tracking, Assessment & Rating System.* https://stars.aashe.org

Stefanovic, I.L., Shefman, Z., & Welch, K. (2016). Paradigms, praxis and environmental phenomenology. In B.E. Bannon (Ed.), *Nature and experience: Phenomenology and the environment* (pp. 129–42). Rowman & Littlefield.

Sterling, S., Maxey, L., & Luna, H. (2013). *The sustainable university: Progress and prospects.* Routledge.

Stewart, K. (2020, 31 August). Big oil backers are jumping ship – and that's good for the planet. *The Tyee.* https://thetyee.ca/Analysis/2020/08/31/Big-Oil-Backers-Jumping-Ship/

Stoknes, P.E. (2015). *What we think about when we try not to think about global warming: Toward a new psychology of climate action.* Chelsea Green Publishing.

Thunberg, G. (2019, 23 September). *Transcript: Greta Thunberg's speech at the U.N. Climate Action Summit.* NPR. https://www.npr.

org/2019/09/23/763452863/transcript-greta-thunbergs-speech-at-the
-u-n-climate-action-summit

ULSF (University Leaders for a Sustainable Future). (2020). *Talloires
Declaration Signatories List*. http://ulsf.org/96-2/

UN Environment Programme. (n.d.). *About education and environment*.
https://www.unep.org/explore-topics/education-environment
/about-education-environment

University of Toronto Asset Management Corporation (UTAMC). (2019).
Toward a greener future: Carbon footprint report. https://www.utam
.utoronto.ca/wp-content/uploads/2020/02/2019-Carbon-Footprint
-Report-FINAL.pdf

Vaughter, P., McKenzie, M., Lidstone, L., & Wright, T. (2016). Campus
sustainability governance in Canada: A content analysis of post-
secondary institutions' sustainability policies. *International Journal of
Sustainability in Higher Education, 17*(1), 16–39. https://doi.org/10.1108
/IJSHE-05-2014-0075

Vaughter, P., Wright, T., McKenzie, M., & Lidstone, L. (2013). Greening the
ivory tower: A review of educational research on sustainability in post-
secondary education. *Sustainability, 5*(5), 2252–71. https://doi.org
/10.3390/su5052252

Vincent, S., & Mulkey, S. (2015). Transforming US higher education to
support sustainability science for a resilient future: The influence of
institutional administrative organization. *Environment, Development
and Sustainability, 17*(2), 341–63. https://doi.org/10.1007/s10668-015
-9623-4

Viner, K. (2020, 5 October). The Guardian's climate promise: We will keep
raising the alarm. *The Guardian*. https://www.theguardian.com
/environment/2020/oct/05/
the-guardians-climate-promise-we-will-keep-raising-the-alarm

Vitello, C. (2020, 22 June). Canadian universities sign charter to tackle
climate change. *Environment Journal*. https://environmentjournal.ca
/canadian-universities-sign-charter-to-tackle-climate-change/

Volcovici, V. (2014, 15 January). UN climate chief urges investors to bolster
global warming fight. *Reuters*, Environment section. https://www
.reuters.com/article/us-un-climate-change/un-climate-chief-urges
-investors-to-bolster-global-warming-fight-idUSBREA0E1KM20140115

Weston, P. (2020, 25 April). "We did it to ourselves": Scientists say intrusion
into nature led to pandemic. *The Guardian*. https://www.theguardian
.com/world/2020/apr/25/ourselves-scientist-says-human-intrusion
-nature-pandemic-aoe

World Commission on Environment and Development (WCED). (1987). *Our common future*. Oxford University Press.

Zambrano-Monserrate, M.A., Alejandra Ruano, M., & Sanchez-Alcalde, L. (2020). Indirect effects of COVID-19 on the environment. *Science of the Total Environment, 728*, 138813. https://doi.org/10.1016/j.scitotenv.2020.138813

"Universities and the Ethics of Environment"

TODD LATHAM
President, ActualMedia Inc.

There is no escape from climate change. Every living thing on earth is affected by this global environmental emergency. It is the existential threat of our lifetime and requires rapid change in policy and human behaviour.

The good news is that the global COVID-19 response has shown that we can act together to overcome challenges. While it may be difficult to avoid the social, financial, and environmental impacts of climate change in the short term, there are exciting opportunities in the long term.

Leading corporations recognize the positive business and societal benefits of "walking the walk" and pivoting green. And when they do not, the markets turn on them. Exxon's value is down by half while Tesla's is up seven-fold. Similarly, universities that are slow to embrace similar practices and curriculum will see student registration dwindle and international rankings and revenue along with them.

Shareholders, like students, are demanding action. Unilever, a global consumer goods company, has plans to cut greenhouse gas emissions from its operations to net zero by 2030 and to halve the environmental impact of its products. A growing coalition of Canadian companies, including Maple Leaf Foods, CN, and Celestica, have committed to reducing carbon emissions, setting science-based targets, resource stewardship, and sustainability reporting and are encouraging other companies to join them. Likewise, the Caisse de dépôt et placement du Québec, the Ontario Teachers'

Pension Plan. and the OPSEU Pension Trust have all committed to carbon-neutral portfolios.

As outlined in this chapter, many universities are also adopting targets that reflect environmental, social, and governance risk-management principles and are moving their learning, personal development, and endowment funds to where they need to be for our global green economy transition. This chapter shows us that, as important contributors to society and nations, and as an ethical imperative, our corporations should, as should our universities, seize *more* of these opportunities to become climate change leaders too.

chapter two

University Responses to and Obligations for Business Air Travel Emissions

JOHN ROBINSON, DIONE DIAS, AYAKO ARIGA, RASHAD BRUGMANN, NICOLAS CÔTÉ, MEGHAN HENDERSON, ANDREA MUEHLEBACH, RUTU PATEL, JENNIFER PUSKAR, AND PETER VUONG

Introduction

Climate change is a defining issue of our time. To address it, the widely recognized Greenhouse Gas (GHG) Protocol requires that institutions reduce their emissions in three categories: scope 1, scope 2, and scope 3. Scope 1 comprises direct emissions from owned assets, scope 2 comprises indirect emissions from purchased energy, and scope 3 includes all other indirect emissions from sources not owned or controlled by the institution, including emissions from academic and business-related air travel.

However, scope 3 emissions are not covered under the United Nations Framework Convention on Climate Change (UNFCCC) and most other GHG reporting frameworks. As a result, formal reporting requirements and national and sub-national GHG emission-reduction targets address only scope 1 and 2 emissions. And it is left up to individual universities whether they will measure and take responsibility for scope 3 emissions.

Through its Low Carbon Action Plan released in September 2019, the University of Toronto (U of T) committed to reducing GHG emissions by 37% below 1990 levels by 2030. In October 2021, the university announced a "climate positive" target for its downtown campus by 2050. This commitment is a big step forward, but neither the plan nor the University of Toronto GHG emissions-reduction commitment includes scope 3 emissions.

What should the university leadership do about scope 3 emissions? In 2019, the President's Advisory Committee on Environment, Climate Change, and Sustainability (CECCS) was approached by stakeholders from the U of T community on the university's plan to address business air travel (the biggest component of scope 3 emissions) and saw the opportunity to develop an approach to measuring and taking responsibility for such business air travel emissions.[1] Tackling business air travel could be a first step to a more comprehensive look at all scope 3 emissions.

In order to take action on climate change and keep U of T on a path to becoming a net-positive institution while supporting necessary business air travel that cannot be mitigated, the CECCS has proposed an institutional plan to capture the size and significance of air travel related scope 3 emissions across the three campuses, and articulate a plan for reducing such emissions. We have adopted a three-pronged approach to address air travel at the university focusing on:

I)   Quantifying air travel scope 3 emissions,
II) Assigning institutional responsibility for business air travel emissions,
III) Reducing business-related air travel, and
IV) Developing an emissions mitigation program at the U of T.

First, quantifying air travel scope 3 emissions is a key infrastructural need to set the context for the scale of emissions that is being discussed. Without a reliable and efficient method to quantify these emissions, the climate impact of U of T's air travel and effectiveness of any future programming cannot be demonstrated. Second, there are different ethical considerations involved in assigning institutional responsibility for business air travel emissions of faculty, staff, and students, and these must be addressed before meaningful action can be undertaken. Third, the most obvious and immediate solution to mitigating emissions from flying is to reduce business-related air travel at the university. Several strategies can be employed to achieve this reduction. One important strategy involves developing virtual conferencing infrastructure at U of T to reduce travel to conferences, lectures, and meetings, and this was the focus of our work on this topic. Last, as U of T is a large public research institution, we accept that not all business-related air travel will be eliminated, and we therefore need to develop methods to mitigate the emissions from the remaining air travel. These methods also raise important ethical questions.

I. Quantifying Air Travel Scope 3 Emissions

Developing a sustainable methodology to quantify business-related air travel at U of T is the first step in addressing the resulting scope 3 emissions. Although scope 3 includes various other indirect sources, the focus for the CECCS has been on air travel, as it makes up the bulk of the scope 3 institutional emissions. A brief analysis of GHG reports of five Canadian institutions (including U of T) reveals that, despite a lack of comprehensive accounting measures by the university, air travel emissions contribute 9% to 54% of an institution's total reported emissions. At the University of British Columbia, another leading research university in Canada, a detailed study found that business-related air travel emissions were as high as 75% of UBC's annual operational emissions (Wynes et al., 2019).

In the fall of 2019, a group of students in ENV461/1103, *The U of T Campus as a Living Lab for Sustainability* course, undertook a project to quantify the emissions from air travel at the university. The living lab course, taught by Professor John Robinson, pairs campus "clients" with students who research and address real world problems and challenges faced by the clients on campus. For this project, the CECCS project manager, Dione Dias, acted as client in the course.

A. Methodology and Results

To quantify the business-related air travel emissions generated by the U of T community, the students used three sources of data:

1 Avenue Travel, U of T's travel booking agency (showing booking data),
2 General Ledger (showing reimbursements for air travel issued through U of T Finances), and
3 A survey on flying behaviour of a sample population.

Data was collected from September 2018 to September 2019. During this time, $2.9 million was spent via Avenue Travel, while $20.9 million was reported in air travel reimbursements in the financial system's General Ledger. This data demonstrates that only approximately 10% of the flights were booked through Avenue Travel. Since the Avenue Travel data shows distances flown, while the General Ledger data does not, a combination of top-down and bottom-up methods were used to investigate U of T's air travel emissions.

For the **top-down approach**, Avenue Travel booking data was used to calculate the kilometres travelled per dollar for short-, medium-, and long-haul flights. Proportions of the three flight categories were then applied to the General Ledger spending data to estimate total kilometres travelled.

Since emission intensity differs by flight distance, the total distance in each flight category was then used to calculate respective GHG emissions. This approach assumes the proportions of flight categories reported in Avenue Travel are true for the full General Ledger data.

For the **bottom-up approach**, a short survey was administered through the CECCS network, which collected 79 responses totalling 115 round-trip flights. Using the origin-destinations reported in the survey, kilometres travelled by short-, medium-, and long-haul flights were classified. The average cost of each flight length from Avenue Travel was applied to estimate total spending and percentage of spending by flight category. These percentages were applied to the General Ledger data to estimate the GHG emissions by respective flight categories. This approach assumes proportions reported in the survey are true for the full General Ledger data.

The two values produced by the two approaches span a range from 26 to 58 thousand tonnes eCO_2, respectively, as shown in

Table 2.1. Estimated Air Travel Emissions at U of T (September 2018–September 2019)

Method	Estimated emissions (t eCO$_2$)	Air travel emissions as proportion of scope 1 and 2 emissions*
Top-down approach	26,028	23%
Bottom-up approach	57,838	51%

* Total scope 1 and 2 emissions in 2017–18 were 114,265 t eCO$_2$.

Table 2.1. When compared to the GHG emissions of the university, these values are significant, as they are equivalent to 23% to 51% of the total 114,265 tonnes eCO$_2$ emitted from scope 1 and 2 sources (2017–18).

B. Limitations and Conclusions

There are several limitations to this approach of estimating air travel emissions. First, the biggest challenge was the lack of representative data. Bookings made through Avenue Travel accounted for only 10% of U of T's total spending on air travel while the survey results (meant originally to generate more representative data) captured only 0.65% of U of T's total air travel spending. Assuming the proportions of short-, medium-, and long-haul flights from these data sources to be valid over the full General Ledger, spending data is the only available methodology; however, the reliability of the emissions estimates is thereby diminished.

Second, the flight classes are not specified in any case, while emissions differ significantly between economy class travel, business class travel, and first class travel. Ultimately, students identified the lack of a comprehensive dataset as the greatest challenge and made recommendations for U of T to establish a centralized and standardized method of collecting air travel data for all individuals travelling. It was recommended that a comprehensive dataset should collect the following information: relation of individuals to the university (staff, student, faculty, and visitor), origin and destination, flight class, cost of flight, who paid for the travel, and purpose of travel (meeting, conference, lecture, etc.).

II. Assigning Institutional Responsibility for Business Air Travel at the University of Toronto

To address scope 3 air travel emissions, it was necessary to determine which U of T air travel emissions constitute the institution's responsibility. A literature review was undertaken to compare the implications of two proposed approaches to assigning responsibility, with differing consequences and ethical commitments:

1 Accepting responsibility for the air travel the university pays for ("University Paid" approach). This would include all business travel, university faculty, staff, and students, and invited guests whose travel costs are paid by the university.
2 Accepting responsibility for all travel undertaken by students, staff, and faculty of the university, whether paid for by the university or not ("University People" approach).

These two options are represented in Figure 2.1. Approach #1 would amount to accepting responsibility for the shaded elements in the figure, while approach #2 would amount to accepting responsibility for the U of T Community (the left-hand side of the figure). Academic literature on this topic is limited, so we sought an answer to the question of *how* to assign responsibility by broadening our research scope and looking also at petitions, pledges, open letters, and institutional publications. The objective of this review was to understand how the approaches compare in their implications, what peer institutions are doing, and how we can improve upon those efforts.

A. Discussion

The University Paid approach was found to be relatively popular among implemented projects and strategies included in the literature review. While it is not the case at U of T, some institutions

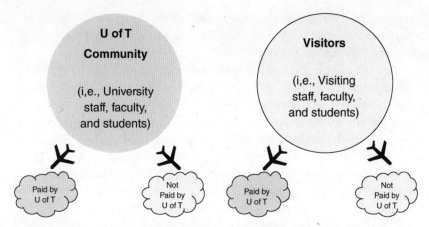

Figure 2.1. Sources of Air Travel Emissions at U of T

centrally process travel booking and/or financial data, making goal setting and monitoring easier. Additionally, adopting this approach makes the business case for financial savings while mitigating travel, which may be convincing for many campus stakeholders. All the initiatives using the University Paid approach relied on financial data to estimate air travel emissions of the institution, implying that the university is responsible only for emissions generated from travel funded by the institution.

The University People approach, on the other hand, was treated inconsistently in the literature. Some initiatives were classified as this approach because they used self-reporting methods in addition to financial data to estimate emissions. This opens the possibility of accounting for staff and faculty air travel that may not have been paid for by the university.

An important difference that emerges from comparing the University Paid and University People approaches is that the latter enables carbon accounting of student air travel. Davies and Dunk (2016) argue that since "(Higher Education Institutions) HEIs are explicitly providing education for overseas students and study-abroad opportunities," universities are responsible for the resultant air travel (p. 235). This aspect of student air travel as institutional responsibility completely disappears when considering the University Paid approach since, in most cases, the university does not pay for this travel.

Another important concern arising from this pursuit of defining boundaries of responsibility is the "double counting" of air travel emissions. This particularly applies to visitor travel, since emissions of their visit may be included in the emissions accounting of both institutions. Most of the initiatives classified as the University People approach do not explicitly address or include the travel of visitors as part of their approach. Many of the initiatives in the University People approach, however, supported the inclusion of all air travel by university personnel, even when it is not paid by the university, in the emissions calculation.

B. Recommendations and Way Forward for U of T on Assigning Responsibility for Air Travel

The main difference between the University Paid and University People approaches is the emission sources for which they account. While the University Paid approach is effective at capturing travel of staff and some visitors to campus, it largely misses the faculty travel that is not paid by the university as well as student air travel (home visits by international students and study abroad opportunities). Even the visitor air travel is only partially captured, since visitors on campus often have their travel paid for by another institution or organization. The University People approach then opens the possibility of accounting for the previously missed faculty and student travel through surveys and self-reporting methods. Here, however, the visitors' air travel is completely ignored since "visitors" are not university personnel. Absolving institutions of responsibility for inducing visitor air travel (e.g., in the form of inviting international speakers and attendees rather than virtual conferencing) does not facilitate transition to a low-carbon university culture.

Therefore, the CECCS suggests that U of T should adopt an ambitious approach that takes ethical leadership and aims at accounting for both sources of air travel emissions (as a combination of the

University Paid and University People approaches). We believe that this combined approach is particularly important, given the current lack of initiative by other institutions to thoroughly count and address their air travel emissions. Double counting of emissions, then, is a future concern, since most institutions still do not count their own share. When accounting and reporting on scope 3 air travel emissions becomes as common a practice as scope 1 and 2, a more selective method can be applied.

While the approach proposed here is ambitious, despite comprehensive methods of accounting, it is very possible that we would miss many sources of emissions, especially visitor travel, which is not paid for by the university. At the core of this comprehensive approach, however, is the intent to adhere to the science of climate change and an acknowledgment of the urgent need for significant emission reductions.

III. Reducing Business-Related Air Travel at U of T

Reducing the number of flights taken is the most effective way of mitigating scope 3 emissions. Additionally, under the COVID-19 pandemic, limits to travel continue to pose challenges to the functions of the university. Influencing behaviour is challenging and requires strong administration, ongoing coordination, and communication. There are two parts to this strategy: to reduce travel via policies, and via virtual conferencing alternatives.

First is to consider applying travel mitigative strategies to limit or discourage unnecessary air travel and to reduce travel GHG emissions. Examples include (Burian, 2018; Wynes et al., 2019):

- eliminating same-day return flights,
- reducing flying for one-night stays,
- reducing group travel,
- favouring direct flights over layovers,
- requiring university personnel to travel by economy class only, and
- altering reimbursement rules requiring travel via the cheapest option only.

Each of these strategies can limit air travel and create measurable emission reductions, among other benefits. Eliminating same-day return flights and one-night stays, for example, can result in financial savings as well as time savings for the travelling individual. In these cases, the individual spends more time and energy in travelling than in the face-to-face meeting. Reducing group travel helps avoid redundant emissions, unless the presence of more than one person has significant work benefits. Direct flights should be favoured over indirect routes, since indirect flights waste more fuel for multiple take-offs and landings, generating more emissions (Lewis, 2013). Travel by economy class is also favourable because the emissions per person are lower. Last, eliminating the requirement of using the cheapest travel option can promote land-based travel or purchase of direct flights, since train travel and direct flights, despite their emission benefits, are often more expensive. The last point was emphasized by both Burian (2018) and Wynes et al. (2019). The "cheapest travel option" requirement at their respective institutions was potentially barring travellers' access to more sustainable travel.

Specific practices within the reimbursement system can create barriers to sustainable travel at U of T. At present, the policy prioritizes financial efficiency to assess eligibility for reimbursement. For example, U of T's Policies and Guidelines for Travel and Other Reimbursable Expenses includes a requirement stating, "Travellers should request the lowest available fare at the time of booking," which likely discourages the use of land-based travel and direct flights. Another example includes the difficulty of combining several visits into one round trip to mitigate travel emissions. For example, a faculty member combining a visit to Hong Kong for a conference and to Taiwan for field work may experience difficulty in being reimbursed for the four days between these two purposes of travel. In this way the reimbursement policy forces the traveller to either emit more with repeated travel or to personally absorb financial costs. In such cases, the current reimbursement policy fails to reward decisions based on sustainability. To mitigate scope 3 air travel emissions, travelling staff and faculty will need appropriate administrative support. Therefore, it is recommended that a policy based on emissions reduction, in addition to financial savings, be considered at the university.

A second strategy is to invest in developing information and communication technology (ICT) infrastructure to increase capacity for virtual conferencing as an alternative to in-person attendance. The success of many of the above travel mitigative strategies depends the availability and accessibility of appropriate ICT infrastructure. If virtual conferencing were accessible and easy to use, much of the staff and faculty's same-day and one-night stay travels could be eliminated.

ICT development requires a central mandated push as part of climate action planning (Wynes & Donner, 2018). One key behavioural motivator is offering equal "credit" for virtually delivered presentations, lectures, and talks for career advancement of younger academics at U of T. Adjustments to merit-based promotion systems for faculty and librarians are arguably required, along with a broader shift in the academic culture.

In the meantime, virtual conferencing can be supported by regularly updating institutional software licences, developing state-of-the-art virtual conferencing facilities, and providing funds as incentives for departments or units that opt for virtual meetings (Wynes et al., 2019). Interest in such initiatives ballooned with the onset of the COVID-19 crisis.

U of T is prioritising the creation of resources for virtual conferencing by providing a menu of virtual conferencing models (see Table 2.2), finding caselets to model as examples at U of T of each option in the menu of options, holding workshops on how to host virtual conferences, providing ICT support and resources, and creating a community of practice to share best practices and encourage innovative solutions for virtual events and conferences.

Table 2.2 shows several approaches to virtual conferencing. These models were conceptualized on the basis of a study of the literature on academic air travel, virtual conferencing, and virtual event case studies. A full list of the literature has been compiled as a resource for use at the university. The models were then applied to events of various sizes and objectives to create a "Menu of Options for Virtual Conferencing." This document was created for those

Table 2.2. Virtual Conference Models

Traditional in-person	Live stream	Teleconferencing (several interacting screens)	Hybrid model (One example below)
Traditional conference with all speakers and attendees meeting at one location for set programming	Largely traditional conference with live-stream/broadcast for virtual attendees	Semi-hybrid programming with several interacting screens of presenters and attendees, which enables bilateral communication	A combination of models fits the specific needs of the programming

planning a virtual event and lays out the pros and cons of each virtual event model, along with hardware and software needs. Furthermore, to complement the "Menu of Options," the CECCS is developing caselets of the different models of virtual events with best practices from and for event organizers. The caselets will be available as a resource for staff and faculty at U of T. These are working documents that are meant to be updated as new models and solutions become available.

IV. Case Study

U of T took the lead with Distribute 2020 – a biennial conference of the Society for Cultural Anthropology and the Society for Visual Anthropology (both sections of the American Anthropological Association) that took place on 7–9 May 2020. Distribute 2020 was a near-carbon-neutral conference, which originally intended to follow a virtual-hybrid model of conferencing (see Figure 2.2).

Distribute 2020 was hosted on a dedicated website, where recorded multimedia presentations were streamed in one continuous, 72-hour live stream. Each panel was streamed three times over the course of three 24-hour loops, allowing viewers from all over the world to view panels at times that matched their time zones. The original hybrid model had groups watching the conference via in-person "viewing nodes" as in 201 (see Figure 2.2), when the two societies pioneered this conference model. Because the pandemic made in-person gatherings impossible, Distribute 2020 designed a "virtual hallway," where participants could gather for discussions with panellists in real time. These discussions exceeded all expectations and were not only lively but also exceptionally inclusive. Many hallway discussions included not just professors but also students from all over the world. This made the virtual hallway not only a space for conversation but unprecedented collective learning and networking.

This model bears many benefits once it can be taken up again in its fully distributed form, i.e., local viewing nodes and elements of the fully virtual version, like the virtual hallway, could be interwoven into the nodal model as well. First, the budgetary savings

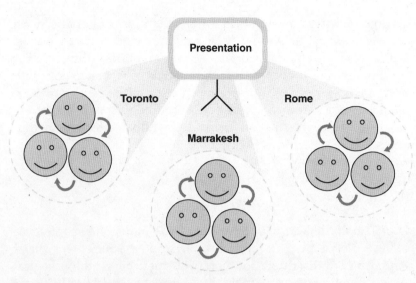

Figure 2.2. Hybrid Conference Model of Distribute 2020

on venue and catering means the conference tickets can be made affordable, increasing accessibility by lowering financial barriers to participation. Distribute 2020 is a case in point: It costs only $10 for individuals and $100–$200 for institutional nodes. A preliminary count reveals that Distribute 2020 saw 1,029 conference participants, with registrations still trickling in as Distribute 2020's film festival continued into May. This far exceeds the 250 registered participants usually attending SCA's in-person conferences.

Second, the virtual hosting of media means people from all over the world – even from the Global South, where participation has been low in the past – can participate, making the conference more equitable. Distribute 2020 saw record participation from over 65 countries and hundreds of cities, a scale and breadth that again vastly exceeded participation in SCA's past, in-person conference.

Last, NCN conference models need not exclude networking opportunities. The virtual hallways (as well as our "Coffee With ..." sessions, which allowed for emerging scholars to meet with established scholars as well as with the editors of several prominent presses, including Duke University Press and Princeton University

Press) were excellent sites for networking, especially for junior scholars. It is hoped that future iterations of this conference will feature local viewing nodes again, which will further solidify the many networking opportunities this conference model can offer.[2]

All conference materials will continue to be stored on U of T's MyMedia space and will still be accessible via U of T's conference domain. Distribute 2020 will serve as a case study and experiment to enable the ICT capabilities of the U of T campus for this purpose. This case study will reveal any technical shortcomings of ICT at the university and illustrate the path to develop the infrastructure to support virtual conferencing. In this regard Distribute 2020 hinged significantly on collaboration with University of California Santa Cruz technology, which provided the platform for the panel-stream (via Ustream).

The sustainability recommendations by the CECCS to quantifiably and significantly reduce air travel and promote virtual conferencing are especially relevant under the COVID-19 pandemic. The CECCS is committed to promoting the sustainability aspects of hosting virtual events, including creating a guide to assess the life-cycle analysis of virtual events.

V. Developing a U of T Emissions Mitigation Program

Reducing air travel at U of T by developing virtual conferencing infrastructure will likely mitigate an avoidable portion of the air travel emissions. However, some air travel will persist, so it is important for U of T to develop a plan to mitigate those emissions.[3]

A. Air Travel Emissions Mitigation Initiative

Operations and Real Estate Partnerships (OREP) has developed an air travel emissions mitigation initiative to accelerate U of T's emissions reduction and to help counter university-related scope 3 emissions, beginning with air travel. This initiative is in line with "green" air travel funds that have been implemented at peer institutions including University of California, Los Angeles (UCLA) and

Duke University, and it is designed to allow U of T to take immediate action towards these goals while discussions and research on scope 3 emissions continue.

While business air travel has been eliminated during the pandemic, as restrictions are lifted this pilot will apply to all air travel by the president, vice-presidents, assistant vice-presidents, and deans, as well as other senior leadership in their offices, including senior administrative staff and all vice-provosts, vice-deans, and associate deans. All covered air travel will be assessed an air travel carbon mitigation charge, ranging from C$15 per North American round-trip flight, to $116 per round trip flight to locations such as Shanghai.

Finance or accounting officers in each unit will ensure that appropriate transfers are made to a central fund on a quarterly basis. These funds will be invested in projects identified and prioritized by the Tri-Campus Sustainability Board for their respective campuses. The results will be verified as part of U of T's annual emissions audit, completed by a third-party emissions auditing firm certified by the provincial Ministry of Environment, Conversation and Parks.

Examples of immediate projects for U of T under the Air Travel Emissions Mitigation pilot include on-site composing, electrification of fleet, on-site renewable energy projects, and forest and land management initiatives.

B. The Ethics of Carbon Offsets

Discussion of the potential of offsetting programs to address U of T's climate change responsibilities led to a request that the ethics of offsetting be examined by CECCS. To understand the ethical implications of using carbon offsets to address scope 3 air travel emissions, a limited literature review was conducted. Seventeen research articles, non-governmental organization publications, and blog posts were reviewed on the ethical dimensions of carbon offsets, of which more than two thirds were from institutions in Europe (Cames et al., 2016; Friends of the Earth, 2009; Lovell, 2008, 2010).

The ethical debates on carbon offsetting can be organized into three areas: fundamental objection (ethics of environmental markets), outcome dependent (ethical challenge of assured emissions reductions), and neo-colonialist (ethics of existing inequalities) (Lovell, 2008).

C. Fundamental Objection: The Ethics of Environmental Markets

Some critiques of carbon offsets stem from an objection to using "fundamentally flawed" economics and markets to address environmental problems (Friends of the Earth, 2009; Lovell, 2008). For instance, one article argues that when offset projects are built, they stimulate development that leads to a net increase in emissions (Anderson, 2012). However, it is suggested that the risk of such a "rebound" effect is low and could be avoided by benchmarking emissions (Kim & Pierce, 2018).

Another common argument against the carbon offset market is that it does not create an incentive to implement policies and transition to new technologies and behaviours that reduce emissions (Anderson, 2012; Bachram, 2004; Brown, n.d.; Friends of the Earth, 2009). In this respect, carbon offsets focus the main responsibility of changing consumption patterns on the individual and do little to encourage political and economic institutions to alter their own behaviour (Smith, 2007). Smith raises further concern that the financialization of carbon emissions is a form of greenwashing as businesses try to convince their customers to buy carbon offsets rather than reducing their consumption.

On the other hand, those who support offsets and other market mechanisms note that Articles 5 and 6 of the Paris Agreement and the Intergovernmental Panel on Climate Change science support offsets as one of many tools in a transition to a lower carbon economy. Article 5 supports the REDD plus (Reduced Emissions from Deforestation and Destruction) with particular focus on respecting Indigenous and local community needs (United Nations, 2015). The preponderance of domestic and global offset projects, they argue, has resulted in measurable climate, environmental, community, and additional sustainability benefits.

D. Outcome Dependent: The Ethical Challenge of Assured Emissions Reductions

Further critique of carbon offsets focuses on the ethics of assured outcomes for emissions reductions (Lovell, 2008). Several articles also conclude that offsets cannot generate the reductions needed to meet climate targets (Anderson, 2012; Brown, n.d.; Friends of the Earth, 2009). In part, this argument questions whether it is possible to accurately predict future emissions reductions, especially for projects in other countries (Friends of the Earth, 2009, Lovell et al., 2009; Smith, 2007). Another issue is that companies can manipulate these theoretical numbers to generate as many sellable credits as possible (Smith, 2007). A broader ethical argument is that it can be extremely difficult to prove that offsetting projects would not have happened without the offset funds, and therefore that the project creates additional emissions reductions to offset the emissions produced (Friends of the Earth, 2009). The long-term impacts of carbon offset projects are rarely studied and incorporated in the process of verification, so if an offset project's indirect effects create more emissions that are not accounted for, the verification conclusions are distorted and inaccurate (Maryanski, 2015).

E. Neo-Colonialist: Ethical Concerns of Existing Inequalities

Carbon offset projects that are implemented internationally, typically in the Global South, are questioned for the ethics of their missions to "develop." This ethical debate centres on the argument that offsets shift the moral responsibility for reducing emissions to countries in the Global South (Bachram, 2004; Brown, n.d.; Friends of the Earth, 2009; Lovell et al., 2009). In this context, emissions-producing behaviours are referred to as "indulgences" that are being allowed at the expense of communities in the Global South (Dhanda & Hartman, 2011; Lovell, 2008; Lovell et al., 2009; Smith, 2007). However, Kim and Pierce (2018) argue that carbon emissions are not inherently bad, because if they could all be offset, we would not have a changing climate. In addition, there is concern that many projects harm the communities in which they are located, and community members are not consulted for the development (Brown, n.d.; Friends of the Earth 2009; Lovell et al., 2009).

VI. Discussion of Findings

The fundamental objection to using carbon offsets as a climate mitigation strategy is part of a broader debate in environmental ethics and economics about assigning a market value to environmental resources, and about the desirability or possibility of continued economic growth. It is argued that GHG emissions cannot be assigned a monetary value. It is worth considering, then, whether the same argument should be held for other carbon pricing schemes such as a carbon tax or cap-and-trade system. If carbon pricing schemes are accepted in principle, the argument that carbon offsets do little to enact institutional behaviour change suggests that the price of (mandatory) offsets is simply not high enough to disincentivize emissions-producing behaviour.

Proponents of green growth argue that carbon emissions (and other environmental impacts) can be decoupled from economic growth, while others suggest that this is an illusion and ultimately we need to adopt some form of steady-state economy to avoid breaching fundamental ecological limits. This raises fundamental questions that go well beyond the carbon offsets issue. However, it could be argued that, if a limits to growth approach is in fact adopted, offsets may still be required to compensate for existing emissions.

The argument that offsetting projects in the Global South should not be pursued because they spur a "rebound" of development suggests that the Global South should not invest in increasing economic development because more emissions would be produced as a result. It also assumes that offsetting projects themselves cannot be an important part of overall sustainability strategies in the South. These arguments raise important international equity issues. They have given rise to a large literature on the international and intranational equity implications of various forms of environmental policy.

If offsets do not create the promised emissions reductions, they compromise the climate action plans of which they are a

part. Labelling carbon offsets as "indulgences" implies that carbon emitting is inherently bad. An alternative view is that many
emissions-producing activities, including flying, are not inherently
bad and should be acceptable if the emissions can be actually and
completely offset.

A working paper on carbon offsets for scientific societies by Kim
and Pierce (2018) recommends carbon offsets as a short-term or
partial strategy for climate mitigation by institutions. Four basic
criteria of robust carbon offsets are identified:

1 **Additionality**: It must be shown that emissions reduction
   projects would not have happened without the offset financing.
2 **Permanence**: Carbon offset projects must be guaranteed to
   remain in place and operational for the life cycle accounted for
   in emission reduction estimates. This is particularly important
   for projects to plant trees, where there is a risk they may be
   harvested prematurely.
3 **Absence of leakage**: It must be assured that emissions
   mitigated do not simply occur somewhere else, such as forest
   conservation resulting in a different forest being logged.
4 **Verification**: These criteria must be confirmed by an
   independent and credible authority.

VII. Ethics Applied to the Air Travel Emissions Mitigation Initiative at U of T

The U of T Air Travel Emissions Mitigation Initiative put forward
by U of T Operations and Real Estate Partnerships addresses many
of the ethical concerns found in the literature about carbon offsetting. Unlike other offset programs, it is designed to incentivize
lower-carbon behaviours and mitigate emissions by supporting
no-travel and low-carbon travel alternatives before imposing an
air travel charge. In addition, it is unlikely that there is any incentive to use the mitigation initiative as an excuse to continue air
travel because the university does not directly profit from air travel
for which it pays. However, it should be noted that international

travel is informally (and in some cases formally) viewed as an indicator of academic success. Reducing air travel therefore challenges institutional norms about academic careers.

The proposal aims to completely offset unavoidable air travel emissions wherever possible and recommends that quantified reduction targets for emissions are set. Such reduction targets could be a percentage of air travel emissions and they may need to be developed and adjusted as funding and availability of projects change. It is broadly acknowledged that emission reduction programs without quantified targets have a significantly lower impact because targets are needed to create emissions reduction strategies and to maintain accountability. If the proposal does not set targets to offset all or a high percentage of air travel emissions, there is a risk that it may become an ineffective climate action strategy.

VIII. Conclusion and Looking Forward

In the coming months, the following developments are expected on the three fronts.

1 **Quantifying air travel scope 3 emissions.** Student research highlighted the need for centralized and representative air travel records at the university to enable accurate calculation of GHG emissions from aviation. To pilot these efforts, the Air Travel Emissions Mitigation Program by University Operations and Real Estate Partnerships was set to collect travel data from the participating offices in 2020. To pilot these efforts, the Air Travel Emissions Mitigation Program by University Operations and Real Estate Partnerships collected travel data from the participating offices in 2020. Implementation of the pilot at the time of this writing. An internal information-collection infrastructure will be tested during this pilot with the help of the U of T Central Finance Team to test for eventual university-wide application. Nonetheless, an internal information collection infrastructure will be tested during this pilot with the help of the U of T

Central Finance Team to test for eventual university-wide application.

2 **Reducing business-related air travel.** The main focus of mitigating travel, at the moment, supports the development of virtual conferencing infrastructure at U of T. Through the continued support of collaborations with offices across campus, the CECCS hopes to create examples of a near-carbon-neutral conference at the U of T and demonstrate the capacity of the university's conferencing technology to increase adoption of such practices. Additionally, using sample conferences, the CECCS, together with conference organizers, will quantify emission savings from avoided travel. A report on learning and findings will be produced. Last, in light of the COVID-19 pandemic, more lectures, meetings, workshops, and conferences were held virtually. We hope to learn from this fast transition by developing a resource documenting best practices at the university that will have implications for future activities once pandemic-related travel restrictions are lifted.

3 **Developing an air travel emissions mitigation program.** The Air Travel Emissions Mitigation Initiative Pilot was approved retroactively from January 2020 until the end of the academic year in August 2020. While air travel data may vary from the initial January to June study plan as a result of the impacts of COVID-19 on air travel and university operations, this pilot is an important case study at U of T.

In closing, the CECCS supports strong action by U of T related to the mitigation of air travel scope 3 emissions. The committee recognizes that this will require a further investment of resources and raises important ethical issues that must be explicitly addressed. Some of the recommendations, particularly the trip reductions and the need to expand the infrastructure that enables the alternative arrangements, call for a cultural shift and support for the need to direct the appropriate level of resources for this considerable and noteworthy responsibility of the university. The COVID-19 pandemic may have started the conversation into rethinking what travel is necessary and what can be accomplished virtually.

Opportunities will arise to determine whether we will keep on this trajectory and reduce air travel or revert to our original pre-pandemic course.

ACKNOWLEDGMENTS

We would like to thank the students, faculty, and staff who engaged with the process to produce this work. We are also thankful for the cooperation and support received from the central administration at the University of Toronto to undertake this study.

The following people worked on the original Business Air Travel Report submitted to president Gertler at the University of Toronto:

CECCS committee and subcommittee members: Ahmed Azhari, Shamaila Bajwah, Aimy Bazylak, Lisa DeMarco, Steve Easterbrook, Aviatar Inbar, Paul Leitch, Shashi Kant, Bryan Karney, James MacLellan, Daniella Mallinick, Liat Margolis, Jan Mart-Smith, Fiona Miller, Jeffrey Miller, Jennifer Murphy, Derek Newton, David Roberts, Ron Saporta, Claire Westgate, John Robinson; Ayako Ariga and Dione Dias (lead)

CECCS research assistants: Rutu Patel (lead), Rashad Brugmann, Nicolas Côté, Meghan Henderson, Lauren McLachlan, and Peter Vuong

Other contributors: Adriana Dossena and Jennifer Puskar (Sustainability Office, St. George campus), and Andrea Muehlebach (associate professor, Department of Anthropology)

NOTES

1 This chapter draws from Office of the President (2020). CECCS research assistants who contributed directly to that report include Rutu Patel (lead), Rashad Brugmann, Nicolas Côté, Meghan Henderson, Lauren McLachlan, and Peter Vuong. Other contributors include Adriana Dossena and Jennifer Puskar (Sustainability Office, St. George campus), and Andrea Muehlebach (associate professor, Department of Anthropology).

2 Distribute 2020 was supported by the following people at University of Toronto: Andrea Muehlebach (Department of Anthropology) is a board

member of the Society for Cultural Anthropology and was a member
of a five-person organizing team distributed across five institutions in
three countries. Other important partners in this conference were John
Robinson and Dione Dias (CECCS), Avi Hyman, Peter Cheung, and James
McAllister (Academic and Collaborative Technology); Stephen Marks
(digital librarian, Robarts Library); Janice Boddy (chair, Anthropology);
Elizabeth Parke (Collaborative Digital Research Space, Office of the Vice-
Principal, Research, at University of Toronto, Mississauga); Kent Moore
(vice-principal, Research, UTM). Farzaneh Hemmasi (Faculty of Music)
and Margaret Wall (communications and research librarian, Robarts
Library) were also active in initial planning meetings.

3 This section on the Air Travel Emissions Mitigation Initiative stems from
the proposal created by the Sustainability Office, St. George campus,
under the direction of Ron Saporta (chief operating officer, Property
Services and Sustainability), and Kenneth Corts, during his term as
acting vice-president, Operations & Real Estate Partnerships Professional
Experience Program, with the support of the Tri-Campus Sustainability
Board.

REFERENCES

Anderson, K. (2012). The inconvenient truth of carbon offsets. *Nature, 484*(7),
7. https://doi.org/10.1038/484007a

Bachram, H. (2004). Climate fraud and carbon colonialism: The new trade in
greenhouse gases. *Capitalism Nature Socialism, 15*(4), 5–20. https://doi
.org/10.1080/1045575042000287299

Brown, V. (n.d.). *Carbon offsets do not work*. Responsible Travel. https://www
.responsibletravel.com/copy/carbon-offsets

Burian, I. (2018). *It is up in the air: Academic flying of Swedish sustainability
academics and a pathway to organisational change* [Master's thesis, Lund
University]. Lund University Libraries. https://lup.lub.lu.se/student
-papers/record/8947780

Cames, M.O., Harthan, R.M., Füssler, J., Lazarus, M., Lee, C., Erickson, P.,
& Spalding-Fecher, R. (2016). *How additional is the Clean Development
Mechanism?* Öko-Insitute.V.

Davies, J., & Dunk, R. (2016). Flying along the supply chain: Accounting for
emissions from student air travel in the higher education sector. *Carbon
Management, 6*, 1–14. https://doi.org/10.1080/17583004.2016.1151503

Dhanda, K.K., & Hartman, L.P. (2011). The ethics of carbon neutrality:
A critical examination of voluntary carbon offset providers. *Journal of*

Business Ethics, 100(1), 119–149. https://doi.org/10.1007/s10551-011
-0766-4

Friends of the Earth. (2009). *A dangerous distraction.* Friends of the Earth.
https://foe.org/resources/a-dangerous-distraction/

Kim, R., & Pierce, B.C. (2018, 24 June). *Carbon offsets: An overview for scientific
societies.* https://www.cis.upenn.edu/~bcpierce/papers/carbon
-offsets.pdf

Lewis, T. (2013). *A life cycle assessment of the passenger air transport system using
three flight scenarios* [Master's thesis, Department of Energy and Process
Engineering, Norwegian University of Science and Technology]. NTNU
Open. https://hdl.handle.net/11250/235319

Lovell, H. (2008, June). The ethics of carbon offsets. Presentation at Carbon
and Communities in Tropical Woodlands: International Interdisciplinary
Conference, Edinburgh.

Lovell, H.C. (2010). Governing the carbon offset market. *Wiley
Interdisciplinary Reviews: Climate Change, 1*(3), 353–362. https://doi.org
/10.1002/wcc.43

Lovell, H., Bulkeley, H., & Liverman, D. (2009). Carbon offsetting: Sustaining
consumption? *Environment and Planning A: Economy and Space, 41*(10),
2357–79. https://doi.org/10.1068/a40345

Maryanski, H. (2015, 1 February). *The ethics of carbon offsets.* Markkula Center
for Applied Ethics, Santa Clara University. https://www.scu.edu
/environmental-ethics/resources/the-ethics-of-carbon-offsets/

Office of the President. (2020). *2020 annual report of the President's Advisory
Committee on the Environment, Climate Change, and Sustainability (CECCS).*
https://www.president.utoronto.ca/2020-annual-report-of-the-presidents
-advisory-committee-on-the-environment-climate-change-and-sustainability
-ceccs/

Smith, K. (2007). *The carbon neutral myth: Offset indulgences for your climate
sins.* Carbon Trade Watch. http://www.carbontradewatch.org/pubs
/carbon_neutral_myth.pdf

United Nations. (2015, 12 December). Paris agreement to the United Nations
Framework Convention on Climate Change. TIAS no. 16-1104. https://
unfccc.int/sites/default/files/english_paris_agreement.pdf

Wynes, S., Donner, S.D., Tannason, S., & Nabors, N. (2019). Academic air
travel has a limited influence on professional success. *Journal of Cleaner
Production, 226,* 959–67. https://doi.org/10.1016/j.jclepro.2019.04.109

"University Responses to and Obligations for Business Air Travel Emissions"

KEVIN NILSEN
President and CEO, ECO Canada

In the face of climate change, organizations are pursuing initiatives to identify and reduce emissions within their sphere of control. Although governments are developing regulations and guidelines to regulate emissions, such initiatives often are not enough to make a tangible impact. This leaves the onus on progressive organizations to not only control their emissions but look to influence the behaviour of their stakeholders to make a measurable impact on their climate initiatives.

Traditionally, organizations have focused on their scope 1 and scope 2 emissions, and rightly so, as they have a greater control over their own activities. As Robinson and his team show clearly, scope 3 emissions, though, have their own challenges associated with indirect emissions, "not owned" by the organization. But if quantified and analysed credibly, these emissions could provide opportunities for significant reductions in the overall emissions.

Business travel, in particular air travel, is often one obvious target when organizations start looking at their scope 3 emissions. However, any such move needs to be carefully assessed both in terms of long-term impact on its business/operational sustainability and the overall economic and social environment where it operates. Pointing fingers and requiring one group to change its behaviour or make sacrifices is likely to have a negative impact as this leads to confrontation and opposition as opposed to generating clear win-win outcomes. The questions an organization should ask are:

1 Are there other emission sources that need to be considered, such as employee (or student) commuting, purchased goods and services, or even capital goods?
2 What are the potential long-term impacts of targeting a particular source of emission (e.g., can significant cuts in travel affect the long-term sustainability)?

In addition, organizations also need to consider the overall impact of the "substituted" activity (i.e., sustainability impact of the alternative activity that replaces the original source).

This chapter shows that academic institutions can minimize their emissions significantly by cutting down on "non-essential" air travel. Other institutions should pay heed to this message, recognizing that emissions overall, caused by travel as well as other energy sources, including even data centres for Teams/Zoom calls, need to be reduced. Finally, everyone could also benefit from working collaboratively with industry in reaching reduction goals. Canada's largest airline, Air Canada, has made bold commitments in its 2021 Sustainability Report to achieve net-zero GHG emissions by 2050 and invest $50M in sustainable aviation fuels and clean energy. A research and development partnership with the aviation industry could be a valuable and effective way of helping minimize scope 3 emissions at a global scale.

PART TWO

Pursuing Excellence and Integrity

chapter three

Resourcing the Pursuit of Academic Excellence

GORDON M. MYERS

The traditional mission of a research-intensive university is the growth and dissemination of knowledge. Success on that mission is important for the well-being of society. One could argue that "what we have learned," broadly defined, is all that separates us from our rather ignoble human past. In this way, resourcing the pursuit of academic excellence becomes important.

This chapter interprets the evolution of important elements in the governance of universities in terms of information asymmetries and the associated academic moral hazard inherent in the nature of universities. Universities face informational asymmetries associated with a lack of intellectual proximity of central administrators (e.g., the president and provost) to the state of the art in teaching and in research in the diverse intellectual disciplines of a modern university. I first build an understanding of information asymmetries to provide an explanation for the partitioning of universities by academic discipline, which began in the late nineteenth century (Cole, 2011). The recognition that no single person could accurately evaluate teaching and research across the breadth of the university made the partitioning necessary to allow the decentralization of academic authority from the president and provost down to the academic discipline level.

That understanding of informational asymmetries will also allow us to understand more recent developments in university budgeting. The traditional approach to university budgeting is incremental, a centralized top-down cost-based approach. The

last 40 years has seen some large research-intensive universities – for example, Harvard in the United States and the University of Toronto in Canada – move from incremental budgeting
to responsibility centre budgeting (RCB). RCB is a decentralized
cost- *and* revenue-based form of budgeting. It puts much more
financial responsibility in the hands of deans. In this way, at a
RCB university there is an alignment of academic authority and
financial responsibility that allows the university to avoid academic moral hazard. Informational asymmetries also allow us to
understand why RCB is successful in generating resources, why
adoption is often partial, and why it is more apt to be adopted
at large, complex, and research-intensive universities (Myers,
2019).

Information asymmetries will also be used to provide an explanation for why the recent trend to performance-based provincial
university grants may be a mistake and something universities
should be working to avoid. It will be argued that if there is an
information gap between a provost and an academic faculty
within the university, then there is an informational gulf between a
provincial government and that faculty. There are better ways for
a government to oversee university performance.

The chapter is organized as follows. The first section makes
the case that universities are about money – in particular, the
wise and responsible use of money in the pursuit of our mission.
The second section explains the inherent and serious asymmetric
information problem that exists in a university environment and
uses that to understand the decentralization of academic authority in a university. The third section describes the traditional
approach to university budgeting – incremental budgeting –
and the problems associated with it, such as March Madness.
It explains the problems as originating in the misalignment of
academic authority and financial responsibility and the resultant
moral hazard. The fourth section describes the recent rise of RCB
as a mechanism to deal with academic moral hazard. The fifth
section discusses the management of the provincial performance-
based grants at a RCB university, and the final section provides
some conclusions.

I. Budgeting Is about Money and Universities Are Not about Money

Consider a university academic administrator (e.g., the provost or dean) concerned with advancing the university's research and educational programs in the pursuit of academic excellence. In this pursuit there are choices: how many research professors versus lecturers versus student advisors versus research services staff to appoint. Within the research enterprise, there is the choice of prioritizing foundational research versus knowledge mobilization, among many others. Within the education enterprise, there are admission standards for applicants and the right continuation standard (retention rate) for enrolled students, to name two important choices.

These choices involve at least three distinct concepts: preferences, feasibility, and the choice. Preferences are about what the academic administrator wants to do. Is the administrator's preference all about great educational programs or all about research or a balance?[1] Feasibility is about what is possible. The preference may well be to hire the best researchers and educators in the world, but that may simply not be feasible. It is feasibility that forces trade-offs in an administrator's pursuit of academic excellence. Trade-offs always exist: for example, lower university admission standards with a given continuation standard trade off more revenue from more students, which can be used in pursuit of the mission, versus more students being unsuccessful once admitted. Lowering continuation standards trades off hurt for enrolled students against all the costs of graduating students who are not qualified, ultimately affecting the student, society, and institutional reputation.

Given a fixed amount of resources, there will be combinations of research quality and education program quality that are feasible. The administrator's preferences are then applied to the set of feasible combinations in generating the choice of the "best" combination. An important component of that choice process is budgeting. Budgeting determines the allocation of scarce resources to competing alternatives: for example, research versus the student education enterprise. Now imagine an exogenous increase of total resources. Compared to the best combination in the absence of the additional money, it should be possible to use the additional money to achieve a higher quality of both research and education and so do even better (e.g., more of both). Finally, in the more complicated case where an increase in resources is not exogenous, but comes instead from increasing a particular activity (e.g., lowering admission standards), the fundamental nature of the choice problem does not change – it is just that one activity becomes more desirable/less undesirable than previously, because it generates resources that can be used to achieve higher-quality research and educational programs.

Universities are not about money directly, but they are about money indirectly. Great universities are about the wise and responsible use of money in the pursuit of academic excellence. I will argue below that an understanding of asymmetric information, moral hazard, and mechanism design are important in achieving success.

II. Asymmetric Information and the Decentralization of Academic Authority

Consider the following simple principal-agent problem as an illustration of asymmetric information and moral hazard.[2] Imagine a nineteenth-century absentee agricultural landowner (the principal) who lives in London and owns land in Scotland. There are very limited modes of communication between London and Scotland and the owner does not want to leave London. The owner employs a farm worker to work the land (the agent). Like anyone, after some point, the worker prefers being in the local pub rather than exerting more effort picking rock in the fields. Further, the worker must receive a minimum salary to participate – that is, the worker must accept the employment contract. The crop yield depends on both worker effort and luck with the weather. If the crop yields are low and the worker claims that bad weather was the problem, given the lack of physical proximity, the landlord does not know whether that is true.

This is an environment of asymmetric information, as the worker knows her or his effort level and the owner does not. Monitoring is not possible or prohibitively costly, and the observed production does not fully reveal the effort due to the vagaries of weather or more generally the inherent uncertainty in the economic environment. Effort is hidden and so the moral hazard is that the worker can falsely claim to have worked hard. For the owner, the mechanism design question is, What type of labour contract would you write with the worker: an annual salary, land rental, or sharecropping?

Now consider the university environment. Professors at the state of the art in their discipline must do the teaching and research. That work requires local knowledge, effort, and trade-offs. The provost could try to monitor and provide oversight on academic decisions, but monitoring teaching and research is very difficult, if not impossible, not for lack of physical proximity, but for lack of intellectual proximity. For example, a provost who is not a biologist has little idea what a state-of-the-art fourth-year biology course looks like, let alone what a great young biologist looks like. The provost could devote a great deal of time and resources to find out, but in a year or two, that knowledge would be largely obsolete. The original partitioning of American universities by academic discipline in the late nineteenth century was connected to the realization that no single person could accurately evaluate teaching and research across the breadth of the university (Cole, 2011). In other words, it was connected to the inherent asymmetric information problem. Today we take that decentralization of academic authority as given.

III. Centralized Incremental Budgeting and Academic Moral Hazard

There are many sources of unrestricted revenues for Canadian universities. These include student tuition fees, provincial government operating grants, funding for indirect costs of research, gifts of unrestricted funds, investment income, and sales revenues from various sources such as student fees, rental from student residences, bookstores, athletic events, and so on. In 2017–18, Canadian governments contributed about $14 billion to Canadian universities (Statistics Canada, 2019). According to Statistics Canada, this is less than half of university total revenue. University budgeting then allocates these revenues to a wide variety of services and academic areas. There are the school/college/faculty (henceforth faculty) budgets. Then there are university-wide services such as finance, insurance, and legal services. Finally, there are expenditures on direct support services for the faculties such as academic facilities, the library, research services, fund raising, and student services. The budgeting question is how to allocate those resources in the pursuit of academic excellence and to advance the university mission.

The traditional approach to university budgeting is incremental. It is a centralized, top-down approach characterized by central control of all unrestricted revenue. For example, budget discussions between the provost and a faculty dean begin with the previous year's budget and then move away from that with incremental adjustments for new developments such as proposed new faculty positions or programs (Curry et al., 2014). Incremental budgeting has strengths, but one difficulty is that doing it well runs up against the asymmetric information discussed above.

In incremental budgeting, the difference between projected revenues and costs generates an expected pool of resources available for incremental adjustments. Faculties and administrative units make cases for resources in a system where there is no clear downside to requesting more. As a result, the pool is oversubscribed and must be rationed among incremental requests. For the provost to make the equitable and efficient allocation of those scarce resources, particularly among faculties, requires an intimate knowledge of departments as diverse as Physics, Philosophy, Engineering, and Music. How much does it cost to teach a good fourth-year course in business versus physics versus English versus music? What does great biology research look like? What are the right trade-offs? As usual, the asymmetric information will map directly into moral hazard. For example, when the head of an academic unit tells the provost that the appropriate curriculum in their discipline necessitates very small classes of very strong students, the administrator, when not a professor from that discipline, does not know whether that is true or simply the academic unit trying to avoid putting time and effort into teaching larger classes of more challenging students.

> In large, complex institutions like the University of Toronto, the president and his Administration had the authority to make specific decisions about the allocation of resources to colleges and faculties but sometimes did not have the requisite sapience (March) or proximity (Whalen) to do so because crucial plans and budgets were often divorced from the reality of scholarship and program delivery. (Lang, 2002, p. 192)

Further, given this severe informational challenge, one worries that units with academic leaders trained in advocacy (e.g., deans of law schools) or relatively experienced leaders (e.g., long-time professional administrators), or those with a lower opportunity cost of time (deans of small faculties), or simply the "bold" will do too well under incremental budgeting. Further, having a surplus at the end of the year could be taken as an indication of an inappropriately large "ask" at the beginning of the year, rather than prudence and cost control. This leads to "getting the money out the door" or "March Madness" spending. Rather than wanting to control costs, the administrative unit may want to fully spend a too-large budget in the hope of maintaining the large budget for the following year. More generally, incremental budgeting is about partially informed, small adjustments to a history-based budget. It could eventually be very far removed from the "right" budget.

IV. Responsibility-Centred Budgeting and the Aligned Decentralization of Financial Authority

In the agricultural example above, what is the right labour contract from the owner's perspective? The salary contract is one extreme, where the owner keeps the crop and pays a fixed salary to the worker. The rental contract is the other extreme, where the worker keeps the crop, and the landowner receives the fixed rental payment for the land. Intermediate is sharecropping, where the landlord and worker keep a share of the produced crop from the year. So, which is it?

First, assume that both the owner and worker are risk neutral.[3] Under a fixed salary, given the lack of monitoring and the costly effort, the worker does not have the incentive to work hard. It turns out that the solution to the landowner's incentive problem is to rent the land to the worker for a fixed payment with the worker keeping all production. The core of the intuition is that this mechanism makes the worker the *residual claimant*. The worker always incurs the full cost of the effort, but only in the rental case does the worker receive the full additional crop/benefit (i.e., the residual) from the additional effort, so only in this case will he or she choose the efficient level of effort in her or his self-interest – in other words, without any need for the owner to monitor effort.[4]

Now assume the more realistic case of a risk-averse worker. A significant problem with the pure rental contract is that in solving the incentive problem, the worker faces all of the risk – that is, the payment to the worker varies with the full swing of the good and bad weather. The problem for the self-interested owner is that, given the risk inherent in the payment, a risk-averse worker would demand a higher yielding (average) contract, that is, a lower rent for the worker's acceptance of the deal (participation). It then makes sense for the owner to take some share of the payment in the year's crop in sharing the risk of bad weather. This is sharecropping. It provides a balance between the owner's desire to provide the worker with the incentive to work hard and the owner's desire to accept some of the risk in lowering the average (expected) payment to the worker.

What is the university budget model (mechanism) that is analogous to the rental contract? Responsibility centre budgeting in its pure form is the analogue. Unlike incremental budgeting, which is cost based, RCB is both cost and revenue based. In its pure form, it assigns all unrestricted revenue directly to the faculties generating the revenues and then assigns both direct costs (e.g., faculty salaries) and indirect costs (e.g., students services or facility costs) to the faculties generating those costs. The assignment of all unrestricted revenue to the revenue/responsibility centres with fixed payments to the administration to cover facilities and other faculty support costs is the equivalent of a rental contract.

RCB has a history going back over 40 years, with early adopters being Harvard, the University of Pennsylvania, and the University of Southern California. Of universities currently employing RCB in Canada, the first to adopt a full RCB approach was the University of Toronto. It experimented with an RCB-type model at its Scarborough campus from 1997 and then went to a full model, in 2005–6. McMaster and Queen's University followed suit in 2013–14 period (Deering & Sá, 2014). In 2010, UBC implemented a model where faculties are partially paid by the revenue they generate. Simon Fraser University in BC began experimenting in 2011 and implemented a partial RCB in 2016–17. For a review of the literature on responsibility centre management, see Curry et al. (2014, chap. 4).

The adoption of an RCB approach at Canadian universities is accelerating, but it has not been quick or widespread. Further, most RCB implementations have been partial (Deering & Lang 2017), and there have been some pullbacks from pure RCB (Curry et al., 2014, p. 123). In fact, the first university to adopt RCB in Canada was the University of Lethbridge in 1993–94. It reverted to incremental budgeting a decade later. For a list of American universities using RCB as of 2013 see Curry et al. (2014) and for a list for North America, see Ziskin (2014). Consideration of the lists leads to the obvious empirical regularity that RCB is more apt to be employed at large, research-intensive, and complex universities (Curry et al., 2014, p. 123).

Myers (2019) formally models asymmetric information in a university and explains the rise of RCB as a mechanism designed to avoid academic moral hazard. RCB allows *aligned* decentralization of decision-making authority and financial responsibility to the faculty level, where the faculty makes the academic decisions but faces the university's financial realities. For example, the faculty chooses the effort to devote to research versus the effort to devote to teaching and revenue generation, but now while facing the financial consequences of those choices. As in the rental case, since the faculty always faces the cost of any additional effort generating resources for the university, it is only when the faculty receives the full additional benefit (MB) of their effort under pure RCB that they will make the efficient effort choice as the residual claimant. Further, a surplus at the end of the year becomes an indication of success generating revenue and prudence on expenditures, rather than budgetary malfeasance.

The article by Myers also shows that RCB interpreted as a mechanism designed to deal with academic moral hazard explains the empirical observations above. Only pure RCB (all revenue to faculties) fully solves the hidden effort problem through the full alignment of incentives. However, in a world of revenue uncertainty and risk aversion, RCB may not be for all universities, and partial RCB (less than 100% of the revenue risk being faced by the faculty) is what you would expect for almost all universities. Partial or impure RCB (like sharecropping) allows the administration to make the right trade-off between providing good incentives and sharing the revenue risk with the faculties. It also explains why the larger, more complex research-intensive universities are the RCB adopters. For example, small teaching-intensive two-year colleges simply do not face the serious asymmetric information and hidden effort problem that makes the adoption of RCB rational. Additionally, to the extent that wealth makes for lower risk aversion, we should expect universities with richer faculties such as Harvard's to employ "purer" RCB.[5] Finally, the pullbacks from pure RCB could be explained by a growing understanding that RCB is not for all universities (smaller, less-complex universities reverting to incremental) or by the revenue environment becoming more uncertain over time, for example, as universities come to rely more heavily on international student tuition.[6]

V. Dealing with Performance-Based Provincial Grants and Asymmetric Information

Canada has a long history of generous provincial grants in public support of universities. Grants can be block grants (unconditional) or performance based (conditional). The latter have become more important over the last 30 years so an important issue for Canadian universities is how to deal with performance-based provincial grants. According to (Lang, 2016), eight of ten provinces had some part of their university grants performance based in 2016. Further, Ontario is going through a major reconsideration of its university grant system to particularly promote differentiation within the university sector. Alberta is also moving more in the direction of performance funding.

There are many different types of performance grants that subsidize particular behaviours and outcomes, such as higher graduation rates or higher employment income of graduates (Lang, 2016). Some involve rewarding desired types of performance or sometimes bundles of desired performance and have budgets that are open ended (performance set-asides and bundled set-asides). Other grants have a fixed budget and provide shares of the budget to a university based on its relative performance on an indicator (competitive performance funding). There are also matching grants, which match funds raised by a university privately. Other grants are aimed at promoting "efficiency" (negative performance funding). How should a RCB university respond to performance-based grants?

First, universities should not take the nature of the performance-based grants as given. Every university has a government relations office, and most are members of government lobbying organizations (e.g., Universities Canada, COU in Ontario, or RUCBC in BC). These offices should be politely making the case to government that, if the government agrees that the mission of a province's universities is the growth and dissemination of knowledge, then they, with good oversight, should trust universities to fulfil that mission. A primary reason is that if there is an information gap due to a lack of intellectual proximity within a university, then there is informational gulf between a provincial government and a given university faculty or department. For example, in Ontario a significant share of grants has been based on student numbers with the per student grants across student types differentiated by the education "costs" per student (basic income units or BIUs). The

BIU weight on an engineering student, for example, is larger than the BIU weight on a philosophy student. The cost estimates for BIU were made over a half century ago and, even then, they were not different costs, they were estimates made by looking at different expenditures per student.[7] Governments do not know the costs of different programs and, in any case, they will vary across universities. A given university will have a sense of its faculties' relative costs, but only a sense.

Further, would any university leader want a temporary, national leader with particular political or personal views playing a central role in deciding desirable, long-term performance indicators for his or her university? If the answer is no, would some of our provincial government leaders be better? The oversight in every province involves government-appointed governors on university boards and academic external reviews, hopefully from the department or school level right up to the central level. Such arrangements make much more sense, in light of the dramatically reduced information asymmetry associated with an external professor or university administrator rather than an external provincial civil servant conducting the reviews.

What type of grant should universities be lobbying for? In other words, what is the nature of the "ideal" provincial government grant, from the university's perspective? The answer is an unconditional block grant. It is simply an amount of money that does not depend on any target or performance.[8] First, the size of the block grants can be chosen to promote equity across universities, such as according to relative size as measured by student numbers. Second, it allows the university to choose its own performance indicators – and notice that it could freely choose whatever indicators the government would have chosen. That option then means that block grants can never be worse, only better, than the government-chosen indicators, from the university's perspective.

For RCB universities, another element of "making the case" to governments can be in regard to the responsible nature of RCB management itself. Anyone who has worked in senior university administration has attended meetings of university, business, and government leaders, in which business leaders occasionally

complain about the "glacially slow" university, full of irresponsible "job-for-life" university professors. First, business leaders
are almost without exception not well informed about the "up or
out" nature of the tenure decision at a good university. For example, at the best universities, most assistant professors, after years
on a probationary contract, are not awarded tenure and so must
leave the university. Business leaders are also usually unaware
of the fact that RCB leads universities to be more responsive to a
changing environment than are most private sector organizations.
They need to be informed.[9]

Nevertheless, once the university's lobbyists have done their
best, there will almost certainly be performance-based provincial
grant structures. For example, the government may desire something other than research and education program excellence. Or
it might reasonably prefer more weight on teaching over research
than would most research-intensive university administrators.
How should a RCB university build the given performance-based
grants into its budgeting? It turns out the answer is simple. As
always, face the deans with the university's *actual* feasibility/bud-
get constraints and then leave it the deans with the local knowledge and academic authority to make the right trade-offs. If the
government offers the university more resources for undertaking some activity that is neutral with respect to the mission of the
university, look at the benefit in terms of providing additional
resources for the mission versus the opportunity cost of using the
time and energy on this activity rather than in directly pursuing
the mission. If the activity is counter to the mission, there will be an
additional cost beyond the opportunity cost of time and effort. Is
it possible that the optimal response for a university is to not pursue that revenue source at all? Universities are not directly about
money, so the answer is yes!

VI. Concluding Remarks

This chapter interpreted the decentralization of academic authority a century ago and more recent trends in university budgeting,

in terms of information asymmetries inherent in the nature of the universities. As discussed, universities face informational asymmetries associated with a lack of intellectual proximity of central administrators to the state of the art in teaching and in research in the diverse intellectual disciplines of a modern university. This meant that universities needed to be partitioned by academic discipline so that academic authority over, for example, appointments, tenure, and course design could be decentralized to the discipline. The chapter then argued that, once academic authority was decentralized, financial responsibility needed to be decentralized to align academic authority and financial responsibility in avoiding academic moral hazard. It was argued that the trend to responsibility centre budgeting over the last 40 years constitutes that decentralization. It puts much more financial responsibility in the hands of deans. It was shown how a deeper understanding of asymmetric information and mechanism design allows us to understand a number of empirical regularities in that evolution, such as why RCB is more apt to be adopted at larger, more complex, and more research-intensive universities.

The final section of the chapter used information asymmetries to argue that the recent trend to performance-based provincial university grants may be a mistake and something that universities should be lobbying to avoid. Given the informational "gulf" between a provincial government and particular academic departments at a provincial university, it was argued that there are better ways for a government to oversee university performance by placing its trust in the university itself, providing oversight by university boards, and in its own external performance evaluations.

NOTES

1 Of course, there could be a preference for having a very fancy office
   or funding an overly large bureaucracy, but this chapter will abstract
   from that generally unrealistic possibility and assume that academic
   administrators are focused on research and teaching. There is a potentially
   important paper to be written on how to appoint great academic

administrators. A very good provost from a very good university once told me that his job was largely done once he had great deans in place.

2 See Varian (1992, chap. 25) for a formal discussion of asymmetric information and moral hazard.

3 Risk neutrality is indifference to being allowed to play a lottery or receiving that lottery's expected value with certainty: for example, indifference to a lottery of $100 if a fair coin comes up heads and nothing if tails, and $50 with certainty.

4 The owner would want effort chosen such that the additional production/revenue generated from a bit more worker effort, or marginal benefit (MB), would equal the additional cost of a bit more effort to the worker or marginal cost (MC). The self-interested owner cares about the cost of the worker's effort to the worker because of the participation constraint. If MB was larger (smaller) than MC efficiency requires undertaking a bit more (less) effort to increase the "pie." This is the economically efficient level of effort, that is, the level that avoids waste and so maximizes the pie, that is, total product net of effort costs. The worker's participation constraint determines the division of the pie between owner and worker.

5 Harvard, with its large endowments, employs pure RCB with faculties largely financially independent. Another reason that there is usually some revenue held at the centre in RCB is to fund central strategic priorities. The president or provost, for example, may wish to support or build some particular research or education program strengths.

6 All of this, of course, should not be taken to imply that RCB is perfect budgeting. RCB is only half of the story within responsibility centre management. There are many important procedures surrounding RCB that are important in making RCB work well. For example, with RCB it is still important to provide oversight on the quality of programs and to provide incentives for interdisciplinary programming.

7 If I take a limo to work every day, that is a commuting expenditure, not the commuting cost. Further, why incentivize universities to attract expensive students? Why not incentivize universities to attract students who the government views as important to society's well being?

8 BC operating grants are, more or less, block grants. They do have student FTE targets associated with them, but within reason: being over or under target has no consequence.

9 If the business leaders are informed that a university uses RCB (which they will not know) and that RCB is the university-sector analogue to profit-centre budgeting (which they will know), their potentially damaging statements in front of government will become more muted.

REFERENCES

Cole, J.R. (2011). The great American university. *Bulletin of the American Academy of Arts and Science, 64*(3), 27–35.

Curry, J.R., Laws, A.L., & Strauss, J.C. (2014). *Responsibility center management: A guide to balancing academic entrepreneurship with fiscal responsibility.* National Association of College and University Business Officers.

Deering, D., & Lang, D.W. (2017). Responsibility center budgeting and management "lite" in university finance: Why is RCB/RCM never fully deployed? *Planning for Higher Education, 45*(3), 94–113.

Deering, D., & Sá, C.M. (2014). Financial management of Canadian universities: Adaptative strategies to fiscal constraints. *Tertiary Education and Management, 20*(3), 207–24. https://doi.org/10.1080/13583883.2014.919604

Lang, D.W. (2002). Responsibility center budgeting and management at the University of Toronto. In D.M. Priest, D.W. Becker, D. Hossler, & P. St. John (Eds.), *Incentive-based budgeting systems in public universities* (pp. 109–36). Edward Elgar.

Lang, D.W. (2016). Incentive funding meets incentive-based budgeting: Can they coexist? *Canadian Journal of Higher Education, 46*(4), 1–22. https://doi.org/10.47678/cjhe.v46i4.186434

Myers, G.M. (2019). Responsibility center budgeting as a mechanism to deal with academic moral hazard. *Canadian Journal of Higher Education, 49*(3), 13–23. https://doi.org/10.47678/cjhe.v49i3.188491

Statistics Canada. (2019, 24 July). Financial information of universities and degree-granting colleges, 2017/2018. *The Daily.* https://www150.statcan.gc.ca/n1/daily-quotidien/190724/dq190724a-eng.htm

Varian, H.R. (1992). *Microeconomic analysis* (3rd ed.). Norton.

Ziskin, M. (2014). *HEQCO project on outcomes-based funding of higher education.* Draft report, Indiana University Project on Academic Success. March.

"Resourcing the Pursuit of Academic Excellence"

ESTHER BERGMAN
Performance Improvement Consultant with Benchmark Performance Inc. and World Class Productivity Inc.

There are clear parallels between resourcing university excellence through responsibility centre budgeting, and efforts aimed at excellent work performance in the corporate world via decentralized resourcing and accountability. In typical decentralized structures, accountability for use of resources (including people and budgets) shifts to the local level, to give greater control over strategy and results.

Ironically, *decentralized* accountability for people's work performance continues to offer less than stellar results, underscoring the need for additional, *centralized* resources and support systems.

We have seen department leaders set objectives aligned with organizational goals, only to struggle to get people to change what they do or how they do it. There are several reasons for such outcomes. For example, leaders may be too far removed from day-to-day work to identify who and what needs to change. They may lack rapport and objectivity to uncover truthful root causes of current behaviours. Leaders may have biases or predispositions around types of interventions and may lack the cross-functional influence to innovate.

Finally, leaders may lack the skills or resources to identify performance gaps in team or role performance and to bring about the needed change.

Effective leaders address some performance gaps from within their own team. Most leaders will get stronger results with support provided by skilled performance analysts and experts who help reframe the problem, gather insights, and find interventions that address drivers of people's performance. This assistance would generally come from a centralized/shared service.

Responsibility centre budgeting at universities shows the importance of allocating accountability to relevant decentralized units. It is important to realize that, as decentralized frameworks evolve at universities and elsewhere, adequate and appropriate support systems should be made available to local units. Those support systems would include experts who can help define performance gaps, recommend interventions at multiple levels and across multiple functions, and see those interventions through to implementation.

chapter four

Aspiring to the Transformational: Building upon a Holistic Approach to Academic Integrity in Higher Education

EMMA J. THACKER

Introduction

Academic institutions thrive on the strength of their role in creating and sharing knowledge. This central role requires that academic integrity define, in an essential way, the research, teaching, and learning fabric of universities – a fabric that is social and political, and interwoven with both local and global power structures. Academic integrity is often used concurrently with the term "academic misconduct." However, they are two separate yet intertwined concepts. Academic integrity speaks to the behaviours and values behind the literacies, scholarly pursuits, and pedagogy of our education systems. In contrast, academic misconduct is an intentional behaviour to undermine this integrity.

To complicate matters, there is the grey area of unintentional or inadvertent academic misconduct, often in the form of plagiarism, brought about by novice writers and newcomers engaging in various forms of academic discourse and assessment. This contested notion of intention, sometimes understood in terms of a "plagiarism continuum" (Sutherland-Smith, 2008, p. 5), is critical to unpacking the complexities of academic misconduct. Educational institutions and their appointed leaders are responsible for ensuring that academic integrity is supported and upheld. Further, those in positions of leadership must be aware of systemic and local issues that challenge faculty and students to uphold the mission of the university. With this awareness comes the responsibility to plan, continually assess, and implement strategies to support an ongoing culture of academic integrity. Without these strategies, the reputation and wellness of institutions, the student experience, and the quality of education and research itself are at risk.

This chapter argues that central to any notion of ethical leadership is the preservation and enhancement of academic integrity. As I intend to show, the matter is more complex than it originally appears, requiring a holistic perspective to ensure that initiatives to preserve academic integrity are truly transformational.

I. Background

Academic integrity and misconduct have been an interdisciplinary focus of study for several decades. More recently, there has been a notable increase of research in the Canadian context (Eaton et al., 2019). Although the COVID-19 pandemic has amplified academic misconduct and brought attention to contentious methods of responding to the issues, such as online proctoring (Langenfeld, 2020), these are not new concerns. Academic misconduct and corruption have persisted for as long as academic institutions have existed (Bertram Gallant, 2008).

Over the past 30 years, research and scholarship have generated a body of work to help us to understand academic misconduct and integrity. For example, studies have helped to explain why students cheat (McCabe et al., 2012). In addition, research has provided insight into the different types of misconduct, such as plagiarism (Carroll, 2013), contract cheating (Clarke & Lancaster, 2006), and collusion (Sutherland-Smith, 2013). Pedagogical considerations, such as how assessment type factors into misconduct (Ellis et al., 2019) and attitudes about cheating (Rodhiya et al., 2020), have also been examined.

Scholars have sought to determine what measures may be implemented to reduce cheating, such as honour codes (McCabe et al., 1999) and text-matching software (Kaktiņš, 2019). Scholars have also explored the many drivers that influence misconduct in higher education, such as academic integrity policy (Bretag et al., 2011), the commercialization of academia (Brimble, 2016; Kezar & Bernstein-Sierra, 2016), and the shift to an increasingly digital education landscape (Deranek & Parnther, 2015). Understanding the influence of technology (Bruton & Childers, 2015) and social media (Lancaster, 2019) on academic integrity is critical, especially as higher education shifts further into the online space in response to the COVID-19 pandemic. The growing body of work on integrity and misconduct continues to expand, and it continues to significantly increase the knowledge available to faculty, staff, and leadership to interpret the complex and evolving issues.

Increasingly, scholars and practitioners are taking a more critical, theoretical approach to academic integrity. This approach has included consideration of academic integrity as a social construct, arguing that cases must be "situated in context" (Price, 2002, p. 88). One can also find academic literacies (Magyar, 2012) and digital literacies (Pfannenstiel, 2010) perspectives in the literature, which view student writing and plagiarism as a literacy practice (McKenna & Hughes, 2013; Valentine, 2016) and socially situated (Barton et al., 2000; Street, 1995). The academic literacies lens moves away from a deficit model of literacy, which attributes academic integrity to a learned skill set, and misconduct as a lack thereof. These critical perspectives frame academia as a complex social institution and provide an opportunity to examine misconduct while paying attention to a student's identity, which is culturally and historically contextualized. Further, epistemological notions regarding writing in the academy allow for rigorous questions about dominant traditions of assessment and knowledge making. These questions provide space to consider who is advantaged and disadvantaged by pedagogical choices made in the academy, and around student expectations.

For example, it is often assumed that disciplinary discourse is stable and that higher education structures are homogenous across institutions and regions. Yet, student migration often requires acculturation to another educational system or community. Students must rapidly build competencies surrounding new models of author attribution, assessment, educational technology, and disciplinary writing. Acculturation takes time and requires the navigation of a new dominant culture, all of which affect engagement and outcomes. All students bring their familiar educational literacy practices with them to higher education, yet some of them are marginalized, or less valued, and may carry less cultural capital (Bourdieu, 1986). Assessments require that students understand more than "surface features of text," such as grammar and spelling (Lea & Street, 2006, p. 369); they must develop assessment literacy (Douglas Smith et al., 2013).

The significance of this body of research, both theoretical and practical, can be measured by the current academic integrity scholars' and practitioners' call to action. The rallying cry is for a holistic institutional approach to address academic misconduct and support academic integrity (Bertram Gallant, 2008; Bretag, 2013; East, 2009; Macdonald & Carroll, 2006). Although this call to action has been heard and echoed by academic integrity experts, researchers in the field, and several national quality assurance agencies (e.g., Quality Assurance Agency for Higher Education, UK), I remain concerned that it seems to have been largely unheard or dismissed by academic leadership and senior administration.

Perhaps lack of attention to academic integrity is related to the prioritization of other pressing issues. For example, many Canadian institutions are focused on addressing student mental health. Student mental health challenges are increasing (COU, 2018), requiring that institutions collaborate with their communities to address access to services. This issue certainly is of critical importance yet may not be unconnected to academic integrity approaches. The literature regarding student mental health and academic integrity is in early stages (Eaton & Turner, 2020; Tindall & Curtis, 2020; Seto, 2020); however, the connections between stress and academic performance have been explored (Ip et al., 2016), including student wellness related to allegations of misconduct (Pitt et al., 2020), confirming the importance of student services and supports as part of an approach to addressing academic integrity.

The COVID-19 epidemic also has pointed to the interconnectedness of the wellness of the institution, its stakeholders, and academic integrity (Eaton, 2020a). The need to focus on academic integrity has therefore never been greater. An institutional approach that will encompass both pedagogy and curriculum and hold regard for other institutional obligations and matters of individual and collective wellness in higher education is critical. This approach is often referred to as "holistic," and although the existing descriptions of the term in the literature have advanced this important discussion, I would argue that to enable stronger uptake from leadership on academic integrity, the scope of a holistic approach must not only be clarified, but also expanded to be transformative.

II. Approaches to Academic Misconduct

Before exploring more about a holistic approach, let us consider some of the dominant approaches to supporting academic integrity and responding to misconduct. Broadly, approaches can be categorized as preventive or responsive. Many institutions use detection as a strategy – for example, the use of text-matching software (Weber-Wulff, 2016), or online exam proctoring tools (Langenfeld, 2020). Faculty discovery and judgment of potential misconduct is also central to the detection approach. In the literature, one can find reference to punitive approaches that typically enact policy to discipline students with penalties when breaches occur (Stoesz et al., 2019). The punitive approach is often quasi-judicial, with sanctions ranging from grade reductions to expulsion. Consequences can also include educative elements, such as attendance at a citation workshop. Sanctions can also be seen as a deterrent, as can legal approaches, such as legislation to regulate the business of commercial contract cheating (Draper & Newton, 2017).

A contrasting, preventive strategy focuses on teaching and learning and emphasizes educational strategies and pedagogy to reduce misconduct (Bertram Gallant, 2008). This proactive approach shifts some responsibility onto the institution, to provide supports, education, and appropriate teaching and learning environments. It acknowledges that students do not arrive with clear knowledge of academic conventions and strategies for success (e.g., time management), and the institution accepts some role in providing this training. Some educative strategies include the offering of academic integrity modules, faculty development, and the inclusion of academic integrity learning outcomes within courses and programs.

The academic integrity movement has long emphasized morals and values (Fishman, 2015) and leaned on the development of students' character as a key to enhancing an institution's culture of integrity. For instance, the use of honour codes (McCabe et al., 1999) and the wide adoption of the International Centre for Academic Integrity's (ICAI) "fundamental values" (ICAI, 2021) into academic integrity policies (Stoesz et al., 2019) are salient examples of this approach. Although ethical awareness and decision-making are critical to research and scholarship, the discourse around student morality as it relates to student misconduct may be limiting (Kaposi & Dell, 2012).

Plagiarism was not always linked to an ethical discourse with moral binaries. Yet, the underlying punitive principals found within academic integrity policy (Stoesz et al., 2019) create little space for students to learn the nuanced practices of writing and citation without consequence (Valentine, 2006). Applying a moralistic standard to the multitude of types of misconduct is problematic when it is known there is a conduct continuum (Sutherland-Smith, 2008), and that students do not come into academic institutions with the same intersectionality or "social location" (Crenshaw, 1991). Students may bring differing value systems and world views, understandings of academic customs, and literacy practices to the classroom. Whilst ethical considerations do buttress academic misconduct policy and process, histories and contexts that guide decision making should be acknowledged.

III. The Holistic Approach in the Literature

The holistic approach to academic integrity considers policy, consequences, teaching and learning, pedagogy, deterrence, and detection as integral to the academic integrity landscape. However, this approach is more than multi-pronged – it is dynamic and considers the *whole* – the whole person/s, interconnected systems, and structures in higher education. Several experts in the field have provided descriptions and direction to support the development of this approach.

Macdonald and Carroll's (2006) call for a holistic institutional approach has a focus on teaching and learning. They note that education must include the teaching of skills and information for students to complete their academic requirements. They stress the importance of appropriate assessment and curriculum design, with support from educational developers. In their view, a holistic institutional approach reflects a shared responsibility for the issue of academic misconduct and leads with a "principled, evidence informed approach" (p. 234). Behind these ideas is the acknowledgment that students do not arrive at their institutions adequately prepared, and that the university must collectively take responsibility to move students to a place where they are aware of the scholarly conventions required for progression with success.

Sutherland-Smith (2008) calls for critical engagement, whereby each university takes responsibility to review, scrutinize, regularly revisit, and update its approach. Institutions must also consider if and how they demonstrate their commitment to academic integrity, share the responsibility between staff, students, and the institution, and ensure that initiatives are prioritized. For Sutherland-Smith, prioritization means funding for educative initiatives to ensure that students have the appropriate skills, and that faculty and staff have the resources and developmental opportunities to take on their portion of the shared responsibility. A university-wide, holistic approach to plagiarism and misconduct also takes into consideration pedagogy and "transformative teaching practices" (p. 198). Critical reflection and a collaborative "challenging of the status quo," Sutherland-Smith advocates, is needed for real change (p. 199).

Bretag's (2013) view of a holistic approach similarly embraces the intentional inclusion of integrity into all aspects of the campus, involving multiple stakeholders. Strategically crafted mission statements, careful admissions processes, apposite policy development, appropriate use of technology, academic skills education, course assessment and judicious curriculum design are all important elements of a broader planning process. Bretag's definition suggests that academic integrity education and support must be embedded within curriculum but also in training and development initiatives for staff and faculty.. Bretag points to a campus culture in which plagiarism "is a symptom of a deeply entrenched academic culture that arguably places tangible rewards (grades, diplomas, publications, promotions, grants) above the intrinsic value of learning and knowledge creation" (p. 2). She calls for an approach that focuses on more than just detection and consequence, but one that fosters the development of a "scholarly community" (p. 3) with shared academic values. Bretag points to the "decades of research that has provided evidence" (p. 2) from which institutions can draw to develop a holistic strategy.

Morris and Carroll (2016) note the importance of resources and a long-term commitment to academic integrity from members across the institution, in particular from senior managers. They note that "connected strategies" (p. 1) involving staff, faculty, students, and the administration that develop and engage a shared understanding are essential, pointing out that "the actions of one group influence the choices of others" (p. 453). They even point to external stakeholders, such as quality assurance specialists, who can play a role in the creation and maintenance of these strategies. They also highlight the opportunity to leverage the policy review process to engage the academic community, and the need for each individual institution to understand its unique context and student body.

Bertram Gallant has written at length on an organizational theory (Bertam Gallant & Drinan, 2006) and systems approach to effect change around academic misconduct and shift an institution's focus to a more robust environment of teaching and learning (Bertram Gallant, 2011). She notes that for institutional change to occur, institutions must confront broader factors, such as "structures, systems, relationships and governance" (Bertam Gallant & Drinan, 2006, p. 841). Bertram Gallant and Drinan argue for holistic strategies "that call for leadership at the highest level of the educational organization and the institution of higher learning" (p. 857) that will "institutionalize academic integrity" (p. 854) and integrity systems within the organization.

Several other scholars make related, salient points. Chankova (2020) argues that the student perspective must be taken into account. East (2009) notes the importance of the alignment of policy with curriculum and highlights a strategy to constructively align academic integrity practices with student learning outcomes. Saddiqui (2016) discusses the importance of clearly defining the institutional stakeholders (both internal and external) and their roles and responsibilities, for better participation and implementation. Serviss (2016) considers faculty development as critical to changing the wellness and integrity culture on campus. She suggests that a holistic approach moves beyond punitive strategies and "brings together data-driven research about student development with identified sites of pedagogical intervention and potential methods (workshops, curriculum redesign, etc.) for engaging faculty" (p. 563). This faculty development perspective brings together teaching, learning, pedagogy, policy, and process, to engage the entire campus academic community. Building on this body of work and the various interpretations of "holistic," let me propose an expanded definition through a discussion of several aspects of higher education less explicitly or commonly understood as linked to academic integrity. This expanded view will, with greater intention, weave equity and inclusion into the approach.

IV. Expanding the Definition

A holistic institutional approach accepts that academic misconduct cannot be reduced to one explanation, and that there is no single, universalizing solution. A complex issue will necessarily require a comprehensive, ongoing response that must take the social, cultural, and human context into account when assessing both the transgression and the repercussions. An expanded definition must acknowledge that our educational systems are not value neutral – they breathe with privilege and power relations and are connected to larger sociocultural practices and institutions. The 2019 American admissions scandal exemplifies this fact (Kates, 2019). To enhance the definition provided by scholars in the field, I will expand upon several issues that require more discussion, all of which share an equity and inclusion theme: precarious academic work, educational development, and the transformative model to teaching and learning.

A. Precarious Academic Work

Long-standing systemic issues of inequity emerge when addressing academic integrity with a critical perspective. For instance, the casual and precarious nature of some faculty hires presents unique challenges (Crossman, 2019; Gagné, 2020a; Walker & Townley, 2012). The "last-minute" nature of part-time faculty work has its consequences for students and faculty (Riaz, 2020). Last-minute teaching contracts mean that part-time faculty are often without the curriculum resources they need, and newer faculty may lack a basic awareness of institutions' processes and practices, leaving instructors to navigate academic integrity on their own.

Research tells us that a students' satisfaction with their teaching and learning environment is a critical variable in some cheating behaviours (Bretag et al., 2019). How part-time faculty are treated and disadvantaged has an impact on the institution, the instructor, and the student experience (Bertram Gallant, 2018). Part-time faculty face barriers in reporting academic integrity issues, such as the additional time commitment and stress. The demands to support academic misconduct processes are often outside part-time contract timelines (Crossman, 2019). Assessment revision and the implementation of high-impact practices related to academic integrity may also fall outside of a part-time teaching role and contract.

Bringing forward breaches of integrity places precarious instructors in a position to upset students, when student evaluations influence the movement into full-time roles, forcing part-time faculty to consider the cost-benefit ratio of turning a blind eye, or managing the incident themselves, which Riaz (2020) argues is even more precarious for Black, Indigenous and People of Colour (BIPOC) instructors. Crossman (2019) notes that for a holistic approach to be effective, the plight of contract faculty and their precarious position must be addressed. She argues that "[a] holistic approach to academic integrity in higher education requires a concerted and integrated effort of all stakeholders across campus, yet the tiered faculty system of most institutions may be at odds with comprehensive approaches" (p. 1).

Eaton (2020b) explained in her review of the intersection of precarious academic employment and the contract cheating industry that attention needs to be paid to an "educational system that propagates precarious academic employment, and its industry counterpart, the commercial contract cheating companies that further exploit unemployed and underemployed academics" (p. 5). Among other suggestions, she recommends that institutions improve their support and commitment to teaching staff, including payment for all "legitimate academic labour," and "increased labour protections" (p. 7). I argue that this support and commitment must also include an equity lens and extend to the consideration of the faculty hiring framework and its associated policies and practices. The landscape of faculty work and the instability of academic employment for non-tenured faculty can be addressed only through collaborative and ethical leadership.

B. Educational Development

In Ontario, Canada, the Quality Assurance Framework (QAF) provides guidance and protocols on degree program development, program modification, and cyclical program review (OUCQA, 2019). The accompanying QAF guide and resources include information on curriculum and assessment design, curriculum mapping, and the development of learning outcomes. Academic integrity scholars and practitioners are calling for the intentional integration of these quality assurance practices, some of which are provincially mandated, with academic integrity initiatives (Gallant & Drinan, 2008; McKenzie, 2018). Centres for Teaching & Learning (CTL) often play a role in these activities, and include educational developers who support quality assurance and provide faculty development, especially on curricular change, and teaching innovation.

CTLs are shaped by their institutions' culture and priorities. More recently, some CTLs include education developers who specialize in academic integrity (e.g., University of Calgary, University of Manitoba) who can implement and embed academic integrity considerations into curricular enhancement activities and processes. For example, curriculum mapping exercises can include the mapping of academic integrity learning outcomes, which are found, for example, in the QAF and the Canadian Degree Qualifications Framework (CMEC, 2007). Faculty professional development can include academic integrity focused instruction on course and assessment design and the implementation of high-impact practices to reduce misconduct opportunities across the disciplines and across modes of delivery. Another increasingly critical element regarding the service of educational developers is their role in supporting inclusive pedagogies and Universal Design for Learning (UDL) (Sanger, 2020). Inclusive and accessible learning environments contribute to increased student engagement, and more satisfaction with the teaching and learning environment.

Research points to a distinct growth in the mission of the Canadian CTL in "playing a larger role in issues of policy and strategy related to teaching and learning" (Forgie et al., 2018, p. 9), although whether this growth includes the proliferation of a robust role specific to academic integrity remains to be seen. Moving from supporting course and assessment design, to using inclusive and UDL frameworks to support academic integrity holds a transformative promise, although this evolution of the CTL structure must be seen as a priority by university leadership and administration to flourish. I have observed that the disconnect between offices of quality assurance, academic integrity, and the CTL is not uncommon. Educational developers are often untapped academic integrity champions in the landscape of academic integrity; however, the COVID-19 pandemic did showcase the critical role of the CTL during the quick pivot to online program delivery (Eaton, 2020c; Gagné, 2020b).

C. Transformational Teaching and Learning

A transformational teaching approach helps to address some of the contributing factors that lead to breaches of misconduct, such as student dissatisfaction with the teaching and learning environment (Bretag et al., 2019), low engagement, and perceptions of unfairness (Owunwanne et al., 2010). Several common teaching strategies, such as active learning, student-centred learning, authentic learning, collaborative learning, experiential learning, and problem-based learning, all fall under the transformational approach (Slavich & Zimbardo, 2012). The basic principles of transformational teaching as defined by Slavich and Zimbardo are (1) to facilitate students' acquisition and mastery of key course concepts; (2) to enhance students' strategies and skills for learning and discovery; and (3) to promote positive learning-related attitudes, values, and beliefs in students (p. 581). Transformational teaching and learning should be active, social, and shaped with and by the students, improving student responsibility for the outcomes of their learning process.

Transformative teaching provides an opportunity to address the roots of plagiarism (Colella & Alahmadi, 2019; Sutherland-Smith, 2008). Sutherland-Smith (2008) rightly suggests that "[as] part of their transformative pedagogical approach, teachers assume a joint responsibility with students and the institution for enabling students to understand plagiarism" (p. 147). One strength of this approach as it relates to plagiarism is that students are expected to adopt a critical stance on their own learning, making broader connections to their lives outside of the academic institution. Transformative teaching also provides an authentic framework for what is being taught and the work that students complete for assessments, and ultimately grades. Transformational approaches allow for real engagement with concepts and the development of a true understanding of why academic integrity matters to their field of study or to themselves. This is counter to a transactional, or "banking" (Freire, 1970) model of learning. Although the choice of teaching approach typically lies with each faculty member and depends upon the discipline and curriculum, teaching approaches still rely upon available resources and reflect an institution's culture and priorities. For example, the CTL has a role in faculty development with teaching approaches, and institutional leadership has a role in decision-making on the design and build of learning environments (e.g., active learning classrooms), as well as class size.

V. Discussion

Addressing academic misconduct and cultivating academic integrity must consider the big picture, while paying attention to context. Although this chapter does not problematize the holistic approach, I propose additional characteristics and expectations of academic leadership, to aspire to a "transformational approach." This approach requires an institution to confront the dominant and privileged systems in higher education, when considering how to strengthen various pathways to support academic integrity and reduce misconduct of all kinds. Such a strategy acknowledges that institutions cannot work alone and must collaborate within the university through interconnected strategies and mandates, across several service units (e.g., CTLs, libraries, governance), and externally, with other institutions and stakeholder associations. This will also include confronting long-standing equity issues, such as racism, access, and gender equity.

A transformational approach includes the tenets of a holistic approach – policy revision, detection and deterrence, fair consequences, and education – but also leverages a commitment to equity and inclusion. I also assert that if a transformational approach is to include equitable and inclusive pedagogy, it should reconsider some aspects of detection, such as digital surveillance to detect and deter academic misconduct. Some have argued that online proctoring systems are biased, invade privacy, and erode a student's trust in the university (Stewart, 2020). We must not divorce approaches to academic integrity from other strategic and academic plans, such as student success, internationalization, responding to the Truth and Reconciliation Commission of Canada (TRC, 2015), or initiatives to support equity, diversity, and inclusion. These are all interconnected frameworks, and they are strategies that scaffold to create an inclusive educational space.

Furthermore, educative approaches need to be created and emphasized with an awareness of colonial history and inclusive practices for all learners. Our colonial history affects students unequally and has an impact on the integrity of the campus fabric. For example, the meaningful social inclusion of Indigenous peoples in higher education is critical for Indigenous peoples to achieve educational success (Pidgeon, 2016) and for the overall wellness of our communities and academic institutions. Indigenous approaches are just one example of several inclusive frameworks that can help inform what academic integrity is or could look like in an institution (see Gladue, 2020). For example, an educational strategist at the University of Toronto created an Indigenous academic integrity resource titled "Seven Grandfathers in Academic Integrity" (Maracle, 2020). Transformational approaches can ameliorate the tension between the student experience and teaching practice.

VI. Conclusion

Development of an institutional, transformational strategy will be challenging and iterative. Leaders and all other stakeholders must support this notion if genuine success is to be achieved. Dominant approaches, such as the punitive and detection models, have been insufficient to address the factors that lead to breaches of academic integrity. Although educational initiatives and policy are necessary and practical, they have limitations when not all students and faculty feel included and engaged in the learning community. What is needed is support from leadership and a willingness to adapt antiquated structures as the academy evolves and respond ethically to changes in the local and global higher education landscape. The transformational approach is offered to cultivate a strong foundation of support across stakeholders to not only reduce academic misconduct, but also to inspire essential transformation within higher education. The strength of this approach lies in its commitment to learning and equity and having all voices in the discussion come together to support the university mission.

REFERENCES

Barton, D., Hamilton, M., & Ivanic, R. (2000). *Situated literacies: Reading and writing in context*. Routledge.

Bertram Gallant, T. (2008). *Academic integrity in the twenty-first century: A teaching and learning imperative*. Jossey-Bass.

Bertram Gallant, T. (2011). *Creating the ethical academy: A systems approach to understanding misconduct and empowering change in higher education*. Routledge.

Bertram Gallant, T. (2018). Part-time integrity? Contingent faculty and academic integrity. *New Directions for Community Colleges, 183*, 45–54. https://doi.org/10.1002/cc.20316

Bertram Gallant, T., & Drinan, P. (2006). Organizational theory and student cheating: Explanation, responses, and strategies. *Higher Education, 77*(5), 839–60. https://doi.org/10.1353/jhe.2006.0041

Bourdieu, P. (1986). The forms of capital. In J.G. Richardson (Ed.), *Handbook of theory and research for the sociology of education* (pp. 241–58). Greenwood Press.

Bretag, T. (2013). Challenges in addressing plagiarism in education. *PLoS Medicine, 10*(12), 1–3. https://doi.org/10.1371/journal.pmed.1001574

Bretag, T., Harper, R., Burton, M., Ellis, C., Newton, N., Rozenberg, P., Saddiqui S., & van Haeringen, K. (2019). Contract cheating: A survey of Australian university students. *Studies in Higher Education, 44*(11), 1837–56. https://doi.org/10.1080/03075079.2018.1462788

Bretag, T., Mahmud, S., Wallace, M.C., Walker, R., James, C., Green, M., East, J., McGowan, U., & Partridge, L. (2011). Core elements of exemplary academic integrity policy in Australian higher education. *International Journal for Educational Integrity, 7*(2), 3–12. https://doi.org/10.21913/IJEI.v7i2.759

Brimble, M. (2016). Why students cheat: An exploration of the motivators of student academic dishonesty in higher education. In T. Bretag (Ed.), *Handbook of academic integrity* (pp. 365–82). https://doi.org/10.1007/978-981-287-098-8_58

Bruton, S., & Childers, D. (2015). The ethics and politics of policing plagiarism: A qualitative study of faculty views on student plagiarism and Turnitin®. *Assessment & Evaluation in Higher Education, 41*(2), 316–30. https://doi.org/10.1080/02602938.2015.1008981

Carroll, J. (2013). *A handbook for deterring plagiarism in higher education*. Oxford Centre for Staff and Learning Development.

Chankova, M. (2020). Teaching academic integrity: The missing link. *Academic Ethics, 18*, 155–73. https://doi.org/10.1007/s10805-019-09356-y

Clarke, R., & Lancaster, T. (2006, 19–21 June). Eliminating the successor to plagiarism: Identifying the usage of contract cheating sites. Proceedings of the Second International Plagiarism Conference.

Colella, J., & Alahmadi, H. (2019). Combatting plagiarism from a transformational viewpoint. *Transformative Learning, 6*(1), 59–67. https:// jotl.uco.edu/index.php/jotl/article/view/184/154

Council of Ministers of Education, Canada (CMEC). (2007). Ministerial statement on quality assurance of degree education in Canada. https:// www.cmec.ca/Publications/Lists/Publications/Attachments/95 /QA-Statement-2007.en.pdf

Council of Ontario Universities (COU). (2018). Ensuring a whole-of -community approach to mental health. https://ontariosuniversities.ca /wp-content/uploads/2018/01/COU_Ensuring-a-Whole-of-Community -Approach-to-Mental-Health.pdf

Crenshaw, K.W. (1991). Mapping the margins: Intersectionality, identity politics, and violence against women of color. *Stanford Law Review, 43*(6), 1241–99. https://doi.org/10.2307/1229039

Crossman, K. (2019). Is this in my contract? How part-time contract faculty face barriers to reporting academic integrity breaches. *Canadian Perspectives on Academic Integrity, 2*(1), 32–39. https://doi.org/10.11575 /cpai.v2i1.68934

Deranek, J., & Parnther, C. (2015). Academic honesty and the new technological frontier. *The Hilltop Review, 8*(1), 1–22. https://scholarworks .wmich.edu/hilltopreview/vol8/iss1/4

Douglas Smith, C., Worsfold, K., Davies, L., Fisher, R., & McPhail, R. (2013). Assessment literacy and student learning: The case for explicitly developing students "assessment literacy." *Assessment & Evaluation in Higher Education, 38*(1), 44–60. https://doi.org/10.1080/02602938.2011.598636

Draper, M.J., & Newton, P.M. (2017). A legal approach to tackling contract cheating? *International Journal for Educational Integrity, 13*(11), 1–16. https://doi.org/10.1007/s40979-017-0022-5

East, J. (2009). Aligning policy and practice: An approach to integrating academic integrity. *Academic Language and Learning, 3*(1), A38–51. https:// journal.aall.org.au/index.php/jall/article/view/66

Eaton, S.E. (2020a). Academic integrity during COVID-19: Reflections from the University of Calgary. *International Studies in Educational Administration, 48*(1), 80–85. https://hdl.handle.net/1880/112293

Eaton, S.E. (2020b). *The intersection of contract academic work and contract cheating: Policy brief.* University of Calgary. https://hdl.handle.net/1880/112662

Eaton, S.E. (2020c, 26 June). Teaching and learning centres are the academic heroes of COVID-19. *University Affairs.* https://www.universityaffairs.ca/opinion/in-my-opinion/teaching-and-learning-centres-are-the-academic-heroes-of-covid-19/

Eaton, S.E., Crossman, K., & Edino, R.I. (2019). *Academic integrity in Canada: An annotated bibliography.* University of Calgary. https://hdl.handle.net/1880/110130

Eaton, S.E., & Turner, K.L. (2020). Exploring academic integrity and mental health during COVID-19: Rapid review. *Contemporary Education Theory & Research, 4*(1), 35–41. https://doi.org/10.5281/zenodo.4256825

Ellis, C., van Haeringen, K., Harper, R., Bretag, T., Zucker, I., McBride, S., Rozenberg, P., Newton, N., & Saddiqui, S. (2019). Does authentic assessment assure academic integrity? Evidence from contract cheating data. *Higher Education Research & Development, 39*(3), 454–69. https://doi.org/10.1080/07294360.2019.1680956

Fishman, T. (2015). Academic integrity as an educational concept, concern and movement in US institutions of higher learning. In T. Bretag (Ed.), *Handbook of academic integrity* (pp. 1–12). Springer. https://doi.org/10.1007/978-981-287-079-7_1-2

Forgie, S.E., Yonge, O., & Luth, R. (2018). Centers for teaching and learning across Canada: What's going on? *Canadian Journal for the Scholarship of Teaching and Learning, 9*(1). https://doi.org/10.5206/cjsotl-rcacea.2018.1.9

Freire, P. (1970). *Pedagogy of the oppressed.* Herder and Herder.

Gagné, A. (2020a). *The Canadian Precariat.* Universitas Press.

Gagné, A. (2020b). Reflections on academic integrity and educational development during COVID-19. *Canadian Perspectives on Academic Integrity, 3*(2), 1–2. https://doi.org/10.11575/cpai.v3i2.71642

Gallant, T.B., & Drinan, P. (2008). Toward a model of academic integrity institutionalization: Informing practice in postsecondary education. *Canadian Journal of Higher Education, 38*(2), 25–43. https://doi.org/10.47678/cjhe.v38i2.508

Gladue, K.. (2020, 25 November). *Indigenous paradigms in practice: Relationships, story and academic integrity* [Video]. Taylor Institute for Teaching and Learning, University of Calgary. YouTube. https://youtu.be/I0ZJl3dLmKg

International Centre for Academic Integrity (ICAI). (2021). *The fundamental values of academic integrity* (3rd ed.). https://academicintegrity.org/images/pdfs/20019_ICAI-Fundamental-Values_R12.pdf

Ip, E.J., Nguyen, K., Shah, B.M., Doroudgar, S., & Bidwal, M.K. (2016). Motivations and predictors of cheating in pharmacy school. *American Journal of Pharmaceutical Education, 80*(8), 1–7. https://doi.org/10.5688 /ajpe808133

Kaktiņš, L. (2019). Does Turnitin support the development of international students' academic integrity? *Ethics and Education, 14*(4), 430–48. https:// doi.org/10.1080/17449642.2019.1660946

Kaposi, D., & Dell, P. (2012). Discourses of plagiarism: Moralist, proceduralist, developmental and inter-textual approaches. *British Journal of Sociology of Education, 33*(6), 813–30. https://doi.org/10.1080/01425692 .2012.686897

Kates, G. (2019, 12 March). *Lori Loughlin and Felicity Huffman among dozens charged in college bribery scheme.* CBS News. https://www.cbsnews.com /news/college-admissions-scandal-bribery-cheating-today-felicity -huffman-arrested-fbi-2019-03-12/

Kezar, A., & Bernstein-Sierra, S. (2016). Commercialization of higher education. In T. Bretag (Ed.), *Handbook of academic integrity* (pp. 325–46). Springer. https://doi.org/10.1007/978-981-287-098-8_59

Lancaster, T. (2019). Social media enabled contract cheating. *Canadian Perspectives on Academic Integrity, 2*(1), 1–18. https://doi.org/10.11575 /cpai.v2i2.68053

Langenfeld, T. (2020). Internet-based proctored assessment: Security and fairness issues. *Educational Measurement, Issues and Practice, 39*(3), 24–7. https://doi.org/10.1111/emip.12359

Lea, M.R., & Street, B.V. (2006). The "academic literacies" model: Theory and applications. *Theory into Practice, 45*(4), 368–77. https://doi.org/10.1207 /s15430421tip4504_11

Macdonald, R., & Carroll, J. (2006). Plagiarism: A complex issue requiring a holistic institutional approach. *Assessment & Evaluation in Higher Education, 31*(2), 233–45. https://doi.org/10.1080/02602930500262536

Magyar, A. (2012). Plagiarism and attribution: An academic literacies approach? *Learning Development in Higher Education, 4*(March), 1–20. https://ueaeprints.uea.ac.uk/id/eprint/61444/1/141_697_1_PB.pdf

Maracle, B.J. Iehnhotonkwas. (2020). Seven grandfathers in academic integrity, University of Toronto, First Nations House. https://studentlife. utoronto.ca/wp-content/uploads/Seven_Grandfathers_in_Academic_ Integrity.pdf

McCabe, D.L., Butterfield, K.D., & Treviño, L.K. (2012). *Cheating in college: Why students do it and what educators can do about it.* Johns Hopkins University Press.

McCabe, D.L., Treviño, L.K., & Butterfield, K.D. (1999). Academic integrity in honor code and non-honor code environments: A qualitative investigation. *Higher Education, 70,* 211–34. https://doi.org/10.1080/00221546.1999.11780762

McKenna C., & Hughes, J. (2013). Values, digital texts, and open practices changing scholarly landscape in higher education. In R. Goodfellow & M.R. Lea (Eds.), *Literacy in the digital university: Critical perspectives on learning, scholarship and technology* (pp. 15–26). Routledge.

McKenzie, A. (2018). Academic integrity across the Canadian landscape. *Canadian Perspectives on Academic Integrity, 1*(2), 1–6. https://doi.org/10.11575/cpai.v1i2.54599

Morris, E.J., & Carroll, J. (2016). Developing a sustainable holistic institutional approach: Dealing with realities "on the ground" when implementing an academic integrity policy. In T. Bretag (Ed.), *Handbook of academic integrity* (pp. 449–62). Springer. https://doi.org/10.1007/978-981-287-098-8_23

Ontario Universities Council on Quality Assurance (OUCQA). (2019). *Quality assurance framework and guide.* https://oucqa.ca/wp-content/uploads/2019/10/Quality-Assurance-Framework-and-Guide.pdf

Owunwanne, D., Rustagi, N., & Dada, R. (2010). Students' perceptions of cheating and plagiarism in higher institutions. *College Teaching and Learning, 7*(11), 59–68. https://doi.org/10.19030/tlc.v7i11.253

Pfannenstiel, A.N. (2010). Digital literacies and academic integrity. *International Journal for Educational Integrity, 6*(2), 41–49. https://doi.org/10.21913/IJEI.v6i2.702

Pidgeon, M. (2016). More than a checklist: Meaningful Indigenous inclusion in higher education. *Multidisciplinary Studies in Social Inclusion, 4*(1), 77–91. http://dx.doi.org/10.17645/si.v4i1.436

Pitt, P., Dullaghan, K., & Sutherland-Smith, W. (2020). "Mess, stress and trauma": Students' experiences of formal contract cheating processes. *Assessment & Evaluation in Higher Education, 46*(4), 659–72. https://doi.org/10.1080/02602938.2020.1787332

Price, M. (2002). Beyond "gotcha!": Situating plagiarism in policy and pedagogy. *College Composition and Communication, 54*(1), 88–115. https://doi.org/10.2307/1512103

Riaz, A. (2020). Manufactured precarity: Some solutions to help mitigate the impacts of precarious employment on Canadian sessional instructors. In A. Gagné (Ed.), *The Canadian Precariat* (pp. 6–22). Universitas Press.

Rodhiya, N., Hermilia Wijayati, P., & Bukhori, H.A. (2020). Graduate students' attitude toward plagiarism in academic writing. *KnE Social Sciences, 4*(4), 206–212. https://doi.org/10.18502/kss.v4i4.6484

Saddiqui, S. (2016). Engaging students and faculty: Examining and overcoming the barriers. In T. Bretag (Ed.), *Handbook of academic integrity* (pp. 1009–36). Springer. https://doi.org/10.1007/978-981-287-098-8_18

Sanger C.S. (2020). Inclusive pedagogy and universal design approaches for diverse learning environments. In C. Sanger & N. Gleason (Eds.), *Diversity and inclusion in global higher education* (pp. 31–71). Palgrave Macmillan. https://doi.org/10.1007/978-981-15-1628-3_2

Serviss, T. (2016). Creating faculty development programming to prevent plagiarism: Three approaches. In T. Bretag (Ed.), *Handbook of academic integrity* (pp. 1009–36). Springer. https://doi.org/10.1007/978-981-287-098-8_73

Seto, A.. (2020, 28 October). The intersection of academic integrity and mental health: From resources to policies [video]. Taylor Institute for Teaching and Learning, University of Calgary. YouTube. https://youtu.be/PjYTH46b6Ks

Slavich, G.M., & Zimbardo, P.G. (2012). Transformational teaching: Theoretical underpinnings, basic principles, and core methods. *Educational Psychology Review, 24*(4), 569–608. https://doi.org/10.1007/s10648-012-9199-6

Stewart, B. (2020, 4 December). Online exam monitoring can invade privacy and erode trust at universities. *Academic Matters.* https://academicmatters.ca/online-exam-monitoring-can-invade-privacy-and-erode-trust-at-universities/

Stoesz, B.M., Eaton, S.E., Miron, J., & Thacker, E.J. (2019). Academic integrity and contract cheating policy analysis of colleges in Ontario, Canada. *International Journal for Educational Integrity, 15*(4), 1–18. https://doi.org/10.1007/s40979-019-0042-4

Street, B.V. (1995). *Social literacies: Critical approaches to literacy in development, ethnography and education.* Harlow, Pearson Education.

Sutherland-Smith, W. (2008). *Plagiarism, the internet, and student learning: Improving academic integrity.* Routledge.

Sutherland-Smith, W. (2013). Crossing the line: Collusion or collaboration in university group work? *Australian Universities' Review, 55*(1), 51–58. https://files.eric.ed.gov/fulltext/EJ1004398.pdf

Tindall, I.K., & Curtis, G.J. (2020). Negative emotionality predicts attitudes toward plagiarism. *Academic Ethics, 18*(1), 89–102. https://doi.org/10.1007/s10805-019-09343-3

Truth and Reconciliation Commission of Canada (TRC). (2015). Truth and Reconciliation Commission of Canada: Calls to action. Retrieved 9

November 2020 from https://www.rcaanc-cirnac.gc.ca/eng /1450124405592/1529106060525

Valentine, K. (2006). Plagiarism as literacy practice: Recognizing and rethinking ethical binaries. *College Composition and Communication, 58*(1), 89–109. https://www.jstor.org/stable/20456924

Walker, M., & Townley, C. (2012). Contract cheating: A new challenge for academic honesty? *Academic Ethics, 10*(1), 27–44. https://doi.org /10.1007/s10805-012-9150-y

Weber-Wulff, D. (2016). Plagiarism detection software: Promises, pitfalls, and practices. In T. Bretag (Ed.), *Handbook of academic integrity* (pp. 625–38). Springer. https://doi.org/10.1007/978-981-287-098-8_19

"Aspiring to the Transformational: Building upon a Holistic Approach to Academic Integrity in Higher Education"

SUSAN McGEACHIE
Head of the BMO Climate Institute

In this chapter, Emma Thacker outlines a transformational approach for addressing academic misconduct and cultivating academic integrity. Her expanded holistic strategy can be applied to many of today's social, environmental, and economic challenges, including the most pervasive: climate change. In 2019, the *Economist* posited that achieving a low-carbon transition will require a complete overhaul of the global economy. Such transformational change entails the same systems approach Thacker (2023) describes, particularly in the fact that these complex issues "cannot be reduced to one explanation, and there is no one, universalizing solution cannot be reduced to one explanation, and there is no one, universalizing solution" (p. 105). Transitioning to a global, low-carbon economy requires appropriate identification of interconnected challenges and solutions across all market players within governments, business, finance, civil society, and academia.

Thacker expands the definition of "holistic" by weaving equity and inclusion into the approach. This concept is an integral success factor in transitioning to a low-carbon economy. A major impediment to this transition has been the perceived negative effect it could have on jobs, economic prosperity, and social inclusion, which can be addressed by integrating social value creation into decarbonization plans. Investments in low-carbon solutions must be linked to business models that promote shared equity opportunities, job creation, and training, particularly for those who are negatively affected by the transition, and those who have been economically excluded as the result of gender, race, or access. This strategy will help tackle the long-standing equity issues that Thacker identifies. If ignored, these issues will be exacerbated by the effects of, and impede solutions to, climate change.

REFERENCES

The Economist. (2019, 20 September). The climate issue. https://www .economist.com/leaders/2019/09/19/the-climate-issue

Thacker, E.J. (2023). Aspiring to the transformational: Building upon a holistic approach to academic integrity in higher education. In I.L. Stefanovic (Ed.), *Conversations on ethical leadership: Lessons learned from university governance* (pp. 97–118). University of Toronto Press.

chapter five

Openness, Responsiveness, and Discomfort: A Relational Approach to Student-Centred Leadership

SARAH J. KING

My students have shown me so many times that it's not always about being the perfect person in the perfect position – it's about showing up when you are needed.

– Jill Biden, US first lady

Biden reminds us that the primary role of faculty, staff, and university leaders is as facilitators of student excellence – facilitators who are responsive to student needs and supportive of learning on a variety of levels. Students stand at the core of the post-secondary vision, mission, and purpose. This chapter argues in favour of a relational approach to student-centred leadership, meaning that universities can benefit only if students themselves are encouraged to step up and have an active voice in decision making, from curriculum design to advancing sustainable operational objectives.

A relational approach to student-centred leadership is characterized, I suggest, by openness to multiple points of view, to many forms of knowledge, and to ideas from all members of a community. It means fundamentally standing *in relation to* those other points of view and taking them seriously. It includes a willingness to change in response to new ideas or information, and to challenge and be challenged. It allows for the possibility of asking questions and being uncomfortable, and it demands an openness to transforming ideas, actions, or institutions based on the community's needs or insights. It values the individual members of a community, and the community itself, and strives not to make one more important than the other.

Relational leadership acknowledges that transformation of relationships within institutions is necessary to create a more effective learning space for all. Relational leaders work towards that transformation, sometimes in incremental ways, navigating the tension between addressing unmet needs in the moment and transforming institutions to meaningfully address student needs in the long term.

This chapter begins in Part I by highlighting elements of the student experience that are increasingly the focus of university leadership, from improving mental health and well-being to encouraging student engagement. The argument will be made that such priorities are most effectively addressed through a relational approach that values student voices. Part II highlights, through a case study at Grand Valley State University, how providing students with actual leadership opportunities results in stronger post-secondary institutions and novel initiatives that emerge if one is able to stand back and invite students to participate as equal partners in shaping universities.

I. Enhancing Student Relations

Ethical leadership invites teamwork, and teamwork thrives when there is trust among the members of the team. Leadership researcher Brené Brown (2018) is right to note that "trust is earned in the smallest of moments ... not through heroic deeds, or even highly visible actions, but through paying attention, listening, and gestures of genuine care and connection" (p. 32). At universities, an open, responsive, and sometimes uncomfortable, disquieting but ultimately productive process requires that decision making involves students – paying attention to them, listening, and genuinely connecting with them. It is, after all, *their* education that drives the institutional mission. They deserve a meaningful voice in their places of learning.

Administrators are faced with numerous challenges in seeking to enhance the student experience. A primary problem is mental health needs that are seen to be "stretching" the capacity of universities to promote care and well-being amongst students (Dixon, 2018). The COVID-19 pandemic has only exacerbated the crisis. "Things were going downhill in mental health for students across North America before COVID," says York University psychology professor Paul Ritvo. "What COVID has done is it has put health and health sciences in the top headlines" (Mastroianni, 2021). In the United Kingdom, according to the National Union of Students, over 50% of students reported a decline in their mental health since the pandemic began (Johnson & Kendal, 2020). The US National College Health Assessment reveals that approximately one in four students "suffers from a diagnosable mental illness, while a much greater proportion report feeling overwhelmed (around 70 percent) or very lonely (around 60 percent" (Whitley, 2020).

In response to such a growing crisis of well-being, some universities – such as Canada's premier University of Toronto – have "dedicated significant funds" to mental health services on campus (Wong, 2021). The vice-provost's commitment to providing additional resources is an important part of addressing such challenges.

However, students themselves provide additional suggestions. For example, enacting an institution-wide policy to lessen the strictness of assignment extensions during the pandemic will relieve stress and accommodate students who, in their own words, sometimes "can't control if one day my mental health is just absolutely terrible" (Wong, 2021). Students tell us that they face significant mental health challenges as a result of the pandemic, with more students screening positive for depression and anxiety than in previous years, and many students who had never accessed campus mental health services now reaching out for help (Anderson, 2020). These students often thrive when given the support and autonomy to manage their workload and deadlines around the challenges of daily pandemic life. Overall, as universities have a responsibility to commit additional resources to such a widespread problem as health and well-being, students can help in identifying useful ways forward. In the words of McGill student Stephanie Zito, "Students say post-secondary institutions should amplify and listen to students to know what initiatives could be revised or newly implemented" (Wong, 2021). University leaders can only benefit from engaging with those student voices and the innovative ideas that arise throughout such dialogue.

In that regard, the American Association of Universities has it right when they describe student-centred institutions as those "which prioritize the needs and interests of ... students, rather than focusing first and foremost on the interests of higher education institutions and the demands of the research enterprise" (AAU 2019). Student-centred learning is similarly understood as a series of related educational approaches focused on mutual, reflexive, active learning.[1] These practices are closely related to "transformative learning" (Attard et al., 2010) and to "high impact practices" fostered and promoted by the work of institutions such as the American Association of Colleges and Universities.[2]

Certainly, student-centred institutions enable meaningful relationships with students in ways that are other than simply incidental or symbolic add-ons. Successful student-centred leadership is profoundly relational, involving practices of mutuality, collaboration, and shared meaning making.

To be sure, one might expect to encounter detractors. Relational, student-centred leadership is not a universally lauded approach. Many are suspicious that such efforts indicate a "pampering" of overly needy students, in "an epidemic of emotional fragility and insecurity of the self among undergraduates" (Gooch, 2019, para. 13). In fact, one might draw interesting parallels through a comparison with some of the common reactions to the current climate emergency and the need for social change. In such instances, there are several common responses:

- Some *deny* or *deflect*: In the case of climate change, some *deny* that global heating is a problem, or that it is caused by humans. There are many more who recognize the threat, but *deflect* responsibility for addressing the emergency to others, often because they feel overwhelmed by the scope of change required.

- Some *perform* and *pretend*: Many groups and organizations (and some individuals) make minor improvements to their sustainability practices and then espouse these initiatives as environmentally significant. This sort of greenwashing is a *performance* of sustainability, pretending to meaningfully address complex issues with overly simplified solutions. Such postures often avoid larger change that may challenge leadership or stakeholders.
- Some *address* and *relate*: Some face the problem, work to identify its origins, and attempt to *address* the emergency. These people consider the larger social *relationships* that have created the climate crisis (at the level of corporations, governments, and other institutions) and the challenges of individual participation in these practices. This relational approach requires a much higher tolerance for complexity and vulnerability, and slow, dogged persistence on the path to transformation.

I would argue that similar responses occur when in the challenges of meaningful student engagement. Some choose to *deny* that the gamut of complex student needs is relevant or real, believing that the academic mission of post-secondary institutions should not indulge in overly "soft," emotional responses. Others acknowledge the needs of students but *deflect* any responsibility for addressing their needs. It is the medical system, for instance, that is seen to hold responsibility for addressing mental health issues. Yet others acknowledge the needs of students, while leveraging them to acquire more resources for the institution. Their approaches are a *performance* intended to look as though they are meeting student needs without transforming the institution or students themselves. Some leaders *pretend* to understand student concerns without being in any meaningful or authentic relationship to students. The cynic in me suggests that some may even leverage their stories to create a false persona of a caring leader. Some faculty leaders go to great lengths to adopt postures as advocates for students, or as uniquely qualified to speak *on behalf of* students, about their needs and experiences, rather than *fostering engagement with* students.

None of these approaches reflect the kind of student engagement that is properly, squarely, meaningfully centred at the core of an institution's vision. None of them reflect the need to engage in a *relational ethic of care* that students deserve.[3] Universities have a moral responsibility to acknowledge student needs, privilege student experiences, and reflect (together with students themselves) on the larger social relationships that shape their lives. As others have shown, true institutional leadership, including senior management and student unions, "are the *sine qua non* of an active and welcoming approach to student engagement" that depend upon "value-based principles...to create a culture of engagement" (Collins & Working Group on Student Engagement in Irish Higher Education, 2016). Those values include democratic principles; viewing students as partners and co-creators of learning experiences; inclusivity and diversity; transparency of process; collegiality and parity of esteem; and overall professionalism (p. 31).

There are so many different ways in which to share leadership responsibilities with students and to meaningfully engage them, both within the classroom and outside of it. In my experience of teaching, this sometimes means facilitating simple practices like student-led discussion, or informal small group work, where students are given the space to develop their own questions and ideas about the course material. Starting from the students' analyses fundamentally affirms that the students' ideas and perceptions are valuable. More often than not, students offer insights from their own experience that enrich the discussion.

Providing students with opportunities to partake in decision making and engage in innovative initiatives enriches the overall university experience. In the following section, I describe a particularly successful case of student leadership in place-based learning that will, I hope, provide additional evidence of the value of privileging student initiatives in university development.

II. The Grand Valley Sustainable Agricultural Project (SAP)

One of the most successful initiatives that I have had the privilege to experience first-hand relates to the student-founded campus Sustainable Agriculture Project (SAP) at Grand Valley State University.[4] Known affectionately as "The Farm," it was launched over a decade ago by six undergraduate students who chose to create a community garden space on their large rural campus. In response, the university provided access to a small parcel of land on the very edge of campus, where there were plans to eventually develop a parking lot for heavy equipment. In the meantime, the thinking went, the students could do little to damage otherwise underutilized land.

Over the years, the Farm has, in the words of one student, "exploded," becoming a vibrant site of collaboration between students, staff, faculty, administrators, the Office of Sustainability Practices, and Facilities Services & Planning. According to the their YouTube video, students feel that "the perception now is 'Oh, this is a successful endeavour ... transforming how we see ourselves and how we see culture.... It's great working for a common goal!'" (GVSU, 2013). Students operate businesses selling produce and honey (during the pandemic, the Farm pivoted quickly to donate produce to the local Community Food Club serving those in need), experiment with practices in sustainable agriculture, participate in field trips and collaborative projects, complete internships, and benefit from volunteer opportunities. There are now more than 5 acres under production, two hoop houses, a successful Community Supported Agriculture (CSA) operation, teaching and research plots, and a new community partnership, alongside the original community garden.[5] To the upper administration, it is an "experiential learning lab," inserting itself into the very sustainability practice of the university as an institution, But for students, it is still just "The Farm" (Figure 5.1).

As a scientific station, this is a place where students can research plants, the environment, human-environment interactions, systems thinking, and the importance of community engagement.

Figure 5.1. GVSU Sustainable Agriculture Project
Source: Photo courtesy Sarah J. King.

SAP is also a laboratory where students can get their hands dirty
while learning quantitative analysis and critical thinking skills
relating to soil, water, plant life, climate change, and the environment. It is a working studio space and gallery for artists, as well
as a field site for research, ranging from the ecological to the socio-
logical (Figure 5.2).

A project of the Brooks College of Interdisciplinary Studies, the
SAP's explicit purpose is to address the triple bottom line of sustainability, engaging the social and cultural, economic, and ecological dimensions of food systems. SAP aims to (1) foster sustainable
farming practices to promote ecological and food literacy; (2) cultivate student leadership and learning; (3) nurture place-based
learning and value ecological integrity; and (4) grow relationships
by "providing a space for dialogue across disciplinary boundaries,
the negotiation of interdisciplinary practices and the contestation

Figure 5.2. SAP Bounty
Source: Photo courtesy Sarah J. King.

of ideas."[6] The mission statement itself was developed in February 2014 as part of a collaborative, participatory community consultation, involving a survey, and a community-wide "Harvest Party" attended by over 100 students, faculty, staff, parents, and even children of faculty and students. The mission statement was revised by the Farm Club, and then again by an Advisory Committee, with a final draft now available online.

The key to the Farm's success has been robust student leadership. With the advice and collaboration of faculty and staff (and, in the later years, of a farm manager), students run the operation. There is a vibrant student community characterized by experimentation and peer leadership, within a relaxed, rural setting. Faculty and staff involved with the farm openly acknowledge that one hallmark of its success is a willingness to fail: student projects are undertaken because they are valuable and interesting, not because they are guaranteed to "work." This openness to failure has led to more risk, and greater success, over the years, and students are clear that they value the Farm as a place where they have meaningful autonomy, together with strong support from faculty and staff.

There are many challenges, and the work is ongoing. But over the years, the Farm has become a vibrant community hub that exemplifies the challenges and rewards of relational leadership. The transformation in this corner of our university community, on this small square of land (no longer slated for paving) is remarkable. Change and growth were often incremental, although sometimes long persistence leads to individual, brilliant breakthroughs. While a major aim of postsecondary education is to enable students to "do it for themselves," the paradox of university life is that our systems of power are entrenched, and it can be challenging for students, faculty, and staff to realistically turn this idea into practice. At the SAP, shared leadership is not simple or clear-cut but, I would argue, it is precisely the complication and contestation of relationships of authority that meaningfully empower students, enabling them to move out of their traditional roles. Such place-based learning is a welcome disruption to the standard dynamics of student–professor relationships, creating new opportunities for engaged pedagogy and lessons in leadership.

More specifically, one of my largest challenges in introductory courses is to encourage freshmen to move beyond their natural deference to my authority as professor and take their own ideas and goals seriously in the content of the course. Working side-by-side on relatively mundane tasks at the SAP mean that these students begin to look at me differently as we haul compost together week after week. And planting the first fruit trees in an orchard or learning to use a pickaxe means that they begin to look at themselves differently as well. Back in the classroom, conversations flow more freely, and students are more confident in the value of their own ideas, engaging the readings – and me – more directly. On the basis of my own experience, I remain convinced that they are more willing to engage in the practice of learning for themselves (and not for me), and to take their own ideas seriously.

This sort of renegotiation of power also happens at a much larger scale at the Farm: not only is it student-founded but, for the first decade of the project, student interns were the only on-site residents. It is students who do the largest portion of the day-to-day labour. When the long-term farm manager left at the beginning of the season a few years ago, the renegotiation of roles and responsibilities was a fascinating process that demonstrated how students, faculty, and staff can step up to jointly participate in the ongoing compromises of shared leadership. The current farm manager, and the two previous people who held this position, are former students who participated in various leadership roles over many years before transitioning into the role of manager.

Emphasizing the value of interdisciplinary learning opportunities, at the 2013 Annual Meeting of the American Academy of Religion, the farmer, author, and community activist Wendell Berry wryly observed that "there isn't any important question that we have to deal with that is in a Department." The Sustainable Agriculture Project embodies a response to this challenge, as students learn how creating sustainable food systems requires the integration of the work of various disciplines, such as:

- ecology and agricultural science to grow food in a manner that accounts for the health of people and the land,
- philosophy to interrogate the principles and values that guide farm practices and goals,
- anthropology and cultural studies to understand the communities that are developing at the farm and that it serves,
- organizational behaviour and risk management to secure on-campus sale of food grown on the farm, and
- marketing and entrepreneurial skills to successfully run the farm stand and CSA.

While individual courses may explore one of these elements in more detail, coming out to the farm means that students experience first-hand how these discrete elements are, in practice, inseparable. Sometimes those connections are obvious to students as they work on site; other times they are made clear in the classroom afterwards. But removing students, at least for a time, from the relative comfort of the classroom and immersing them in the complexity of living agricultural systems makes Berry's observation even more potent, enabling these kinds of interdisciplinary connections.

In fact, over the years, I have found that there can be unexpected insights. In a course entitled "Food for Thought," my students completed 15 hours of service work on the farm as a part of their coursework. While the purpose was to learn about ecological farming practices specifically, there were other unanticipated benefits. Some of them found the labour challenging – all of them realized the skill involved in farming, and the physical strength and endurance necessary to make a go of it. When we returned to the classroom later in the semester to discuss Tracie MacMillan's book about food justice in the United States, *The American Way of Eating*, the tiny taste that they had had of farm work made them much more able to understand the demands placed on farm labourers in the United States, many of whom are also undocumented. Simply knowing the number of hours worked a week, or the number of bushels of garlic planted or picked per worker per day is intellectually interesting, but the numbers were much more easily contextualized when students had planted garlic themselves and felt the challenges of this labour in their own inexperienced muscles.

Overall, successive generations of student leaders at SAP have shared a clear vision and invested much energy in each small step towards positive change, taking years to get approval for bee keeping; the additional years to prepare to sell produce to Campus Dining; the longing, still, to raise and care for chickens! There are still many unmet needs. But slowly, step by step, the community moves forward and, looking back, the tremendous accomplishment of genuine institutional transformation through meaningful student engagement, is clear.

III. Closing Reflections

In a regional public university, students come from a wide variety of backgrounds. On Zoom or in the classroom, I see students facing and navigating profound human challenges. Some are without food, adequate health care, or safe shelter. Many are working full-time jobs to pay for their full-time student tuition, often also raising children and/or caring for aging parents. Some navigate racialized and gender identities, sexual orientation, disability, and more in an unequal society. They are not exempted from being human in the world simply by their status as students, and the costs of navigating these issues do not disappear at the classroom door. Those who suggest these learners are overly "delicate" or demanding of their universities seem to be suffering under the false assumption that university students are all young people, universally well supported by their families, who have not faced any challenges in their lives before arriving at our institutions. This notion that life happens to people only after they receive their degrees, or get full-time work does a profound disservice to young adults everywhere. These students are tremendously capable and can handle great challenges, especially when they have the relational support to do so.

The Sustainable Agriculture Project at Grand Valley State University clearly illustrates the importance of bringing some of these diverse student voices into the organizational structure of the university. Community engaged learning is one way in which education becomes true to the interdisciplinary, wicked problems of the day that we all must face.

I am reminded of a case of a university, recently searching for a vice-provost of teaching and learning. Early in the search committee deliberations, it was decided to reverse the order of the terms and define the position instead as one dedicated to "learning and teaching." For some, such a move may appear trivial but the important moral dimension here is the affirmation that universities are not one-way delivery systems, imparting knowledge through teaching. Instead, the priority of student (and faculty!) learning must be explicitly and deliberately acknowledged at all levels.

Of course, such learning can take many forms. The SAP is one way in which to engage student learning and leadership responsibilities. Another way is to invite non-academic, community stories into the classroom, as a reminder that academic learning is more than a matter of imparting theory and should never be unidimensional. For instance, in the fall of 2015, Jonestown survivor Laura Johnson Kohl visited my university and spoke to my students about her experiences. In the early 1970s, Johnson Kohl was a social activist and an early member of Jim Jones's Peoples Temple community in California. In 1974, when the community moved to Guyana, Johnson Kohl joined them. Four years later, she was one of very few people who survived the mass suicides that Jones initiated. More than 900 people died at Jonestown, many of them children. Only 87 survived. In its day, Jonestown was the largest civilian casualty event in US history. Many years later, Johnson Kohl is an educator and a speaker with the Speakers Bureau of the Jonestown Institute, who connects with many communities to tell her story and help people understand the events at Jonestown.

Laura Johnson Kohl joined 25 undergraduate students in a course where we used philosophy and literature to explore the value of education. She spoke directly, honestly, and clearly to my students about her experiences. She told of the initial appeal of the Peoples Temple Community and its social justice focus, of the realities of life in the Guyana compound, and of the deaths of her entire community when Jim Jones called for "revolutionary suicide." She spoke of her life afterwards, of the decades she spent trying to come to terms with these experiences and with her loss, and of how she understands those events with 40 years of hindsight.

And while she spoke, she wept. She told the students that her tears were normal and that they should not worry; when she speaks of these events, they bring tears, but the tears do not stop her from speaking. And the students responded wordlessly – with open faces, and attentive eyes, listening closely and carefully, holding themselves as witnesses to her story. When Johnson Kohl finished speaking, they spoke quietly with her, and when it was time to leave, they could not bring themselves to go. They picked up their belongings and gathered around her, standing silently in a deep, wordless response of solidarity and care. They were relating to her, standing with her, on the most profound level.

That day I was privileged to witness deeply caring, honest sharing about the most difficult issues. And the impact of that approach on my students lasted throughout the rest of the semester and certainly beyond. This kind of community-based conversation is rarely comfortable or easy. There were tears, but the tears were not the point, nor did they prevent us from moving into the difficult stories. It was not comfortable, but there was willingness of everyone in the room to sit with that discomfort, allowing us deeper understanding of a difficult past.

Students thrive in environments where learning moves beyond theory – where complex human experiences can be shared, where diverse insights and knowledge are recognized, questions are welcome, and there is a willingness to change in response to new ideas. So do leaders. Students thrive when given space to navigate their identities, needs, and challenges, in the context of community. So do leaders. Relational approaches to leadership are transformative – not only for students and communities, and institutions, but also for leaders themselves. These approaches are successful when they can foster openness to new perspectives, a willingness to change, to challenge, to be uncomfortable, and to be open to the hard work of transformation. These things cannot be forced. But they can be cultivated, often incrementally and sometimes with brilliant breakthroughs.

NOTES

1 The concept of student-centred learning traces back through Friere, Rogers, and Dewey and includes:
   - The reliance on *active rather than passive learning*;
   - An emphasis on *deep learning and understanding*;
   - *Increased responsibility and accountability* on the part of the student;
   - An *increased sense of autonomy* in the learner;
   - An *interdependence between teacher and learner*;
   - *Mutual respect within the learner–teacher* relationship; and
   - A *reflexive approach to the teaching and learning process* on the part of both the teacher and the learner (Lea et al., 2003, as cited in Attard et al., 2010).

2 This characterization of relational classrooms as playful, accepting,
   curious, and empathetic comes from *Belonging: A Relationship-Based
   Approach to Trauma-Informed Education* (Phillips et al., 2020).
3 For more on the ethics of care, see Sander-Staudt (n.d.).
4 For more information, see Sustainable Agriculture Project (2022).
5 For more on CSA, please see Community Supported Agriculture (n.d.).
6 Please see the project's mission statement and an introductory video
   (Sustainable Agriculture Project, 2019).

REFERENCES

American Association of Universities. (n.d.). *Student-centered: Reorient the
   educational environment to prioritize students as individuals with diverse
   educational and professional interests, needs, and challenges.* Retrieved on 20
   February 2021 from https://www.aau.edu/education-community
   -impact/graduate-education/phd-education-initiative/student-centered
Anderson, G. (2020, 11 September). *Mental health needs rise with pandemic.*
   Inside Higher Ed. https://www.insidehighered.com/news/2020/09/11
   /students-great-need-mental-health-support-during-pandemic
Attard, A., Di Iorei, E., Geven, K., & Santa, R. (2010). *Student-centred learning:
   Toolkit for students, staff and higher education institutions.* European Students
   Union and Education International.
Brown, B. (2018). *Dare to lead: Brave work, tough conversations, whole hearts.*
   Random House.
Collins, T., & Working Group on Student Engagement in Irish Higher
   Education. (2016, April). *Enhancing student engagement in decision making.*
   https://nstepsite.files.wordpress.com/2018/07/enhancing_student
   _engagement_in_decision_making_report.pdf
Community Supported Agriculture. (n.d.). National Agriculture Library,
   USDA. Retrieved 14 March 2021 from https://www.nal.usda.gov
   /farms-and-agricultural-production-systems/community-supported
   -agriculture
Dixon, G. (2018, 2 November). Growing mental-health needs of students
   require creative solutions. *The Globe and Mail.* https://www
   .theglobeandmail.com/canada/education/canadian-university-report
   /article-growing-mental-health-needs-of-students-require-creative
   -solutions/
Gooch, P. (2019, 20 November). *Is the modern university now all about students?*
   University Affairs. https://www.universityaffairs.ca/features
   /feature-article/is-the-modern-university-now-all-about-students/

Grand Valley State University. (2013, 15 January). *The Sustainable Agriculture Project* [Video]. YouTube. https://youtu.be/Dow13Yi4mCA

Johnson, D., & Kendall, C. (2020, 9 December). *Student mental health: "I am living in a bubble of one."* BBC News. https://www.bbc.com/news/education-55105044

Mastroianni, J. (2021, 25 January). The pandemic has made post-secondary students' mental health even worse. *Now Magazine.* https://nowtoronto.com/lifestyle/education/covid-19-pandemic-post-secondary-students-mental-health/

Phillips, S., Melim, D., & Hughes, D.A. (2020). *Belonging: A relationship-based approach to trauma-informed education.* Rowman & Littlefield.

Sander-Staudt, M. (n.d.). Care ethics. In *Internet Encyclopedia of Philosophy.* Retrieved 9 March 2021 from https://iep.utm.edu/care-ethics/

Sustainable Agriculture Project. (2019). *Mission.* Grand Valley State University. https://www.gvsu.edu/sustainableagproject/history-mission-14.htm

Sustainable Agriculture Project. (2022). Grand Valley State University. https://www.gvsu.edu/sustainableagproject/

Whitley, R. (2020, 19 March). Improving student mental health during the COVID-19 crisis: Six ways students can promote their mental health in the coronavirus pandemic. *Psychology Today.* https://www.psychologytoday.com/us/blog/talking-about-men/202003/improving-student-mental-health-during-the-covid-19-crisis

Wong, M. (2021, 9 January). *Morale at an "all time low": Post-secondary students grapple with COVID-19 fatigue.* Global News. https://globalnews.ca/news/7564247/student-mental-health-pandemic/

"Openness, Responsiveness, and Discomfort: A Relational Approach to Student-Centred Leadership"

LOIS LINDSAY

Executive Director, Strategic Initiatives, Evergreen

At Evergreen, the Canadian non-profit where I am part of the Leadership Team, we aim to make cities better – cities that are low-carbon, inclusive to all, and sustainable at their core. It is an ambitious goal, and its expression has taken myriad forms over our 30-year history. In that time, we have navigated profound changes in the environmental movement, the fundraising landscape, and the very definition of "green" cities. We pride ourselves on being nimble, responsive, and opportunistic, while retaining a steady focus on our mission. In this era of ongoing environmental reckoning, as well as recovery from COVID-19, we are presented a new kind of uncertainty – a suite of challenges that is perhaps overdue and has the potential to transform our organization and sector.

Sarah King's characterization of relational leadership manifests as being "student-centred" in the academic context, but could the concept also help us, in the non-profit sector, respond to the current moment? It seems to me that the opportunity for non-profit leaders now is to rededicate ourselves to the notion of responsive listening and leading *in relationship* with the communities we serve and the colleagues at all levels who bring our work alive. We may not know exactly where such a leadership approach will lead – and the journey may prove to be uncomfortable – but openness to change is surely what progressive, non-profit leadership is all about. This is a moment, if there ever was one, for steadfast curiosity about how we could do better, how we might learn from community and colleagues, and how our "institution" may need to change in order to remain faithful to its mission.

PART THREE

Community Engagement and Diversity

chapter six

Leadership, Vision, and the Role of Chancellor in University Governance

ANNE GIARDINI

As chancellor of Simon Fraser University from 2014 to 2020, I witnessed first-hand the complexities of university governance, and the benefits of systems that best promote the goals of the institution. While the titles, culture, norms, and distribution of power and authority vary from university to university, post-secondary institutions everywhere are multifaceted places in which to set strategy and make decisions. Students, staff, administrators, tenured and non-tenured professors, sessional instructors, graduate students, unions, parents, athletes, donors, alumni, governments, communities, and others all expect to be consulted on university decisions and look for evidence that their views have been given appropriate weight and will be duly reflected in how the university behaves. Balancing these interests is a difficult and ongoing project for university administrators. Institutions of higher education are complex organizations at the best of times and can be complex *dis*-organizations during times of change, stress, and challenges. Equilibrium – and trust – are years in the making and can be dissipated in a day. On the positive side, the structures and habits of good governance that are laid down during times when issues are few can help ensure institutional strength and resilience when the university is tested.

The leadership role of university president is particularly vexed because the key university "workers" are tenured professors, who can readily withstand direction, suggestion, correction, and ejection. Tenure reflects the recognition that faculty need security of employment if they are to have the freedom to ensure the level of academic freedom of thought that is or should be the hallmark of a university. Tenure provides the freedom necessary to search for knowledge fearlessly, to challenge accepted understanding, and to contribute to the evolution of ideas. In a tenured system, the possibility of dismissal for cause or any level of interference with or evaluation of faculty members' performance is low. Once tenure is granted, faculty members can take unpopular positions without fear of loss of employment. Dismissal can in most instances be based only on gross misconduct, incompetence, or persistent failure to discharge academic responsibilities. Collegial governance is a safeguard of academic freedom. Promotion, pay increases, appointments, and eligibility for research grants are subject to peer oversight, rather than the wishes of the president.

In Commonwealth and former Commonwealth nations, it is common for the senior role at comprehensive and research universities to be held by an appointed, unpaid chancellor, a titular or ceremonial head of the university, and for the president or chief executive of the university to have the additional title of vice-chancellor.

The defining role of the chancellor at these institutions is the authority to recognize and confer degrees. In practice, in addition to recurring roles presiding at university ceremonies, the chancellor often serves in an official or ex officio function on the university's governing body or bodies, its council or board of governors, and/or senate. He or she may also participate in or chair committees such as the search committee for a new president or chief executive, the honorary degree selection committee, and others.

In British Columbia, Canada, where I served as chancellor at Simon Fraser University for 6 years, from 2014 to 2020, the role of chancellor has been viewed as important enough to be codified in Part 5 of the *University Act*, RSBC 1996, Chapter 468. The *University Act*, which has counterparts in other provinces, sets out detailed provisions for the chancellor's election and term in office, but makes scant mention of the purpose of the role apart from the duty "to confer all degrees." In some ways, the role mirrors (albeit on a smaller scale) the roles of the Canadian governors general and provincial lieutenant governors, who preside at or participate in ceremonies and rituals, and support and recognize important causes and individuals. In so doing, they deepen and strengthen pro-social bonds. The role of chancellor encompasses analogous aspects of representation, support, connection, amplification, and encouragement. One important difference is that governors general and lieutenant governors have limited but important decision-making powers that provide certain rarely invoked, democratic safeguards. Modern chancellors have few, if any, such powers. While the role of a chancellor is limited, the selection of a chancellor sends a message to the university and wide communities about what that university is and how it wishes to be perceived.

This chapter considers how a chancellor's leadership and vision can go beyond ceremonial and ritual support, can enhance how the university is viewed by stakeholders within the context of broader university governance, and can serve to make the university more trusted and more resilient.

I. Historical Roots

The word "chancellor" comes from the Latin word *cancellus*, having the sense of lattice or railing, bars or enclosures. In church (Christian) architecture, the chancel (or presbytery) is the space around the altar in the sanctuary at its liturgical east end. Before relatively modern changes in practice, only clergy and choir members were permitted to be in the chancel, in part to ensure that the sacrament was protected from irreverent access. The area of the church used by the clergy was screened off from that used by the congregation; hence, a lattice or chancel rail set the area apart but still permitted the congregation to see what was happening on the other, sacred side. Today, churches may have neither screen nor rail, but the area is still called the chancel, or choir (since this is where the choir often sits) or sanctuary, a word that gestures back to the intended holiness and consecrated nature of the area.

Cobban (1988) points out that the great universities of England and elsewhere in Europe arose when they were sorely needed. The time of marauding Vikings was ending. Kings and popes were meting out state- or nation-sized areas for permanent settlement. These societies needed financial, political, and other organizational systems. Ruling was becoming more complex. Church, state, educational, training, and professional structures and systems were necessary in order to build and deploy intellectual capacity. The start of the great universities of the Western world, including among them Bologna (1088), Paris (1150), Oxford (1167), and Cambridge (1209) – these dates are all approximate and open to debate – was not what we might today call top down. Rather (with parallels to the creation of guilds), they formed as students began to gather around noted scholars and learned teachers, and teachers moved to where they would encounter students. Organization and attempts at regulation soon followed.

Stresses and conflict have always marked relations between state and religious authorities, relating to control and ownership of the trappings of power: money, decision-making, taxation, rule-setting, cultural norms and more. In the eleventh, twelfth, and thirteenth centuries, and since, church and crown each perceived that it might be in its best interests to strive to regulate the nascent and thereafter growing universities; rather than risk leaving it to the other to do so. Papal and civil authorities pursued the prerogative of regulating the incipient universities, although from very early days the new institutions of learning sought to defend autonomy from incursions by ecclesiastical and secular rule-makers.

The names and dates of appointment of the first chancellors in England are debated. Oxford University asserts that Robert Grosseteste was its first chancellor, appointed in about 1214 (University of Oxford, n.d.). Cobban (1988) thinks the date is between 1214 and 1216, although it is possible, he says, that Master John Grim held an analogous role by as early as 1201. There is consensus that the first chancellor of Cambridge was Richard of Wethringsett, who was appointed by the bishop of Ely by about 1222. Cobban (1988) says that Wethringsett "was conceived of as an episcopal agent, exercising delegated powers of the bishop of Ely" (p. 57). The appointment was thus an exercise of religious jurisdiction.

At that time, and for a considerable period thereafter, chancellors held enormous power. This was in part because chancellors were already powerful church officials, but also because universities themselves wielded sudden authority. In addition to governing all aspects of the university's operations, the university held sway over many aspects of the town in which it was resident, without having to defer to civic authority or adhere to local rules. As a result, tensions over who had the power to appoint the chancellor arose almost immediately. Cobban thinks it possible that the masters assembled at Oxford in 1214 tried to elect Robert Grosseteste with the title of "chancellor" but were prevented from using that term by the bishop of Lincoln, Hugh of Wells, who would allow only the title of "magister scolarum," likely because the title of chancellor was formidable and because of a desire to maintain ecclesiastical control over the power of appointment and the exercise of powers by the person appointed.

Whatever the dates and names, chancellors already existed in an ecclesiastical capacity. In the case of the first chancellor of Cambridge, it appears that the bishop simply repurposed his duties, while at Oxford, it seems, at least for a time the church resisted the title of chancellor, given the breadth of the powers of ecclesiastical chancellors.

Church chancellor as a role arose out of recognition that bishops tended to be educated and, at least sometimes, wise, so the state had devolved to them jurisdiction over certain matters – marriage, divorce, wills, and so forth. But bishops had many matters to attend to and could not resolve all questions that were brought before them, so other educated men were appointed to serve as chancellors: advisers to the bishop within the rail. At first, chancellors likely simply advised and assisted the bishops, but they then often took on greater roles in resolving disputes, and they may have served variously in such roles as librarian, archivist, superintendent of schools, and lecturer on ecclesiastical matters.

Popes and bishops alike sought to ensure that what was taught at the universities had the stamp of church approval. There were rewards for compliance. In 1233, for example, Pope Gregory the Ninth awarded to the chancellor and scholars of Cambridge the right not to be sued in the courts outside the diocese of Ely so long as they submitted to the rule of the chancellor or bishop. Oxford was granted similar rights a few years later, in 1254.

Importantly and not obviously, the delegation of the bishop of Ely's powers to a chancellor may have represented the first steps towards independence of the scholars. In the late fourteenth century, John of Donwich, elected twice chancellor of Cambridge by the masters, sought to avoid the oath. Following a lawsuit by the bishop, he was compelled to swear it. Thereafter, cagily, the bishop decided not to insist on the oath of obedience, while reserving the right to require it. Cobban (1988) reports that the last chancellor to provide an oath of obedience, willingly or otherwise, was Richard Billingford, confirmed as the chancellor of Cambridge by the bishop of Ely, John Fordham, in 1400. The next year, Pope Boniface IX dispensed with need for the bishop of Ely to confirm the appointment of chancellor, a privilege Oxford had acquired some years earlier.

As English chancellors began to be chosen and confirmed by the university instead of the church, they came to embody the growing powers of the university itself and exercised extensive civil and even criminal authority. A chancellor could impose fines, expel students, ban people from town and university, even excommunicate anyone associated with the university. Powerful chancellors were essential to the development of universities, since their powers displaced civil and church authority and, most importantly, accreted to the university as an institution, rather than to the roleholder or his family, since the role was not personal and could not be passed down or inherited. As universities gained their own status and power separate from the church, in part with the assistance of the role of the early chancellors, the authority of the chancellor per se dwindled. By the late 1400s, chancellors were increasingly deployed as non-resident power brokers, and the role of chancellors at the university became centred on the core role most familiar today: granting and recognizing degrees. As a corollary, over the same period, as the resident, active, senior officer of the university, the role of vice-chancellor acquired more scope, authority, and significance.

II. The Contemporary Canadian Landscape

In British Columbia, the *University Act* requires that there be a chancellor of each university, who is to be appointed by the board on nomination by the alumni association and after consultation with the senate or, in the case of the University of British Columbia, after consultation with the council. The chancellor holds office for up to 6 consecutive years.

The chancellor's intended independence is underscored by a rule that he or she must not be employed by a university.

In practice, in my experience, in British Columbia and elsewhere in Canada, the university chancellor's role includes:

- Conferring degrees;
- Representing the university in an official capacity within the larger community, as one of the university's chief ambassadors;
- Serving on committees, the governing board, and/or senate;
- Hosting events;
- Serving as a confidential advisor to the president;
- Connecting the university to other stakeholders in the community;
- Bringing external interests and concerns to the attention of the university;
- Supporting, amplifying, and encouraging university projects and scholars; and
- Giving and securing gifts to the university.

The role of chancellor can therefore be seen, more broadly, to amplify the president's use of persuasion and vision-setting to direct the university, and to support trust in the role and work of the university.

Over the last three decades, Western countries have witnessed an erosion of trust in the old repositories of confidence, including universities. This is not to say that employers, religious leaders, professionals, experts, universities, and so on are less honourable now than they once were. Collective trust has eroded during a period when the skillset we can draw on has improved, if only because providers of services and others are better educated, more specialized, and under greater and better-informed scrutiny. A chancellor serves a role in supporting trust in universities. Because he or she is both part of the governance of the university and independent, he or she can provide or embody counsel that takes into account interests that are not readily identified as those of the university.

A chancellor has the opportunity in giving advice and making external connections to bring into discussion interests and issues that may not be evident to others at the university, and to encourage the consideration of ways to meaningfully address the interests of others in university decision-making, particularly the interests of people and groups and interests that may have both less power and something at stake. Organizations generally do better when they engage meaningfully with other parties who not only share the mission, but also see the world differently. Entities that do so are more informed, more robust, more engaged, and ultimately more trusted. In the same way that companies do better with a diverse board of directors, a university can expect to engender greater trust with a chancellor in place who can provide fresh perspectives or at least pathways towards them.

Former University of Alberta chancellor Douglas Stollery (2016–20), for example, had, among many prior and ongoing achievements and roles, served on the legal team that argued *Delwin Vriend v the Province of Alberta* [1998] 1 SCR 493, among the first successful LGBTQ rights cases to come before the Supreme Court of Canada. His appointment thus, among other things, signified the university's commitments to human rights broadly, and to sexual and gender rights more particularly.

The installation of Indigenous chancellors at many Canadian universities over the past several years demonstrates an ongoing and growing commitment to reconciliation and to indigenization of the university environment and curriculum.

In 2015, when the University of Northern British Columbia announced that former Conservative cabinet minister James Moore (a UNBC alumnus) would be its next chancellor, some UNBC senators and students objected on the grounds that Mr. Moore's political affiliation conflicted with the university's stated values, including its claim to be "Canada's Green University." The university's senate passed a non-confidence motion and the Confederation of University Faculty Associations of British Columbia and the Canadian Association of University Teachers called on BC's Advanced Education Minister Andrew Wilkinson to investigate Moore's selection. There were also complaints that staff had not been consulted before or after the appointment. Brian Menounos, a faculty senator and the Canada Research Chair in Glacier Change, was reported to have asked that the board reconsider the appointment or that Moore step aside, saying, "A chancellor is supposed to unify a community, not divide it" (Kane, 2015, para. 13).

Columnist Peter Ewart (2015) agreed, arguing that, in light of what the role of chancellor represents, and his or her potential influence,

> members of the university community, as well as the community at large, are fully justified in weighing in about who does become chancellor, and whether or not the views of an appointee such as Moore are consistent with the core values and principles of the university as expressed in its mission statement and official description of the chancellor position. (para. 5)

Moore's appointment in this manner was made on the heels of then-recent changes to provincial law changing how chancellors at UNBC and several other British Columbia universities were to be selected. Before the amendments, the affected universities seem to have followed the general practice in Canada, including at Simon Fraser University, for the chancellor to be elected with broad support from various university bodies, referred to as "members of the university convocation." After the legislative changes, however, chancellor appointment power at UNBC (and the other affected universities) was vested in the Board of Governors. Ultimately, and doubtless because the legislation squarely gave the Board of Governors the appointment power, Moore's installation as chancellor proceeded and he served until 2019.

In May 2019, Joseph Arthur Gosnell became the seventh chancellor of the University of Northern British Columbia. A Nisga'a hereditary chief, Dr. Gosnell had helped to finalize the Nisga'a

Nation Treaty, the first modern treaty with the BC and Canadian governments. He was the first Indigenous leader to take on the role at the university. His appointment was without public controversy and seems to have met Brian Menounos's benchmark for a chancellor as someone who unifies a university rather than divide it. (Sadly, Dr. Gosnell's term ended prematurely on his death in spring 2020.)

III. Concluding Reflections

An ideal chancellor – like the ideal university – may not exist, but we get closer to the ideal when both are informed, attentive, adaptable, creative, keenly curious, patient, and resilient, and demonstrate genuine, authentic care for the university's mission and for the range of views and needs of others who benefit from the roles of the university.

During my term as chancellor of Simon Fraser University, I was often asked how much time the commitment took up. My answer was usually "as long as a piece of string." During weeks when the Board of Governors met, and during convocations, the role was more than full time. At other times, the intensity depended on which committees I volunteered for, and at which events I attended or presided. Because of my background and interests, I paid particular attention to environmental and cultural meetings and events. Prior chancellors have focused on athletics, donors, philanthropy, and other areas of particular interest.

During my first convocation, I noticed that one undergraduate award-winner had made their way through their degree without family support. No relatives were in attendance to witness the attainment of their degree with distinction. I told them that I would be honoured to serve as their surrogate family that day, and I undertook to beam the kind of love and pride towards them that I would for my own children. After that day, realizing that I could not know every graduand's story, or as much about their losses, sorrows, needs, struggles, joys, and supports as I would have liked, I strove to engage with every individual who crossed the convocation stage – to give each and every one my wholehearted attention along with a bolt of parental pride. This could become exhausting several days into convocation weeks, but it was, I found, rewarding beyond measure.

One value a chancellor should, in my view, represent and support is the principle that campuses should be a place where a wide range of viewpoints can be aired and explored, within the limits of legality and safety. At SFU, from time to time, as on other campuses, contesting viewpoints on, for example, abortion, gender politics, Middle Eastern policies, foreign state influences, the environment, religious expression, and other issues became flashpoints. While I cannot remember ever disagreeing with SFU's president on how any of these issues should be handled, I can easily envision that a president and chancellor holding two viewpoints could be a valuable way of signalling to stakeholders that there are many issues on which informed, educated, and right-thinking individuals may disagree.

A chancellor can express or exemplify views that might be at odds with that of university leadership in ways that can make the university a richer, more dynamic place in practice and how it is seen. For example, a university chancellor may serve during their term on the board of a mining or forestry company, as I did, thus highlighting that those industries – done well – can be compatible with a university's values.

Has the role of chancellor outlived its usefulness? Should the duties of chancellor be wrapped up into those of the president or provost or some other salaried university employee? I believe that the loss of a chancellor would be a real loss to the university and to its communities. Well chosen, chancellors bring an outside perspective while having the university's best interests at heart. They have connections that can be pursued and strengthened to the benefit of the university. They serve without remuneration and in fact often make significant personal financial contributions to the university's endowment. They remain in many cases committed to the university mission long after their term of service. During this time of worldwide political and social upheaval, I have often mused on the relative stability of models that include that of a governor general or chancellor; in short, such appointments, wisely exercised, seem to sustain a broader view, longevity, and resilience. I sometimes compare this kind of system to a bicycle, which works brilliantly while continuing to defy full scientific and mathematical explanation.

My view is that a system of university governance that includes a chancellor selected with the support of the university convocation will be more robust and more likely to hold and retain trust in part because the chancellor can exemplify the university's values with a perspective from outside the university itself.

REFERENCES

Cobban, A.B. (1988). *The medieval English universities: Oxford and Cambridge to c. 1500*. University of California Press.
Ewart, P. (2015, 7 December). *To be or not to be chancellor of UNBC*. 250 News. http://250news.theexplorationplace.com/www.250news.com/56677.html
Kane, L. (2015, 10 December). *James Moore appointment as UNBC chancellor didn't get consultation: Senate*. CBC News British Columbia. https://www.cbc.ca/news/canada/british-columbia/james-moore-unbc-senate-1.3360137
University Act, RSBC 1996, c 468. https://www.bclaws.gov.bc.ca/civix/document/id/complete/statreg/96468_01
University of Oxford. (n.d.). *Past chancellors*. Retrieved 8 January 2023 from https://www.ox.ac.uk/about/organisation/university-officers/chancellor/past-chancellors
Vriend v Alberta, [1998] 1 SCR 493. https://scc-csc.lexum.com/scc-csc/scc-csc/en/item/1607/index.do

"Leadership, Vision, and the Role of Chancellor in University Governance"

B. ALEXANDER LEMAN
Co-founder, Vitruvian Group

Giardini's chapter locates the author's personal experience in the role of chancellor in its ecclesiastical origins. Are there similar roles beyond the academy and, if so, what mandate do they fulfil?

The Canadian vice-regal roles are perhaps the most direct analogue. Given the ceremonial nature of such roles, arguably the choice of the incumbent and the values that are signalled through that choice, are just as important as the duties subsequently performed. The case of Canada's resigned governor general is a case in point: originally appointed for her profile as a symbol of scientific achievement, she was ultimately pressured to resign for failing to represent other values expected of public figures.

Having served on various corporate boards, the closest analogue that I see to the role of chancellor in the corporate, NGO, or broader public sector context is the non-executive chair – a respected and senior person outside the formal chain of management, who brings a different perspective, may represent the organization with outside stakeholders, and, crucially, performs a key independent governance function. In these contexts, the efficacy and accountability of governance has primacy, and the demands and scrutiny in these dimensions is ever-increasing. The choices on board composition and non-executive chair selection are increasingly based on skills and focused on mandate, although the need to reflect a system of values that aligns with the corporate culture remains important as well.

While Giardini notes how the chancellor role evolved 800 years ago, the mid-twentieth-century concept of board roles as ceremonial sinecures has long ago been dispelled in the corporate world and is quickly being extinguished in non-profit and broader public sector contexts as the demands of rigorous, independent governance transform the nature of these roles. In Canada, government agencies that fail to prevent the inadvertent funding of corrupt practices in foreign countries, and charities that face scrutiny for failure of their boards and leadership to exercise their fiduciary duties over funds and relationships with government, are cautionary tales about why governance roles are more than simply symbolic or ceremonial.

Giardini concludes that, freed of the demands of everyday administrative duties, the chancellor's duties are to reflect a system of values, rather than a narrowly prescribed skills matrix. In the corporate and NGO context, seeking an alignment of values among a diversity of perspectives and experiences is an intrinsic benefit to the quality and character of board decision-making and should not be neglected. Giardini's perspective is an important reminder and reference point in that conversation.

chapter seven

Equity, Diversity, and Inclusion: Closing Gaps and Opening Minds

TRICIA GLAZEBROOK

Some of the most fraught decision-making in academic units takes place against a muffled background of equity, diversity, and inclusion (EDI) when gatekeeping practices and attitudes intervene during hiring and graduate-student admission. This chapter identifies strategies for "educating the educators" and opening the gates more widely, and subsequently for strengthening a unit's capacity to be inclusive and equitable every day. A key takeaway is that inclusive environments are fragile and need ongoing care. There is no silver bullet or one-size-fits-all solution. Surprisingly simple practices can displace long-standing disagreement to enable decision-making, but only long-game approaches can support a sustainable ethos of EDI that recognizes the strength that difference brings to a community. This chapter goes beyond how-to advice to deeper questions of values, identity, and self-and-other that are best engaged episodically, both alone in reflection and together in conversation. That is, EDI is not just about policy and compliance. EDI is fundamental to what kind of person each of us is and chooses to be.

This chapter starts by showing that what counts as an EDI issue is not often agreed upon, and EDI is a fragile work in progress. Section II provides experience-based evidence of treatment of diversity colleagues, advances in EDI education of higher-learning educators, EDI differences across disciplines, and finally, who carries the harms and how well-meant support can be toxic. Section III provides overview and comparative analysis of EDI in European Union (EU), US, and Canadian universities. The INVITED project assesses EDI in higher education in 48 EU countries, and its widespread and systematic assessment provides a unique, thorough, and useful data collection for grounding subsequent analysis. Section IV identifies EDI challenges. Section V discusses EDI in university governance and leadership. Section VI is a transition from information and explanation into discussion of strategies to increase EDI implementation in higher education. Sections VII and VIII address hiring and retention, respectively, and Section IX concludes that EDI in academic units depends almost entirely on faculty members and their commitment to EDI.

Bias and underrepresentation are long-standing injustices in higher education. This chapter takes EDI to be a historical issue and draws from literature as far back as the thirteenth century and as recently as 2021 to convey a sense of the recalcitrance of the challenge, the exception of individuals who broke the EDI barrier, and the differential advance of EDI academics. For example, disproportionate discussion of gender in this chapter is due to the substantial and well-researched entry of women into academic employment, though, as shown in this chapter, a barrier to women of colour is the incapacity of EDI systems to address intersectionality.

I. EDI in Education and Civil Society

What counts as an EDI issue is not always agreed upon and the defining of EDI is a fragile work in progress. This uncertainty is a strength, however, as it allows introduction of emerging issues – e.g., age, culture, marital status, LGBTQ+, education, ethnicity, language, appearance, and political perspective – that, using the United States as an example, do not appear in the 1964 U.S. Civil Rights Act (CRA) but do in some organizations' diversity policy. The CRA is included in Table 7.1 as an example of legislation in contrast with policy. Colour is the CRA's only category

Table 7.1. Diversity Categories Acknowledged by Organization

Categories	University of Michigan	The eXtension Foundation	Code for America	US Civil Rights Act
Age	*	*	*	–
Colour	–	–	–	*
Culture	*	–	–	–
Disability	*	*	*	*
Education	–	–	*	–
Ethnicity	*	*	*	–
Gender	*	*	*	*
Gender identity	*	–	*	–
Language	*	*	*	–
Marital status	–	–	*	–
Nationality/origin	*	*	*	*
Physical appearance	–	–	*	–
Political perspective	*	*	–	–
Race	*	*	*	*
Religion/commitment	*	*	*	*
Sexual orientation	*	*	*	*
Socio-economic status	*	*	*	–

Sources: Code for America (n.d.); eXtension Foundation Impact Collaborative (2020); University of Michigan (2021); US Equal Employment Opportunity Commission (1964).

not addressed by any of the three organizations named in Table 7.1, while the Act does not include ethnicity, language, or socioeconomic status. Current policy is accordingly well advanced to more inclusive diversity categories than in the 1964 law.

Taking diversity alone as an example of different approaches in EDI policy, Table 7.1 lists recognized diversity categories in three different kinds of organization: an institute of higher education (University of Michigan); a civil society organization (Code for America) that works to **improve government service of Americans; and an organization that is** both academic and civil-society (The eXtension Foundation), a consortium of 49 US Land Grant Institutions that connect academics with agricultural practitioners to conduct research on new technologies. Nationality and national origin have been combined into one category based on assumption that these terms intend the same group, as have religion and religious commitment. Gender and gender identity remain distinct as impacts are on different groups, though there can be overlap.

The table of 17 diversity categories shows 10 recognized across the board: age, disability, ethnicity, gender, language, nationality, race, religion, sexual orientation, and socio-economic status. The remaining are somewhat chopped up. The Civil Rights Act includes 14 categories, the University of Michigan 13, and The eXtension Foundation 11. The University of Michigan is the only one to include culture. The Civil Rights Act is the only one to include education, marital status, and physical appearance. The University of Michigan and Civil Rights Act include gender and gender identity, but The eXtension Foundation only gender. Presumably only the Civil Rights Act includes education because the other two are educators, and the Civil Rights Act likely excludes political perspective to avoid partisanship. Other differences are harder to explain. It may well be that selection of categories depends upon an individual's or organization's decision-making.

Rather than choosing defined lists, I understand all three parts of EDI as broadly and practically as possible in this analysis, and to be significantly different from each other, but also in close relation, in academic disciplines and teaching units. "Diversity" means, generally in this account, any identity underrepresented or person marginalized in any context, recognizing that each experience of diversity is unique for each person. "Equity" means being treated the same as everyone else when in that unique experience, e.g., equal pay for equal work and equal opportunity. "Inclusion" is the goal in this account because it is taken to mean that the individuality of intersectional diversities no longer affects anyone's prospects, benefits, or feeling of place in the work environment. That is, diversity is who we are, equity is how we are treated, and inclusion is how we feel we belong in our context.

These terms inform any analysis of EDI in the workplace of educators in institutes of higher education. For students and faculty, the first moment that EDI issues arise is upon accessing the university, i.e., upon a student's acceptance into a program and a faculty member's hiring. The second major moment, for both students and faculty, relates to retention. Institutions have invested in significant support systems for students, but faculty are largely expected to navigate their context on their own. This means that

EDI is not fixed in academic units but disparately understood and differentially implemented across disciplines and departments.

II. Lessons from Experience: An Anecdotal Account

I have been employed in various leadership positions in my role as an academic. In one of them, at one point the other chairs and I were given a book on how to succeed as an effective department chair. The book had been published in its second edition four years before we received it, and its first edition is still less than a decade old. So I assume it is widely read, or at least widely provided to chairs to read. There is no chapter or section on diversity or inclusion. These two words, in fact, do not appear in the book's index. This is a surprising omission when institutions of higher education today typically invest substantially in EDI programs and units. As I show below, evidence indicates that faculty hiring and retention of diversity personnel are largely left to faculty decision-makers with, in some cases, little understanding of the justice and benefits of EDI in the teaching, research, and service workplace.

There have been significant advances in understanding EDI as values in themselves. Diversity of the student body has increased through substantial financial investment and structural changes to attract and retain students. Amongst the teaching faculty, however, EDI has not always grown. For example, when I have moved to new institutions, I have increasingly been required to watch a one-hour video on diversity in the workplace and successfully answer related, multiple-choice questions. Usually, the issues addressed in this process are narrowly limited to racism and sexism in the workplace. Yet, it is important to realize that diversity faculty are autonomous agents and expert, competitive scholars rather than victims of prejudice. Those who carry biases that were entrenched in their training and discipline are responsible for moving themselves beyond such biases for the benefit of everyone in the unit and all our stakeholders.

Moreover, because my research is inherently interdisciplinary, my leadership has not been limited to one discipline. I have thus experienced protocols, by-laws, and other discipline- or department-specific traditions and policy approaches in Canada and the United States in the humanities and social sciences. There are also differences across disciplines in how EDI are integrated; for example, in STEM disciplines, women are still underrepresented (AAUW, n.d.; WEF, 2021), though they have advanced in other areas; women are also underrepresented in philosophy (Lombrozo, 2013), though more integrated into other humanities disciplines (Anderson, 2015). It seems that faculty have largely been left to themselves to manage the composition of their unit. Advances in EDI have varied broadly across disciplines, with my primary discipline, philosophy, lagging substantially behind. This state of affairs is counterproductive, because EDI progress is largely an "all-hands-on-deck" affair in which central administration provides leadership and resources, and an increasingly diverse student body and non-academic staff populate the classroom, hallways, and departmental administrative offices.

However, the brunt of EDI amongst the faculty is carried by students and young colleagues. A monolithic faculty face does students a disservice. EDI faculty are necessary to serve an EDI student body appropriately. Students need role models who will help to ensure that the academic classroom feels like home to each student, rather than as someone else's home into which they are invited.

Similarly, with faculty, a comment such as "I'm so glad you are here" might appear to be an appropriate welcome when one meets a new colleague in the hallway for the first time. But, in reality, the message that is actually communicated can feel like "This is my space, but I'm a generous person and will share it with you." The better statement might rather involve a question such as "Finding your way around OK?" or just a plain "How's it going?" – an expression of support and an interest in talking with a new colleague. Inclusion is precluded when equity is compromised by differential treatment for those identified as diverse by even the most well-meaning around them. EDI failures affect students without role models and faculty reminded that they are "diverse" from their colleagues' perspective. In such cases, they are made to feel that they do not belong, and they are vulnerable to imposter syndrome. Young faculty particularly may expect a glass ceiling.

III. EDI in Europe and the United States: In the Data and in the Trenches

In 2015, the European Union states agreed on the Paris Declaration, in response to race-targeted terrorist attacks in France and Denmark. It was aimed at K–12 education, encouraging teaching EDI values early in life, but it also prompted attention to EDI in higher education. In 2019, the European University Association (EUA) conducted significant research, known as the INVITED project, into EDI commitments and strategies in higher education for students, faculty, and non-academic staff (EUA, n.d.). The EUA represents the universities and their leadership in 48 European countries and plays a crucial role in the Bologna Process, which promotes intergovernmental coordination and shared recognition of degree qualifications. INVITED surveyed 159 universities, conducted a peer-learning seminar with participants from 23 universities in 13 countries, and hosted in-depth discussions with 12 universities across Europe (Claeys-Kulik et al., 2019, pp. 45–50). Throughout analysis below, "faculty" means teaching personnel and "staff" means departmental administration.

Since the EU was established, with The Schengen *Acquis* (1999), internationality has been a driver for EDI in higher education in Europe (Sursock, 2015, pp. 28–33). After the Schengen Convention abolished systematic border control between the 26 Schengen countries so people could easily move throughout the area, the Bologna Declaration (1999) and Bologna Process (European Commission, n.d.) enabled recognition of degree qualifications across borders. Canada and the United States recognize degrees across their shared border but without the Schengen area's capacity for cross-border employment that has helped Europe drive EDI development. EU progress on EDI in higher education is thus likely to be more organized and advanced than it is in Canada and the United States because Europe has practical need for, and benefits from, coherence in higher education across its smaller, neighbouring countries, and its explicit recognition of the role of education in EDI as cultures mix across borders. The 2019 EUA INVITED report is accordingly worth examining as a substantial, recent, systematic assessment of EDI approaches, successes, and challenges in higher education.

INVITED shows that, for faculty, the two issues most commonly addressed by institutions are disability (76%) and gender (83%). As in the United States and Canada, a significant number of institutions address diversity more for students than for faculty, and more for faculty than for staff. The proportion of institutions addressing gender is virtually the same for students (82%) and faculty (83%), while age and "caring responsibilities" are addressed more for faculty than students (Claeys-Kulik et al., 2019, p. 25), presumably because faculty are often older and more likely to have family responsibilities.

Canada combines partial salary with employment insurance to support parental leave for new-born care throughout the first year. The United States provides virtually no post-partum support but allows women's use of accumulated sick-leave allowances to maintain income. Nearly one in four women returns to work within two weeks of birthing while one in five retires, though Biden's American Families Plan proposing paid parental leave may lower these rates and reduce racial disparities in wage loss if it succeeds (The White House, 2021).

INVITED found that 83% of institutes addressed gender for faculty, though 9% fewer (74%) addressed gender among students or non-academic staff. Similarly, 55% addressed ethnic/cultural/migration-background diversity amongst faculty but only 45% did so among students and staff – a difference of 10%. The INVITE project indicates three further significant outcomes on EDI in European higher education concerning faculty:

1 Students, for the most part, get more EDI support than faculty, and faculty more than staff;
2 Many more institutions address gender issues among faculty than address ethnic, cultural, or national-origin diversity; and

3 Gender is in fact addressed for faculty in significantly more institutions than any other EDI issue, with even disability showing 7% less institutional attention.

Yet gender bias remains in higher education, right down to student evaluations of faculty teaching (Boehmer & Wood, 2017; Huston, 2006).

Bingham and Nix (2010) surveyed women employed in higher education (88% faculty and 12% administrators) to identify their perceptions of women's treatment in hiring, promotions, salary, workload, and institutional support. Respondents overwhelmingly agreed that women did not get fair treatment. The longer interviewees were at the institution, the more they agreed that women were treated unfairly (p. 4). Inequities include a pay gap and women's little use of sick leave in order to store time for maternity, because parental leave is not available (p. 8). Bingham and Nix (2010, pp. 5 and 7) also report a mass of literature recording women's stress created by trying to balance a family with a career; higher likelihood of male counterparts, who became fathers at the same career point, achieving tenure; and issues such as larger teaching and service loads, and less access to research resources. Women also believed that women's work is valued less than men's and that women are perceived as less career committed. Evidence confirms the reality of both women's commitment and their persistent stereotyping as less professionally competent when identified with reproductive or care roles (p. 6).

Respondents were mostly Caucasian (92%), with only 6% either African American or Hispanic (Bingham & Nix, 2010, p. 4). As discussed below, women faculty of colour face significant and disturbing challenges to which white women are not exposed at the same level or rate. At the faculty level, where unit hiring and retention decisions are usually made, EDI may have improved with respect to gender, but decision-makers may not grasp the biasing impact of intersectionality on decision-making.

Justification of diversity hiring based on student impacts is common but tokenizes and defers justice issues at stake in EDI if credentials and achievement are side-lined. In the United States, the Office for Civil Rights of the Department of Education collaborated with the Department of Justice to provide a *Guidance on the Voluntary Use of Race to Achieve Diversity in Postsecondary Education* to replace a 2008 letter limited to student admissions. It was last updated in 2020 but has been under investigation since July 2021, perhaps because of an implied distinction between "our nation's students" and "students of diverse backgrounds" and a suggestion that diversity inclusion is "not just a lofty idea" (Department of Education 2020, para. 2). Its guidance was primarily how to navigate law when proactively pursuing diversity and, like the letter, did not address faculty.

A 2016 report likewise based on students discusses "extraordinary and significant" strategies to increase their diversity (Department of Education 2016, p. 35) but then notes that diversity amongst faculty "plays an important role in achieving an inclusive institution" (p. 37). Students report a "sense of belonging and inclusion … [when] they see themselves reflected in the faculty" (p. 37). To increase faculty diversity, the report recommends wide hiring pools and mentoring and support programs to retain underrepresented minority faculty with high rates of turnover (pp. 37–8). Despite risks of tokenism, this is a large step forward at the federal level in acknowledging bias and need to integrate EDI into higher education as a social issue of quality of education beyond the legal issue of constraints on what can be done.

The 2016 report includes 2013–14 data on faculty diversity collected by the DoE's National Center for Education Statistics (NCES), an independent research centre in the Institute for Education Sciences. The survey of 600,000 non-tenure track, pre-tenure, and tenured faculty showed that fewer than one in ten was either Black or Hispanic; overall, 74% were white, 9% Asian, 5% Black, and 4% Hispanic, and 7% Other (Department of Education 2016, p. 73). Among tenured faculty, the percentages were the same as above except for a 3% shift in which white faculty rose to 77% and Other dropped to 4%. "Other" includes "American Indian/Alaska Native, Native Hawaiian/Pacific Islander, two or more races, nonresidents, and unknown" (p. 73). As discussed below, retention is a significant challenge in EDI.

Pre-tenure faculty showed the lowest proportion of whites at 65%, while Asians were 11% – their largest proportion at 2% more than among the tenured – and Blacks and Hispanics were each only 1% more than among the tenured, i.e., 6% and 5% respectively. These numbers undermine the idea that increasing diversity hires that then work their way through the system addresses EDI. The largest change was a pre-tenure increase to 13% among Others.

This research is, however, undermined by the Other category that at 13% of pre-tenure faculty is more than twice the proportion of Blacks (6%), almost three times the proportion of Hispanics (5%), and more than both combined. Even the proportion for pre-tenure Asians (11%) is uncertain against a 13% Other proportion. Yet this report shows undeniably that diversity is sorely missing in US higher education unless there has been substantial effort to increase it since 2014. This seems unlikely, given how limited prior progress was.

Nonetheless, the report notes that the proportion of faculty of colour gradually increased over 20 years using a study by the Teachers Insurance and Annuity Association measuring diversity faculty between 1993 and 2013 (Department of Education 2016, p. 74). Asians almost doubled from 5% to 9% between Fall 1993, when whites accounted for 81% of full-time faculty, and the 2013–14 academic year. During this time, Blacks went from 4% to 6% and Hispanics from 3% to 5%. That is, yearly for two decades, Asian gains in faculty positions averaged at 0.2%, while Hispanic and Black gains averaged at 0.1%. At this rate, Asians would be 20% of faculty by 2076, Black by 2161, and Hispanics 2171. The report notes further that the fastest growth in diversity faculty between 1993 and 2013 was in non-tenure track and part-time positions. There was little movement towards diversity representation in higher education prior to the 2013–14 academic year, and what progress was made was primarily in the lowest-paying and most insecure faculty positions.

A 2019 report provides useful data for comparison of 2013–14 and Fall 2018 (IES/NCES, 2020, Fig. 2). As Table 7.2 shows, there was small progress.

Table 7.2. Faculty Diversity Compared in 2013–14 and 2018 (%)

Group	Total faculty		Tenured		Pre-tenure		Not tenure-track	
	2013–14	2018	2013–14	2018	2013–14	2018	2013–14	2018
Hispanic	4	6	4	5.5	5	6	4	8.0
Black	5	5	5	4.0	6	8	6	6.5
Asian	9	12	9	10.5	11	14	7	7.0
White	74	75	77	77.5	65	73	74	77.0
Other	7	0	4	0	13	0	8	1.0

Source: IES/NCES (2020, Fig. 2).

Retention remains an issue. If some pre-tenure diversity faculty in 2013–14 had been tenured in the next four years, the diversity proportions of the tenured in 2018 surely have grown as did the white proportion by over 12%.

The NCES report also disaggregates gender. Looking down the ranks from professor to non-tenure track faculty, white women increasingly overtake white men. Overall, of the 75% of white professors, 40% were men and 35% women. In the 80% of white professors, 53% were men and 27% women. Of the 75% white associate professors, 40% were men, 35% women. Assistant professors are, however, a turning point for gender as 73% of the white junior faculty are 39% women and 34% men. Likewise, for the 75% of white instructors, women are 42% and men are 33%, and for lecturers, women are 44% against men's 35%. What this data shows is that white women have been substantially more successful than any other diversity group in entering higher education as faculty. Concerning race and intersectionality, the slow progress shows that EDI still faces significant barriers.

IV. EDI Challenges

Intersectionality is a factor in bias that has been largely unaddressed because policies are unprepared and uniquely unable to address intersectionality because of category design. When gender is itself identified as an EDI issue, it is segregated out from other identified categories. Most women also belong in another category, though impacts are different, given that categories exist because bias privileges some over others, and impacts vary in complex ways. For example, even if an institution includes gender identity in its EDI issues, a trans woman can experience bias differently than other women.

Because the generalized need for policy change commonly initiates activities intended to resolve issues addressed in that very policy, without proactive intervention by implementers, blindness to intersectionality can be carried over into implementation. The consequence is that, for example, women who are white, cis, and not otherwise "Othered" become privileged over other women. That is, EDI policy formulation addressing "gender" is *always already* inherently biased towards a small group of privileged women and thus functions contrary to its very aim of achieving gender EDI. This helps to explain why white, cis, and not otherwise "Othered" women have achieved more success as academics than their counterparts.

The INVITED project identified several issues that hamper progress on EDI (Claeys-Kulik et al., 2019, p. 37). The most common and hardest to solve were lack of awareness among the university community, lack of funding and other resources, difficulty identifying target groups, lack of consensus and support within the community, difficulty in collecting data on issues, and lack of information and training for personnel. There is no reason to believe these are not also significant challenges to EDI in Canadian and US universities.

V. Leadership

Though a small group of women has been privileged in EDI strategies, women still face a glass ceiling and are strongly underrepresented in the highest echelon of university leadership. Historically, women entered universities as students some time ago. Betissia Gozzadini received a degree in law at the University of Bologna in 1237 CE and is reputed to have been the first woman to get a degree in higher education.

The first two women to receive a university degree in the United States did so at Mississippi College in 1831 (Cooper, 2011, p. 23). Grace Lockhart was the first in the British Empire to receive a bachelor's degree, in 1874 from Mount Allison University in New Brunswick, Canada (Reid, 2015).

Since 2000, women's enrolment in higher education has outpaced men's (IES/NCES, 2019, p. 3). In 2016, 54% of university students in Europe were women (Borell-Damián & Rahier, 2019). A 1984 report by the Commission on Canadian Studies called discrimination against women in Canadian universities a "national disgrace" (Gaskell, 2014). By 2013, however, 56% of students enrolled in Canadian colleges and universities were women (Ferguson, 2016, 6).

Women's performance as educators and leaders in colleges and universities has not, however, followed this development path in Europe, Canada, or the United States. In Europe, only 24% of full professors are women. In 2017, only 22% of heads of institutions in higher education were women (EUA, 2019; European Commission, 2019, p. 128). In 2019, 22 of 46 European countries had no female rectors – equivalent to "president" in North America – at all, and only 14.3% of rectors in the remaining countries were female (Borell-Damián & Rahier, 2019). Ten had no female vice-rectors, and only 27.8% (up from 24.3% in 2014) of vice-rectors in the remaining 36 countries were female, with 3 countries moving towards gender parity and 4 having achieved 45% to 55% (Borell-Damián & Rahier, 2019).

In the United States, the first women instructors at a US college or university began teaching in 1783, much earlier than Canada, at the Washington College in Maryland (Kohl Gallery, 2013). In 2017, though numbers of women in university presidencies had grown over the previous three decades, women were still underrepresented and had typically followed a different path to the role than men (ACE, 2021). Moreover, 78% of women presidents were serving their first presidency, and only 8% were leading doctorate-granting institutions (ACE, 2021).

The first time a woman became a full professor in Canada was in 1912 (McGill, 2021). Almost a century later, in 2011, 37% of professors overall were women, making up 46% of assistant professors but only 23% of full professors; women account for 54% of non-tenure-track teaching staff (Ferguson, 2016, p. 17). Collective data on women leaders in institutes of higher education in Canada is hard to find. There are 103 universities, and a Wikipedia compilation last edited in October 2021 of 70 universities shows women holding just 18% of vice-chancellor and president positions (List of Canadian university leaders, 2021).

Gender bias clearly has a long-standing history in higher education and remains throughout leadership, which likely contributes to the smaller proportion of women in higher ranks and larger proportion in non-tenured positions.

VI. Strategies Towards EDI

To address egregious privileging of some women over others in academic units, EDI policy could serve women more effectively by including intersectionality as a unique EDI category, and by embedding statements on gender into other categories. For example, race- and religion-based practices could be acknowledged as varying, and gender identity could be more widely acknowledged and discussed as a gender, intersectional, and independent issue. Moreover, women who have benefitted from non-intersectionality because of EDI policy structure could acknowledge this privilege and practise support and solidarity across intersectionality.

EDI is a legal obligation wherever legal recourse is available to those who feel they have been wronged because of bias. Performance-based funding or quotas can also be EDI incentives. Diversity is also, however, an asset because it produces more creative working environments. It is not solved by filling quotas or implementing strong, unilateral measures. Such approaches are inadequate for achieving the cultural change that recognizes the value of EDI and equips personnel with tools and skills to embrace diversity (Claeys-Kulik et al., 2019, p. 18). Effective EDI strategies

- are led by institutional leaders who promoted diversity rather than simply aiming to prevent discrimination and harassment;
- included supporting actions to help underrepresented, disadvantaged, or vulnerable groups; and
- monitored and evaluated actions, from simple mention of need for accountability to explicit key performance indicators (p. 19).

The top three EDI success factors identified in INVITED are leadership commitment, involvement of target groups in developing and implementing approaches, and committed involvement from the university community (p. 31). Additional resources, government support, and enhancement of the quality of learning, teaching, and research through diversity are also useful drivers of institutional action on EDI.

Cooperation with external stakeholders to overcome barriers is another strategy; e.g., Germany's Excellence Initiative that funds institutional strategic development has helped several universities advance EDI (Claeys-Kulik et al., 2019, p. 17). The EUA recommends a system-wide, holistic approach that strengthens dialogue between universities, policymakers, funders, public authorities, and organizations supporting underrepresented, disadvantaged, and vulnerable groups (p. 44). The Bologna Process enabled such dialogue across Europe. A similar collaboration in North America would likely be productive, though agreement might be uniquely challenging.

Canada and the United States have other EDI challenges in higher education not shared with Europe. For example, at least half (52%) of INVITED respondents reported addressing five of nine diversity issues among academic staff. In Europe, teaching staff are responsible for 26% of implementation of EDI activities (Claeys-Kulik et al., 2019, p. 21), but other than grading and engagement in the classroom and office hours, or by mail, there is little else in EDI that instructors in Canada and the United States are expected to do. This is changing, however: increasingly, universities in Canada and the United States ask applicants for a teaching position to provide an EDI statement. Faculty are constrained by institutional policies and guidelines, though, in my experience, faculty manage compliance and decision-making amongst themselves, though interventions are triggered if decisions or behaviour become actionable.

Faculty independence is especially the case concerning hiring and retaining faculty. There is accordingly significant disparity of diversity representation between academic units (Abdul-Raheem, 2016; Stout et al., 2018). The next two sections discuss gender and other EDI issues in hiring and retention of faculty and provide suggestions for managing persistent bias amongst faculty colleagues.

VII. Hiring

A 1997 study on hiring law school faculty noted that affirmative action remained controversial and that "white women and men of color, but surprisingly not women of color, began teaching at somewhat more prestigious schools than white men with comparable credentials" (Merritt & Reskin, 1997, p. 199). This gain was attributed to credentials and work experience, as well as job search strategies and personal characteristics such as age or marital status that accounted for three times more of the explained variance than gender or race. Much can be unpacked here, starting with the point that age and marital status are inherently gender-biased factors.

Concerning women of colour, Bingham and Nix (2010) show that a decade later, women were still subjected to gender bias, marginalized in academic contexts, and treated inequitably. However, as noted above, their survey reported 92% Caucasian respondents, while in 2019 only 55% of INVITED institutions reported addressing ethnic, cultural, or migration-background EDI issues. That women at the intersection of gender and race had not begun to teach at prestigious schools at the end of the last century is in fact hardly surprising at all, given gender bias and seemingly more deeply embedded race bias that, even in 2019, in a multicultural Europe, is addressed at two-thirds the rate of gender issues. Two conclusions must be drawn here. In the universities of the Global North, strategies, investment, and structural supports addressing race and ethnicity, at the same level as have been widely implemented on gender, is long overdue. And women faculty of colour will continue to be subjected to intersectional bias until racism in the academy is addressed.

The need to increase diversity of race and ethnicity amongst faculty in higher education is a long-standing and still live issue in the literature (Abdul-Raheem, 2016; Merritt & Reskin, 1997; Stout et al., 2018). In departments, changing recalcitrant minds during hiring processes is not easy. Some of the most fraught collective decision-making in academic units takes place against a muffled background of EDI when gatekeeping practices and attitudes intervene during hiring and graduate-student admission. Strategies suggested here apply primarily to hiring but can also be applied to graduate-student admission diversity issues.

Simple methods to reduce or change bias include intentionally building a more positive environment before hiring becomes an active process. Sometimes, regular depersonalization in conversations is one small way to defer and weaken long-standing, habitual disagreements between senior colleagues. Diverting the discussion from people to roles can begin to break habitual conflicts: for example, focusing on what the committee decided, rather than what the individuals said, can be productive for undermining long-standing disagreement that has shifted focus, and thus response, from the issue to the person.

More specifically, in defining the key characteristics of a future position in the earliest moment of hiring, one might collect suggestions by email, transfer them to small pieces of paper, and circulate them in a hat at the search committee meeting, to be pulled out one by one and read by people in the room. While the process may appear silly at first, there is a tendency for those who report a particular suggestion to make it their own. Alternatively, I find that someone will typically ask who submitted this particular suggestion. A useful strategy in such a case is to enquire whether it matters and, if so, what they themselves think about the idea.

In my experience, in such cases, people in the group tend to claim the suggestion as a version of what they themselves have recommended, and thus offer reasons to support it. Usually, someone else will likewise present their own reasons for why they made the recommendation. Typically in such circumstances, surprisingly quickly, people are discussing issues on which they agree, rather than focusing on points of disagreement. This provides the opportunity for colleagues who are accustomed to withdrawing in the face of the expected conflict, to lean into the unexpected experience of agreement.

Such simple strategies for educating the educators open the gates more widely for colleagues to align their views, thereby strengthening the unit's capacity to be more inclusive. Environments are fragile and need ongoing care, but these sorts of simple practices are often fruitful and well suited to promote respect for different viewpoints. There is no silver bullet or a one-size-fits-all solution, but small, regular instances of change can ultimately be responsive to unique contexts while also being impactful. There are many different ways to displace conflict in favour of agreement, but such incremental strategies have served me well in contexts known for their contentiousness. Such in-house experience and progress towards increased openness and collegial inclusion builds a more functional atmosphere, although these instances can be futile if not followed up by more substantial approaches.

It is important not to wait until a hiring process is underway to begin raising awareness of the value of diversity and educating colleagues on EDI hiring policies, but it is also hard to initiate such conversations with no hiring on the horizon. As soon as a hiring is authorized, HR personnel can be invited to talk about EDI in hiring and the institution's relevant policies, including what hiring criteria are standard in the institution's expectations. Generally, people know what should not be considered, but not necessarily what should. When it comes to actual interviewing, whether online or on campus, HR can return to discuss what is and is not appropriate to ask of a candidate.

The advantage of inviting qualified third parties is not simply that they are presumably expert but, also, that they are able to insert information into the subsequent conversation that goes beyond a particular colleague's perspective when the expert has left the meeting and the real discussion begins. The experts need not come just from HR, however. Universities often have non-academic staff managing diversity policy and issues for students and are well prepared to talk to faculty about EDI attitudes, practices, and resources for faculty.

Colleagues supporting diversity will also have collected tools and ideas to strengthen the unit's diversity practices, perhaps through such simple means as searching for places to advertise to attract diversity applications beyond HR's required diversity hiring sites. Issues that have arisen throughout the hiring process can also be discussed in hallways, offices, or department meetings, once the hiring is complete. The more colleagues understand about diversity strategies and practices, the better equipped they are to develop EDI in the unit, in more than just hiring practices. When diversity looks to be exclusively a hiring issue, or worse, becomes seemingly a compliance issue that prompts the recalcitrance, EDI goals cannot be achieved. The conversation and culture change in which diversity emerges is part of the unit's foundational ethos that can be grown over time as long as each participant feels included and respected in a process that is actually aimed at developing everyone's perspective to the positive factors of EDI.

VIII. Retention

In Europe, despite the large numbers of institutions addressing gender, the "long-standing problem" (Claeys-Kulik et al., 2019, p. 29) of women leaving the profession has not been resolved. Moreover, poor retention rates prevent women from achieving high rank, both as faculty and in administrative leadership. High-end leadership roles are typically given in universities to those who complete a PhD, are hired as faculty, and move up into successive administrative leadership roles. This glass ceiling is hampered by poor retention rates in cases where an institution releases women or because they choose to leave for family and/or child-care reasons – or simply because the job is not sustainably tolerable.

Agathangelou and Ling (2002) called the situation of women faculty of colour unten(ur)able. Long-standing and longitudinal research has documented that they receive lower course evaluations from students than white faculty and male faculty of colour (Dukes & Gay, 1989; Fries & McNinch, 2003; Hamermesh & Parker, 2005). Ability as a teacher is an evaluative criterion in tenure application. For women facing intersectionality, the situation can be even more dire.

On a personal level, I recall a department meeting in my early teaching days where a senior colleague, a woman originally from Puerto Rico, presented a course proposal to the department on Latin American philosophy. No one was offering such a course in any philosophy program in Canada or the United States. The syllabus listed several books that she had herself translated. Our colleagues, who themselves knew little about Latin American philosophy, began to criticize the proposal over trivial details, with no regard to the course's originality, or her efforts and expertise as someone who had been teaching for more than 20 years and researching Latin American philosophy even longer. When she responded to their comments, she was asked by a senior female colleague why she was being so defensive. I could not restrain myself from blurting out that her response was certainly a normal reaction to being attacked. The bell rang at just that moment, interrupting the discussion as everyone left for the next class. My colleague eventually took the course to the multicultural program and was soon teaching it there.

On another occasion, a Pakistani woman who had taught on a one-year contract for us was interviewed for a tenure-track position. When the interviews were finished and we met to rank the candidates, a senior colleague – a pastor and expert on Asian religion, who did not support her candidacy – angrily asserted, "I know these Asians, they can't be trusted." Likewise, when a man of Puerto Rican descent was interviewed, he was similarly rejected, though several faculty members thought he was far better qualified than other applicants. His hiring was petitioned to higher administration by several of us and members of the multicultural program. Eventually, he was hired and housed in the Philosophy Department. I suspect that readers from academia could share similar experiences.

Intersectionality can locate a person beyond an unten(ur)able situation into an untenable situation. Women of colour teaching at primarily white research institutions have described gendered racism in their classroom interactions with students, specifically indicating that white, male students challenge their authority, question their teaching competence, and disrespect their scholarly expertise, often behaving in ways that are intimidating and either subtly or overtly threatening to their person or career (Pittman, 2010, pp. 187 and 191–2). Given continuing, widespread dominance of white males in university education and leadership, at the same time that white, male students may themselves feel under threat if they are in the minority, it is challenging to imagine how and when this kind of vindictive behaviour, and the stress, fear, and harm it can bring, will go away. The consequence can be not just loss of a job but demoralization and loss of hard-earned goals and future self- and life-visions.

Diversity faculty might also leave a job because they were denied tenure. This denial can mean inadequate performance or bias that skews decision-makers' preferences or, more insidiously, impacts of bias on performance throughout the years leading up to tenure application. One way to manage bias in retention is to provide the kind of support one might give to all junior faculty. Bringing people together at social events can weaken bias, not necessarily by explicitly promoting EDI, but by prompting colleagues with bias, whether implicit or intentional, to consider the person an exception to biased expectations. Discretely ensuring that achievements are announced and noticed can also support junior faculty, as does co-authoring when research interests overlap. In the classroom, formal introduction of a new faculty member to students, with explicit acknowledgment of degrees, publications, and other highlights, can be more impactful coming from a department chair or senior faculty than from the person alone and can counter students' implicit or explicit bias. One can also participate in organizations typically within the university that represent and support diversity groups. These groups provide community, and introducing new faculty can lead to important mentors and advocates who help build a sense of inclusion and autonomy.

It is also important that senior faculty take responsibility for initiating and contributing to EDI discussions, rather than leaving the initiatives to the more vulnerable, i.e., diversity faculty, and pre-tenure and non-tenure-track department members. Diversity faculty should not be put in the position of having to choose between being the only ones supporting diversity – as if speaking for all diversity everywhere and, in deep infringement of personal identity, defending themselves – or giving up their voice. Admittedly, pre-tenure and non-tenure-track colleagues may be more EDI savvy than senior colleagues after being educated in more diverse classrooms and in institutions that have made significant advances in recent decades. Diversity faculty, pre-tenure or non-tenure-track faculty, are perhaps never really comfortable to speak freely, but they are certainly better able to do so when the conversation includes voices of the less vulnerable. For pre-tenure faculty, especially pre-tenure diversity faculty, risk that tenure may be denied is a heavy burden, and agreeing with senior faculty rather than introducing a controversial point puts less at stake.

At the same time, it is important not to over-compensate – diversity is not an inadequacy that needs to be compensated for, and neither is singling out diversity colleagues helpful. Such actions simply "other" a colleague by reinforcing alterity. Concerning retention, junior faculty should be treated equally, though that does not necessarily mean the same, given differences in the experience of being junior faculty. The crucial point is that no one should feel like an outsider invited in, but not really belonging. Those who have spent a week in a country where people for the most part are not speaking their language, well understand that feeling of estrangement.

Retention is not just about the formalities of the tenure process. It is also about the atmosphere and experience between hiring and tenure application that can support or undermine. Typically, anyone pre-tenure experiences something of both support and undermining. In functional departments, tenured faculty do not withdraw when a colleague intentionally or unwittingly exercises bias-based power that the targeted faculty, especially if pre-tenure, cannot respond to without expectation of future harm to job security, reputation, or other factors that contribute to success. Confrontation does not, however, change minds. It is especially difficult to build an EDI atmosphere in teaching units populated by well-established scholars who are protected by tenure, used to being an authority, and sensitive to change.

Yet there are strategies and practices over the longer term that can bring change. Ongoing listening and sharing views in group discussion – deliberately diverted from direction at particular participants – is a start. Social events outside formal contexts can lower walls between colleagues and build relationships by increasing a sense of mutual humanity and person-being that exceeds "colleague" identity. This is slow work that takes effort and patience and is not always easy. But without such work, it is extremely likely that much longer will pass with no growth in EDI development.

IX. Conclusion

My experience teaching over three decades in Canada and the United States is that EDI interventions into hiring rests in the Human Resources office requiring advertising on specific diversity-oriented job-posting websites – unless a unit asks for more support. Concerning retention, universities have increased pre-tenure support, e.g., my current employer requires an advisory committee, and an annual review that includes broader career progress reporting. These supports, however, are unrelated to EDI issues and buffer the university against litigation in case of tenure denial. The advisory committee consists of tenured faculty in the department, and the annual review is also conducted by the tenured faculty. As is the case at many universities, EDI, in both hiring and retention, is left to a department's own devices. Movement towards EDI in academic units, for both faculty and staff, can happen only when faculty members pro-actively work towards it. Making change is thus hard and slow.

Yet this shortcoming also provides a reality check. EDI practices that bring real change cannot be achieved simply by writing them into policy and governance. Where job ads are posted can be governed, but hiring and retention require complex conversations and group decision-making based largely on voting. It is virtually impossible to identify EDI breaches with certainty or respond in ways that do not divide the unit, while reversing such a decision would put the person at the centre of discussion in an extremely difficult situation. EDI development thus depends almost entirely on the faculty themselves.

This means that introducing and building EDI in a department cannot be about compliance or behaviour but is, for every faculty member, about who you are and who you choose to be in your professional capacity. Every department faculty member is at a unique stage in EDI consciousness development – sometimes we teach, sometimes we learn. Gaining and passing on EDI awareness and commitment are long-game practices of mindful action, honesty, and relationship growth across difference.

The "-isms of prejudice," e.g., racism, sexism, ableism, etc., are a cartography in which no one is entirely free or entirely constrained. Locations on the map define proportions of dominance and oppression. You cannot escape the map, but you can move around on it and make choices about where you are as oppressor or oppressed. Where will you stay? If you see this map as helpful and envision your mobility, you are quite possibly privileged and have little experience of how choice belongs to privilege, and how your resistance to marginalization, underrepresentation, or bias may be an accelerant rather than a solution. The first step to enact change towards EDI justice is acknowledging one's own privilege.

REFERENCES

Abdul-Raheem, J. (2016). Faculty diversity and tenure in higher education. *Journal of Cultural Diversity*, 23(2), 53–6. https://doi.org/10.1097 /ACM.0b013e31822c066d

Agathangelou, A.M., & Ling, L.H.M. (2002). An unten(ur)able position: The politics of teaching for women of color in the US. *International Feminist Journal of Politics*, 4(3), 368–98. https://doi.org/10.1080 /1461674022000031562

American Association of University Women (AAUW). (n.d.). *Explore the issues*. Retrieved 3 March 2021 from https://www.aauw.org/issues/

American Council on Education (ACE). (2021). *Path to the presidency*. *American Council on Education*. https://www.aceacps.org/women-presidents/

Anderson, N. (2015, 28 April). Philosophy's gender bias: For too long, scholars say, women have been ignored. *The Washington Post*. https://www.washingtonpost.com/news/grade-point/wp/2015/04/28/philosophys-gender-bias-for-too-long-scholars-say-women-have-been-ignored/

Bingham, T., & Nix, S.J. (2010). Women faculty in higher education: A case study on gender bias. *Forum on Public Policy*, 1–12. https://files.eric.ed.gov/fulltext/EJ903580.pdf

Boehmer, D.M., & Wood, W.C. (2017). Student vs. faculty perspectives on quality instruction: Gender bias, "hotness," and "easiness" in evaluating teaching. *Journal of Education for Business*, *92*(4), 173–8. https://doi.org/10.1080/08832323.2017.1313189

Bologna Declaration. (1999). *The Bologna Declaration of 19 June 1999: Joint declaration of the European ministers of education*. http://ehea.info/Upload/document/ministerial_declarations/1999_Bologna_Declaration_English_553028.pdf

Borell-Damián, L., & Rahier, M. (2019). *Women in university leadership: Subtle leaks in the pipeline to the top*. Retrieved 12 February 2021 from https://eua.eu/resources/expert-voices/94:women-in-university-leadership-subtle-leaks-in-the-pipeline-to-the-top.html

Claeys-Kulik, A.-L., Ekman Jorgensen, T., & Stoeber, H. (2019). *Diversity, equity and inclusion in European higher education institutions: Results from the INVITED project*. European University Association. https://eua.eu/downloads/publications/web_diversity%20equity%20and%20inclusion%20in%20european%20higher%20education%20institutions.pdf

Code for America. (n.d.). *Our vision for DEI*. Retrieved 22 February 2021 from https://www.codeforamerica.org/diversity

Code for America. (n.d.). *Values*. Retrieved 22 February 2021 from https://www.codeforamerica.org/values

Cooper, F.L. (2011). *Looking back Mississippi*. University Press of Mississippi.

Department of Education. (2016). *Advancing diversity and Inclusion in higher education*. Office of Planning, Evaluation and Policy Development, Office of the Under Secretary, US Department of Education. https://www2.ed.gov/rschstat/research/pubs/advancing-diversity-inclusion.pdf

Department of Education. (2020). *Guidance on the voluntary use of race to achieve diversity in postsecondary education*. US Department of Education; US Department of Justice. https://www2.ed.gov/about/offices/list/ocr/docs/guidance-pse-201111.pdf

Dukes, R.L., & Gay, V. (1989). The effects of gender, status, and effective teaching on the evaluation of college instruction. *Teaching Sociology*, 17(4):447–57. https://doi.org/10.2307/1318422

EUA. (n.d.). *INVITED*. https://www.eua.eu/101-projects/737-invited.html

EUA. (2019, 11 March). *The hard numbers on female university leaders in Europe*. Science | Business. https://sciencebusiness.net/network-news/eua-hard-numbers-female-university-leaders-europe

European Commission. (n.d.). *Education and training: The Bologna process and the European higher education area*. Retrieved 22 February 2021 from https://ec.europa.eu/education/policies/higher-education/bologna-process-and-european-higher-education-area_en

European Commission. (2019, 8 March). *She figures 2018*. https://research-and-innovation.ec.europa.eu/knowledge-publications-tools-and-data/publications/all-publications/she-figures-2018_en

eXtension Foundation Impact Collaborative. (2020). *Diversity, equity, and inclusion*. https://dei.extension.org/

Ferguson, S.J. (2016). *Women and education: Qualifications, skills and technology*. Catalogue no. 89-503-X. Statistics Canada. https://www150.statcan.gc.ca/n1/en/pub/89-503-x/2015001/article/14640-eng.pdf?st=d54KDgrU

Fries, C.J., & McNinch, R.J. (2003). Signed versus unsigned student evaluations of teaching: A comparison. *Teaching Sociology*, 31(3), 333–44. https://doi.org/10.2307/3211331

Gaskell, J. (2014). Women and education. In *The Canadian Encyclopedia*. https://www.thecanadianencyclopedia.ca/en/article/women-and-education

Hamermesh, D.S., & Parker, A.M. (2005). Beauty in the classroom: Instructors' pulchritude and putative pedagogical productivity. *Economics of Education Review*, 24(4), 369–76. https://doi.org/10.1016/j.econedurev.2004.07.013

Huston, T.A. (2006). Race and gender bias in higher education: Could faculty course evaluations impede further progress toward parity? *Seattle Journal for Social Justice*, 4(2), 591–611. https://digitalcommons.law.seattleu.edu/sjsj/vol4/iss2/34/

IES/NCES. (2019). *College enrollment rates*. https://nces.ed.gov/programs/coe/pdf/Indicator_CPB/coe_cpb_2019_05.pdf

IES/NCES. (2020). *Characteristics of postsecondary faculty*. https://nces.ed.gov/programs/coe/indicator/csc?tid=74

Kohl Gallery. (2013). *Timeline of the arts at Washington College*. https://archive.is/20130403112714/http://www.washcoll.edu/about/buildings/kohl-gallery/history.php

List of Canadian university leaders. (2021, 10 October). In *Wikipedia*. https://
en.wikipedia.org/wiki/List_of_Canadian_university_leaders

Lombrozo, T. (2013, 17 June). *Name five women in philosophy. Bet you can't.*
Cosmos and Culture, NPR. https://www.npr.org/sections/13.7
/2013/06/17/192523112/name-ten-women-in-philosophy-bet-you-can-t

McGill. (2021). *Blazing trails: McGill's women.* About McGill. https://www
.mcgill.ca/about/history/features/mcgill-women

Merritt, D.J., & Reskin, B.F. (1997). Sex, race, and credentials: The truth about
affirmative action in law faculty hiring. *Columbia Law Review, 97*(2),
199–210. https://doi.org/10.2307/1123365

Pittman, C.T. (2010). Race and gender oppression in the classroom: The
experiences of women faculty of color with white male students. *Teaching
Sociology, 38*(3), 183–96. https://doi.org/10.1177/0092055X10370120

Reid, J.G. (2015). Grace Annie Lockhart. In *The Canadian Encyclopedia*.
https://www.thecanadianencyclopedia.ca/en/article/grace-annie
-lockhart

The Schengen *Acquis*. (1999). *Official Journal of the European Communities.*
https://eur-lex.europa.eu/LexUriServ/LexUriServ.do?uri=OJ:L:2000:239
:0001:0473:EN:PDF

Stout, R., Archie, C., Cross, D., & Carman, C.A. (2018). The relationship
between faculty diversity and graduation rates in higher education.
Intercultural Education, 29(3), 399–417. https://doi.org/10.1080/14675986
.2018.1437997

Sursock, A. (2015). *Trends 2015: Learning and teaching in European universities.*
European University Association. https://eua.eu/resources
/publications/388:trends-2015-learning-and-teaching-in-european
-universities.html

University of Michigan. (2021). *Diversity, equity & inclusion: Defining DEI.*
https://diversity.umich.edu/about/defining-dei/

US Equal Employment Opportunity Commission. (1964). *Title VII of the Civil
Rights Act of 1964.* https://www.eeoc.gov/statutes/title-vii-civil-rights
-act-1964

The White House. (2021). *Fact sheet: The American Families Plan.* https://
www.whitehouse.gov/briefing-room/statements-releases/2021/04/28
/fact-sheet-the-american-families-plan/

World Economic Forum (WEF). (2021). *3 things to know about women in STEM.*
https://www.weforum.org/agenda/2020/02/stem-gender-inequality
-researchers-bias/

"Equity, Diversity, and Inclusion: Closing Gaps and Opening Minds"

MARGARET (MARGIE) ZEIDLER
President, Urbanspace Property Group

This chapter is a wonderful invitation to us all to get creative about enabling and nurturing inclusive, diverse, and equitable environments in academia. Professor Glazebrook's ideas can and should be applied in any community or institution.

When we created an arts hub – 401 Richmond – in downtown Toronto in 1994, diversity was a goal from the beginning because we knew that diverse systems are strong ones. If we wanted this project to be successful and thrive, it had to be inclusive and equitable as well.

Jane Jacobs's writings about cities, economies, and social structures gave us the inspiration. She suggested that we look at ecosystems in nature for relevant clues. We all know that monocultures in nature are precarious systems. Diversity brings healthy and robust environments that are able to overcome threats to their survival. What we now know about the reciprocity among different organisms of different species to contribute to the health of all and to help organisms at risk, drives home the point. Diverse economies can withstand threats, transform themselves, and heal when one sector becomes weak or dies. Think of the uniformity of the car-making mecca, Detroit, since the middle of the last century and compare it to the richness, dynamism, and variety of New York City.

A strong, healthy innovative university – one that hopes to advance thinking and scholarship – must be diverse, just as our cities and neighbourhoods must be also inclusive of different voices and promote equitable, just environments. Enjoy the clever and inventive ideas that Glazebrook employs in the service of making that a reality.

chapter eight

Critical Issues in Architecture: Engaged, Ethical Architectural Education

THOMAS BARRIE

I. Introduction

As a professor of architecture, I often tell my students that what I mostly teach are values. I do not expect that they will remember much of what I tell them but hope they will retain how I emphasize the responsibility of architects to improve lives, facilitate community, and support human flourishing. I encourage students to consider their own values and develop them throughout their professional education. The crucible to do so is community-based service-learning design studios, where students engage with critical issues of the built environment that can be effectively addressed by schools of architecture.

This chapter focuses on leadership in architectural education and the capacity and responsibilities of universities to apply research and design excellence to issues such as affordable housing, cultural and environmental sustainability, and meaningful place-making. Four subject areas that provide frameworks for ethical practices are summarized, and case-study projects illustrate the educational and advocacy outcomes of engaged architectural education. It argues that a focus on addressing critical issues and envisioning

solutions that exceed isolated problems is fundamentally ethical.[1] Ethical questions provoke reflections regarding who is most
served by architectural and built environment projects, and who is
ignored or harmed (Fisher, 2019, pp. xxiv–xxv). Ethics provides a
framework and praxis for how to best serve the greatest good and
includes *virtue ethics* of personal development and actions, *duty
ethics* of serving others, *social contract ethics*, which seeks equity and
justice, and the *utilitarian ethics* of policies and their enforcement.
All of these aspects inform the studio projects I choose, the ethical
positions I model, and the pedagogical methods I employ.

I founded the Affordable Housing and Sustainable Communities Initiative at North Carolina State University in 2007 to research,
document, and disseminate innovative and applicable solutions to
the housing and urban challenges that North Carolina communities
face. The initiative's mission is primarily educational – to educate
future leaders in the profession and provide research and design
resources for government, non-profits, community leaders, and the
general public.[2] Similar to Public Interest Design[3] (a participatory
design practice that emphasizes social, ecological, and economic
priorities), our projects and partners illustrate the ethical responsibilities of architects and the profession by providing design expertise to the underserved. In addition to these three priorities, our
projects also incorporate spiritual orientations, which together comprise a quadruple bottom line (Walker, 2014, p. 55). The spiritual
component draws from the material culture of religious traditions
and built heritages, and their meaningful and affective place-
making. It also aligns with "engaged spirituality," which emphasizes developing one's character (*virtue ethics*) while serving others
for the common good (*duty ethics*), and comprising practices centred
on effecting social change (*social contract ethics*).[4] Contrary to popular notions of spirituality, which typically emphasize personal benefits, in engaged spirituality, personal development is the outcome
of providing service to others.[5] The Zen priest Bernie Glassman
described it as follows: "We commit ourselves to healing others at
the same time that we heal ourselves" (Glassman, 1998, p. 84).

I am also committed to employing the design capacities of
a research-intensive, land grant university to serve its state and

citizenry. As Jason Pearson argues, "Design innovation is inseparable from social engagement, and thus is inseparable from public
service" (Pearson & Robbins, 2002, p. 5). Design excellence includes
activism to effect lasting, positive change. Projects typically
include public fora where students present to and interact with
stakeholders, professionals, and public officials. Consequently,
while students learn about the power of design to effectively solve
problems, they also learn how to be "citizen architects," who, in
the words of architect and educator Samuel Mockbee, "stand for
solutions that service a community's physical and social needs,
and not just the status quo" (Bell, 2004, p. 153). In addition to studio service-learning projects, I am also active in local education
and advocacy efforts. As a tenured, full professor, I recognize that I
not only have the ability to speak out publicly about controversial
issues and challenge those in power, I have a responsibility to do
so (Fisher, 2011).

The "ethical turn" in architectural education and the profession
arguably began in the 1990s with the publication of *Building Community: A New Future for Architecture Education and Practice, A Special Report*, often referred to as the Boyer Report, as its lead author
was Ernest Boyer.[6] Its recommendations included re-engaging the
profession with the public and contemporary issues and providing the greatest good to the broadest constituencies. This approach
called for schools of architecture to "increase the storehouse of
new knowledge to build spaces that enrich communities, prepare architects to communicate more effectively the value of their
knowledge and their craft to society, and practice their profession
at all times with the highest ethical standards" (Boyer & Mitgang,
1996, p. 28). Since then, the priorities and pedagogy of architectural education have more substantively incorporated sustainability, equity, and even spirituality. However, even though this "turn"
has significantly changed architectural education, it is not without
detractors who accuse it of moral majorityism, and concerns that
expanded agendas will lead to diminished design, aesthetics, and
intellectual excellence.

Clearly, there are daunting issues facing humanity in the
twenty-first century, many of which are directly related to built

environments. These include: (1) the effects of global economies on cultural identities that are often potently embodied and expressed through built form and heritage; (2) policies of land use and transportation planning and their relationship to inequality and systemic racism; (3) settlement and transportation patterns and energy-intensive building materials, construction, performance and life cycles related to global climate change, and (4) the diminishment of places that affects how they serve social, ontological, and spiritual needs. Salient aspects of each of these four areas follow, serving to contextualize the issues germane to engaged, ethical architectural education.

II. Cultural Identities

Built environments have crucial roles to play in cultural memories and identities. They can embody and communicate diverse cultural histories, from national and world heritage sites to places that recall and re-evaluate suppressed, marginalized, or erased histories. Understanding the communicative agency of the built environment is central to recognizing its roles in preserving and transmitting cultural histories. As a cultural artefact, the material culture of architecture and places has a particularly potent capacity to reveal and reflect the culture that produced it, including social, political, economic, and environmental contexts and a complex matrix of beliefs, aspirations, and imperatives (Barrie et al., 2016, pp. 65–66). The mnemonics of place aid cultures in an ongoing process of remembering what they value, and their loss can induce a certain kind of amnesia and dislocation.

The impacts on regional identity by the placeless sprawl, chain and big-box development, and economically stratified monoculture housing of market urbanism,[7] and the car-dependent transportation infrastructure that serves it, have been regularly bemoaned. W.G. Clark wrote in 1991, "The American landscape is being sacrificed to building. The result is dismal, adding nothing satisfactory or even significant except as an accurate self-portrait of cultural ethical dissolution" (Clark, 1991, pp. 3–5). It has been a regular and sardonic observation that subdivisions are often named after what they destroyed. Lost are not only physical places – townscapes, farms, and natural areas – but also the cultural memory of a society's built heritage. Destroying the material cultures of the past is similar to the loss of textual histories, scripture, and literature, and is equally disorienting. As Tony Hiss recounted in 1990, "These days people often tell me that some of their most unforgettable experiences of places are disturbingly painful and have to do with unanticipated loss" (Hiss 1990, p. xiii). Place attachment theory reminds us that humans can make deep emotional connections with place, even a love of place, reflecting the importance of *topophilia*, as outlined by the geographer Yi-Fu Tuan (Smith, 2018, p. 4; Tuan, 1974).

Contemporary globalization presents diffuse challenges to place and cultural identity. Built environments reflect and advance emerging global cultures – from ubiquitous branded artefacts and "non-places" (Augé, 1997) of global capitalism, to international corporations and institutions. In the global economy, some places and people are simply left behind – manufacturing is off-shored, local businesses subsumed by big-box stores, and ubiquitous housing built by multinational firms. The impacts of predatory retail, loss of economic anchors, and diminishment of civic, cultural, and religious institutions can produce ontologically disorienting built environments. The oft-cited axiom that histories are written by the victors also applies to the historical texts of the built environment. What gets preserved and how it is preserved remain crucial issues.

Globalization also presents unprecedented issues regarding personal and professional ethics, especially in the case of high-profile projects (and architects) commissioned by repressive regimes and utilized as state propaganda (Owen, 2009, pp. 1–2). However, similar vexing issues are present locally, such as developments set in gentrifying communities, which provoke questions regarding who is best served (and not) by particular projects. Where and how we build, complying with or challenging regulations, or whether a commission should be accepted at all are ethical questions. The professional emphasis of architectural education often prejudices the serving of clients, not the public at large. Buildings and planned developments may effectively provide for private needs, but too rarely significantly contribute to the public good. Together, these compelling and complicated subjects frame some of the conditions and imperatives of how to safeguard contemporary cultural identity and the built environment – important issues that should be considered in architectural education.

III. Spatial Justice, Access, and Participation

The built environment has often served the powerful and been a means to enforce social and economic hierarchies. As Deyan Sudjuk states, "Architecture is about power. The powerful build because that is what the powerful do" (Sudjuk, 2005, p. 2). The use of architecture as propaganda by repressive regimes is well documented; less so are the subtle ways in which the values and authority of dominant cultures are materialized in the built environment. According to Henri Lefebvre, "The spatial practice of a society is revealed through the deciphering of its space" (Lefebvre, 1991, p. 38). Deciphering built geographies can disclose social and political histories, and cultural, political, and legal determinants. "Reading" the form and organization of the built environment can reveal the motivations of its builders and enablers – histories of spatial injustices, how market forces dictate what gets built and where, and how zoning laws determine location, height, form, fenestration, and relationship to context. All exert implicit or explicit control over the built environment and whom it serves – as well as whom it does not. The complicity of architecture in supporting structures of control illustrates its authority and, paradoxically, its potential to do good. The power of the built environment can be applied to egalitarian or exclusive goals – to enabling or repressing; that is its promise and peril.

Studies on the power of the built environment generally focus on the affective and communicative capacities of singular buildings. However, spatial structures have arguably been more consequential. From hierarchically organized traditional villages to European Jewish ghettos, the built environment has expressed and enforced the wills of the powerful. The design of built environments coupled with social roles dictated by dominant cultures have typically determined who has access to public space and in what manner. The spatial control of women is interwoven throughout history, and in the Jim Crow South, the use of the public realm by Blacks was explicitly circumscribed.

However, there are more subtle means by which the built environment supports hierarchies of access that significantly affect people's lives. The commodification of housing has produced unequal access to this essential need or, as some have insisted, has compromised basic human rights. Transportation modalities, priorities, and accessibility determine the mobility of people and communities, and their ability to access jobs, schools, and services. Unequal distribution results in missing, scarce, or inflated goods and services in low-wealth communities. As the urban planner Edward Soja insists, "Justice and injustice are infused into the multi-scalar geographies in which we live" and "significantly affect our lives" (Soja, 2010, p. 16).

One compelling history of spatial injustices is racist policies in America. Richard Rothstein has documented de jure racist government policies that controlled the built environment to suppress Black Americans. He asserts that they were just as much civil rights violations as was Jim Crow segregation (Rothstein, 2017). During the post–Second World War housing boom, the Federal Housing Administration and GI Bill supported homeownership, but mostly for whites, which significantly contributed to generational economic disparity. Redlining by banks and government agencies denied loans to Blacks, and deed restrictions limited the purchase and sale of housing to whites only. Today, Black Americans are much less likely than whites to own their home. For those who do, exclusive zoning laws artificially suppress property values in low-wealth areas while inflating those in higher-wealth ones. Single-family zoning and minimum lot sizes also erect economic barriers that prevent lower-income people from accessing schools, employment, and services of higher-wealth areas. The Civil Rights and Fair Housing Acts of the 1960s were designed to eliminate racism but did not address zoning laws, which have often accomplished what the acts made illegal – racial segregation and economic marginalization.

Consequently, recognizing the exclusive and privileged history of the profession of architecture is essential to creating a more inclusive and ethical future. For most of its history, Western architecture has been dominated by privileged white men who either prohibited women and minorities to train or enter the profession or excised them from its histories. In America, it has taken a couple of generations for women to substantially enter the profession of architecture, but leadership positions are still predominantly held by white men.[8] Blacks have faced significant challenges and comprise just 2% of the membership of the American Institute of Architects (AIA). The exclusivity of the profession is also reflected in its fee-based model that makes architectural services economically inaccessible to many (Fisher, 2008, p. 15). Consequently, architectural discourse remains stunted and its capacity to create structural changes to how the built environment gets designed, and who has a voice and influence in the process, truncated. The "silent complicity" (Dovey, 2005, pp. 283–96) of the built environment in supporting power structures and its potential to change regressive and repressive systems are essential issues in architectural education.

IV. Sustainable and Regenerative Built Environments

Climate change is a significant challenge and also a remarkable opportunity for human cooperation. We are in a pivotal period where dominant world views, patterns of production and consumption, priorities, and policies can be transformed. However, the transition from the *technological* to *ecological* period depends on dramatic shifts in human consciousness and responsibility (Berry, 1988, pp. 36–49; see also Berry, 1984). Some insist that capitalist, consumerist economies and their dependent political structures will need to transform, and energy sources and use, food production, manufacturing, and transportation modalities shift from carbon dependent to carbon positive (Jackson, 2009, pp. 157–69). Challenges to be addressed include theist religious beliefs in a god that oversees and controls the world, despite human initiative; scientific hegemony that positions science as the pre-eminent solution; neoliberal politics that depict alternatives to individual and national autonomy and unfettered growth as restrictive and regressive; power structures with vested interests in maintaining the status quo; and economic globalization that favours competitive markets over local economies and global cooperation.

The carbon age (Rosten, 2008) has produced remarkable advances in technology, science, and prosperity, and has also resulted in unprecedented degradation of the natural world and risks to human flourishing. The Paris Agreement of 2016 sets clear goals and warns of catastrophic impacts if those goals are not met. Many argue that creating a carbon-positive future will require revolutionary changes to the design of built environments, which produce significant greenhouse gas emissions.[9] The path to decarbonization includes rethinking buildings, settlement patterns and density, transportation modalities for people and goods, energy production, consumption, and regeneration, embodied energy in building materials, and the use, and reuse, of buildings.

Architecture 2030 was founded by architect Ed Mazria in 2002 to provide resources and strategies to "achieve a dramatic reduction in the energy consumption and CO_2 emissions of the built environment by 2030," and "advance the development of sustainable, resilient, equitable, and zero-carbon buildings communities and cities" (Architecture 2030, 2023a, paras. 2 and 3). Other initiatives address a broad range of issues and provide playbooks for creating carbon-neutral/positive, equitable, healthy, and beautiful built environments, including LEED, The Living Building Challenge, Green Globes, and the WELL Building Standard.

Architect and urbanist Peter Calthorpe argues that, for the past 50 years, decentralized, carbon-based energy and transportation systems and economically stratified settlement patterns in North America have created unsustainable built environments. He proposes a "passive urbanism" of density as a sustainable alternative to dominant, land-intensive patterns. He cites New York City as a place with one of the world's smallest per-capita carbon footprints, and insists that compact urbanism, in conjunction with active energy-efficient technologies, such as local energy co-generation and distribution and buildings as energy producers, are the most effective means to address the multiple issues of global climate change (Calthorpe, 2011, pp. 8–24).

Some recommend re-wilding cities as an effective means of passive carbon sequestration, supporting biodiversity and mitigating sea rise and storm surges through natural barrier habitats. Many suggest that to achieve a sustainable future, an evolution of human consciousness, and conscience, must occur. Urban planner Tim Beatley proposes comprehensive ways to reintroduce natural habitats into urban environments and cites their benefits, including supporting wildlife and, perhaps most importantly, reintroducing humans to their co-inhabitants on the planet (Beatley, 2011, pp. 14–15; Newman et al., 2017, pp. 129–30). The Living Building Challenge and WELL Building Standard propose similar strategies and make analogous claims regarding their benefits. A sustainable future depends on these and other means and will require accepting responsibility for our actions and cultivating, through education and practice, compassion, and care for all life on earth and respect for the interconnected web of existence.

V. Spirituality and Built Environments

The history of architecture is dominated by buildings built to serve the practices, institutions, and territorial claims of religions. Understanding their pre-eminent status throughout history, and their diverse cultural, communicative, ritual, and affective agendas, is crucial to designing spiritually informed built environments. Religious buildings demonstrate the power and influence of the built environment. They have often been bounded and imbued with power and designed to affect individuals and groups – to inspire, educate, uplift, encourage, and, in some cases, convince and coerce.[10] High state architecture was typically hierarchically organized, its spaces leading from lesser to higher sacrality, with a rich choreography of path configurations, spatial sequences, and symbolic narratives. They accommodated the rituals essential to completing architectural settings – from individual and group devotions and communal processionals and observances to mysteries performed by the priesthood.

The dynamic and discursive interactions of leaders, participants, and architectural settings are central to the didactic and affective capacity of sacred places. Ritual movements to and through architecture are often interactive, where "entanglements" of our bodies with place provoke connections between participants and settings (Barrie & Bermudez, 2019). Religious buildings and their "atmospheres" were often designed to engage one somatically and emotionally. The contemporary architect Peter Zumthor describes atmospheres as the emotional, sensual, and spiritual experiences of architecture and places (Zumthor, 2006). A scientific study conducted by architect and educator Julio Bermudez documented how architecture can induce spiritually significant experiences that take place mostly in spaces dedicated to religious practices (Barrie & Bermudez, 2019, pp. 349–50; Bermudez, 2009a, pp. 46–9; Bermudez, 2009b, pp. 8–13).

Some have argued, however, that the affective and transformative qualities of architecture are not limited to places dedicated to religious practices. Instead, it is in the regular experience of ordinary built environments where the sacred is more readily experienced. The Finnish architect and educator Juhani Pallasmaa (2015) argues,

> More than ever before, the ethical and humane task of architecture and all art is to defend the authenticity and autonomy of human experience, and to reveal the existence of the transcendental realm, the domain of the sacred. This calls for the identification of the spiritual and holy, not only in deliberate devotional contexts, but in the ordinariness and humility of daily life. (p. 32)

Phenomenologists such as Gaston Bachelard valorized the spiritual and ontological qualities of the everyday, especially the domestic. For Bachelard, the first home of childhood, what he termed the "unforgettable house," had lasting ontological – and nostalgic – significance (Bachelard, 1969). As a distinct cultural artefact, the domestic has been essential to environmental definition and identity. The domestic is our homes, but also the towns, cities, and regions we call home (Barrie, 2017). The architectural theorist Christian Norberg-Schulz (1979), whose scholarship often focused on the ontological and spiritual significance of place, stated that "place is the concrete manifestation of man's dwelling, and his identity depends on his belonging to places" (p. 6). Architecture is a primary figure that emerges from the ground of the communal construct of culture. From the spiritual hub of home to settlements and cities, and civic, institutional, and religious buildings, the built environment has served to materialize and situate humans in place and time.

As meaning-seeking beings, humans have perennially searched for understanding the world and their place within it. The built environment has often served pre-eminent roles in explicating the world and supporting the all too human desire for certainty and control. The enduring materiality of architecture has often symbolized permanence in a world imbued with fragility, decay, and mortality. Asserting the endurance of places through territorial claims was as if to say, "This is our place and will always be – by building it we have made it so." From sacred geographies to high state architecture and the grandiose tombs of leaders, the built environment has materialized such claims. Understanding and explicating what architecture is tasked to do, and the meanings it is assigned, are crucial to understanding its spiritual agency and its community impact (Barrie, 2017, p. 15). At best, humans build to create places that give form to communal values and articulate the meanings and purposes assigned to them. As such, the capacity of the built environment to ennoble existence and uplift the human spirit depends on the intentions and skills of its designers. Recognizing architecture's historical agency provokes questions regarding how to build today and how to meaningfully educate our students.

VI. Responses, Actions, and Trends

In 2014, the City of Raleigh (NC) Planning and Development Department asked me to create a studio project focused on backyard cottages, which had been illegal since the 1970s. We carefully vet requests for service to ensure that they meet educational goals, are appropriate to our expertise and mission, and do not compete with our professional colleagues. In this case, the project's city and neighbourhood support, emphasis on research, and the design of prototypical units on demonstration sites satisfied our criteria. The Mordecai Backyard Cottage Project, named for the inner-city neighbourhood where the project was set, was a graduate, research-intensive, service-learning project, conducted during the fall semester of that year. Students researched and analysed national precedents of backyard cottages (also known as accessory dwelling units, or ADUs), past and current city codes, historical, political, and environmental contexts, and potential risks and benefits. Each collaboratively designed prototypical units for homeowners who had volunteered to participate in the project. The students learned research and advocacy methods, applied design skills to a rigorous housing type for real clients, and observed the impacts that design research and advocacy can have.

Project partners comprised the Raleigh Planning and Development Department, the Mordecai Citizen Advisory Council (CAC), and a local business association. City councillors and other public officials, housing advocates, and members of the community were also project participants. The project included numerous community presentations and workshops, and an exhibition at the annual North Carolina Housing Coalition Conference (in Raleigh). It concluded with a public forum at the state AIA Headquarters, attended by a capacity crowd. In 2015, the Mordecai CAC petitioned Raleigh City Council to create an ordinance to allow backyard cottages. I continued to advocate for its adoption, eventually co-chairing a task force composed of local housing and community advocates. Numerous public fora, op-eds in the local newspaper, regular media coverage, and political activism eventually resulted in a city-wide, by-right ordinance in 2020.

Other, more recent projects have included the 2018 Micro Housing for Homeless and Disabled Veterans Project (Figure 8.1), sponsored by the North Carolina Coalition to End Homelessness, which included research on veteran homelessness and support services, documented precedents, and best practices of supportive micro housing villages, engaged with various constituencies

Figure 8.1. The Mordecai Backyard Cottage Project
Notes: The project included numerous public presentations and programs.
Thomas Barrie FAIA kicking off the project at the Mordecai Citizen Advisory Council.
Source: Photo courtesy Thomas Barrie.

and designed prototypical micro housing villages for statewide implementation. Results included a project report and professionally produced video, both of which have been extensively used for educational and fundraising efforts.[11] In 2019, the Affordable and Supportive Housing for NC State Students Project was conducted in support of campus-wide efforts to address student housing insecurity and homelessness. The project engaged members of a faculty task force and university administration, and its outcomes comprise an essential component of ongoing advocacy efforts.

Projects like these are chosen to provide enriched educational experiences for students, and scholarly and design research for sponsors, partners, and the public. They provide potent settings for teaching the capacity of design excellence to address the kind of issues discussed earlier in this chapter, and to integrate cultural, justice, environmental, and spiritual issues. For example, the Micro Housing for Homeless and Disabled Veterans Project demanded substantive understanding of military culture, the sustainable potential of micro housing villages, the need for affordable housing, and the roles that stable supportive housing can play in economically, physically, emotionally, and spiritually restoring those who have experienced homelessness. Most of these projects also illustrate the multiple challenges that citizen architects face, and the sustained efforts needed to achieve results. The Mordecai Backyard Cottage Project (Figure 8.2) required understanding historical housing types and the dominant culture of the single-family house, negotiating the range of opinions about backyard cottages from those who envision them as models of affordable, equitable, sustainable, and even personally transformative housing, to others who view them as little better than invasive, glorified shacks. Students learned about typical opposition to affordable, alternate housing and increasing the density of residential districts and observed the broad range of motivations and opinions of individuals, neighbourhood leaders, city staff, and elected officials. In time, we came to see ADUs as one means to restore neighbourhoods (by reintroducing traditional housing and density), provide affordable and sustainable housing options, and even foster more heterogeneous, identifiable, and supportive communities.

The Prologue to the 1992 *The Hannover Principles*, prepared by architect William McDonough and partners as a submission to EXPO 2000 in Germany, simply states, "Human society needs to aspire to an integration of its material, spiritual and ecological elements" (McDonough & Partners, 1992). The report argues that nature and humans are interdependent and have equal rights of co-existence; spiritual and material consciousness and environments and health and well-being are interrelated; shortsighted planning, short-term products, and the concept of waste should be eliminated; energy should be renewable; nature is a model to be emulated; and the sharing of knowledge is crucial to "link long-term sustainable considerations with ethical responsibility, and re-establish the integral relationship between natural processes and human activity" (McDonough & Partners, 1992). The "ethical turn" at schools of architecture, though not universal, has led to

Figure 8.2. The Micro Housing for Homeless and Disabled Veterans Project
Notes: The project demanded substantive understanding of military culture and the roles that stable supportive housing can play in economically, physically, emotionally, and spiritually restoring those who have experienced homelessness.
Sources: Project by Austin Corriher. Photo courtesy Thomas Barrie.

shifted priorities and programs to address the critical issues of our time and serve those underserved by the design professions. The visionary artists of modernism and the connoisseurs of the styles that followed, though not absent, have been joined by citizen architects committed to serving the greater good. I tell my students that architecture is a social art and that each project should satisfy the needs of the client, be contextually sensitive, equitable, sustainable, and meaningful, and aspire to provide public benefits beyond the project itself. In this way, we can shift from the reactive conventions of a "service profession," to one of proactive leadership.

Like architects, doctors and lawyers work with individuals and apply professional expertise to solve their problems. However, they have also addressed systemic causes of disease and injustice and advocated for change, such as public health efforts in the medical profession (Fisher, 2019, p. 55). Architects have adopted aspects of public health through university-based programs and community design centres. Public Interest Design aspires to serve the 98% of citizens excluded from architectural services and broaden citizen participation in shaping their communities (Bell, 2004, p. 13).

Others have advocated for land-use reforms, such as eliminating exclusive zoning,[12] or legislating sustainable development and preserving natural and built cultural heritages.[13] Some have pursued the creation of ennobling, meaningful, and spiritually informed buildings and places.[14] However, much remains to be done to find solutions to the critical issues of our time and create more culturally responsive, equitable, sustainable, and spiritually supportive built environments for the future. I remind students that advocacy demands expertise, and that design excellence is the means to envision new solutions to the most pressing challenges faced by society today.

NOTES

1 Ethics, often referred to as moral philosophy, is a branch of Western philosophy concerned with whether human actions are beneficial or destructive in their personal and group contexts. Thomas Fisher defines

ethics as a "way of seeing things from the perspective of those most affected by our decisions and of taking into account their interests and needs in every action we take" (Fisher, 2019, p. xix).

2 All projects are documented on the initiative's website as an open-source, educational archive: https://outreach.design.ncsu.edu/ah+sc/.

3 Public Interest Design began with community design centres in the 1960s and was popularized by the Rural Studio at Auburn University founded in 1993.

4 Engaged Buddhism, as articulated by the Vietnamese Zen monk Thich Nhat Hanh, and the Liberation Theology Movement in the Catholic Church, are contemporary examples.

5 According to Gregory Stanczak and Donald Miller, "In order to fully understand the relationship between spirituality and social change, we must discuss spirituality in ways that are more complex than the stereotypes of individual transcendence or reflection" (Stanczak & Miller, 2004, p. 5).

6 The report, co-authored by Lee Mitgang, was commissioned by the AIA, American Institute of Architecture Students (AIAS), National Council of Architectural Registration Boards (NCARB), National Architectural Accreditation Board (NAAB), and ACSI, and published in 1996.

7 Market urbanism is generally minimally regulated commercial development that responds to, capitalizes on, and expresses market forces.

8 Currently, over 50% of architecture students are women, but just over 20% are members of the AIA (Nicholson, 2020).

9 According to Architecture 2030's (2023b) "2030 Challenge," the built environment is responsible for over 75% of greenhouse gas emissions, 39% of which are attributable to buildings.

10 High state Christian architecture was often deliberate in its pedagogical and evangelical goals, especially during the medieval period where the church served as a materialized *biblia pauperum* and exhortatory text.

11 The project was a winner of the 2019 Architect Magazine Studio Prize and the film a finalist in the 2019 AIA Film Challenge (NC State, 2023).

12 In 2018, Oregon eliminated single-family zoning for mid-size to large cities. The recently adopted Minneapolis 2040 Plan changes zoning citywide to allow duplexes and quads in all single-family-zoned areas, to address histories of racism and exclusion enforced by zoning laws.

13 Such as the Congress for the New Urbanism (Leccese & McCormick, 2000).

14 Such as The Architecture, Culture and Spirituality Forum (2023), co-founded by the author.

REFERENCES

The Architecture, Culture and Spirituality Forum. (2023). https://acsforum
.org
Architecture 2030. (2023a). *Our mission.* https://2030dev-architecture-2030.
pantheonsite.io/our-mission/
Architecture 2030. (2023b). *The 2020 challenge.* https://architecture2030.org
/2030_challenges/2030-challenge/
Augé, M. (1997). *Non-places: Introduction to an anthropology of supermodernity.*
Verso.
Bachelard, G. (1969). *The poetics of space* (M. Jolas, Trans.). Beacon Press.
Barrie, T. (2017). *House and home: Cultural contexts, ontological roles.* Routledge.
Barrie, T. (2020). *The architecture of the world's major religions: Themes,
similarities and differences.* Brill.
Barrie, T., & Bermudez, J. (2019). Spirituality and architecture. In L. Zsolnai
& B. Flanagan (Eds.), *The Routledge international handbook of spirituality in
society and the professions* (pp. 345–55). Routledge.
Barrie, T., Bermudez, J., & Tabb, P.J. (Eds.). (2016). *Architecture, culture, and
spirituality.* Routledge.
Beatley, T. (2011). *Biophillic cities: Integrating nature into urban design and
planning.* Island Press.
Bell, B. (Ed.). (2004). *Good deeds, good design: Community service through
architecture.* Princeton Architectural Press.
Bermudez, J. (2009a). Amazing grace: New research into "extraordinary
architectural experiences" reveals the central role of sacred places. *Faith &
Form, 42*(2), 8–13.
Bermudez, J. (2009b). The extraordinary in architecture: Studying and
acknowledging the reality of the spiritual. *2A – Architecture and Art
Magazine, 12,* 46–9.
Berry, T. (1984). *The twelve principles.* http://thomasberry.org
/publications-and-media/thomas-berry-the-twelve-principles
Berry, T. (1988). *The dream of the earth.* Sierra Club Books.
Boyer, E.L., & Mitgang, L.D. (1996). *Building community: A new future for
architecture education and practice, a special report.* Carnegie Foundation for
the Advancement of Teaching.
Calthorpe, P. (2011). *Urbanism in the age of climate change.* Island Press.
Clark, W.G. (1991). Replacement. In W. Redfield Lathrop (Ed.), *Modulus 20:
Stewardship of the Land* (pp. 2–5). Princeton Architectural Press.
Dovey, K. (2005). The silent complicity of architecture. In E. Rooksky &
J. Hillier (Eds.), *Habitus: A sense of place* (pp. 283–96). Routledge.

Fisher, T. (2008). *Architectural design and ethics: Tools for survival*. Elsevier.

Fisher, T. (2011, 17 August). Tenure: Use it or lose it. HuffPost. https://www .huffpost.com/entry/tenure-use-it-or-lose-it_b_929238.

Fisher, T. (2019). *The architecture of ethics*. Routledge.

Glassman, B. (1998). *Bearing witness: A Zen master's lessons in making peace*. Bell Tower.

Hiss, T. (1990). *The experience of place*. Vintage Books.

Jackson, T. (2009). *Prosperity without growth: Economics for a finite planet*. Earthscan.

Leccese, M., & McCormick, K. (Eds.). (2000). *The charter of the new urbanism*. McGraw Hill.

Lefebvre, H. (1991). *The production of space* (D. Nicholson-Smith, Trans.). Blackwell.

McDonough, W., & Partners. (1992). *The Hannover principles: Design for sustainability*. https://mcdonough.com/wp-content/uploads/2013/03 /Hannover-Principles-1992.pdf

NC State. (2023). *Micro housing for homeless and disabled veterans*. https:// outreach.design.ncsu.edu/ah+sc/?portfolio=microhousing-for-homeless -and-disabled-veterans

Newman, P., Beatley, T., and Boyer, H. (2017). *Resilient cities: Overcoming fossil fuel dependence* (2nd ed.). Island Press.

Nicholson, K.A. (2020). *Where are the women? Measuring progress on gender in architecture*. ACSA. https://www.acsa-arch.org/resources/data -resources/where-are-the-women-measuring-progress-on-gender-in -architecture-2/

Norberg-Schulz, C. (1979). *Genius loci: Towards a phenomenology of architecture*. Rizzoli.

Norberg-Schulz, C. (1991). *Genius loci: Towards a phenomenology of architecture*. Rizzoli.

Owen, G. (Ed.). (2009). *Architecture, ethics and globalization*. Routledge.

Pallasmaa, J. (2015). Light, silence, and spirituality in architecture and art. In J. Bermudez (Ed.), *Transcending architecture*. (pp. 19–32). The Catholic University of America Press.

Pearson, J., & Robbins, M. (Eds.). (2002). *University-community design partnerships: Innovations in practice*. The National Endowment for the Arts.

Roston, E. (2008). *The carbon age: How life's core element has become civilization's greatest threat*. Walker and Co.

Rothstein, R. (2017). *The color of law: A forgotten history of how our government segregated America*. W.W. Norton.

Smith, J.S. (Ed.). (2018). *Explorations in place attachment*. Routledge.

Soja, E.J. (2010). *Seeking spatial justice*. University of Minnesota Press.

Stanczak, G., & Miller, D. (2004). *Engaged spirituality and social transformation in mainstream American religious traditions*. Center for Religion and Civic Culture, USC College of Letters, Arts & Sciences.

Sudjik, D. (2005). *The edifice complex: How the rich and powerful – and their architects – shape the world*. Penguin Books.

Tuan, Y-F. (1974). *Topophilia: A study of environmental perception, attitudes, and values*. Columbia University Press.

Walker, S. (2014). *Designing sustainability: Making radical changes in a material world*. Routledge.

Zumthor, P. (2006). *Atmospheres: Architectural environments; surrounding objects*. Birkhauser.

"Critical Issues in Architecture: Engaged, Ethical Architectural Education"

SABRINA LEMAN
Architect

Barrie's article argues for the importance of "ethics and responsibility" in the education of future architects by drawing a connection between an individual's core values and the premise that it is the primary responsibility of the architectural community to better the lives of others. And though the article focuses on the four areas of ethical decision making – historical/cultural identity, socioeconomic/ethnicity-based justice, environmental sustainability and spiritual contextualism – Barrie makes an interesting point when he notes that the means by which his students are introduced to notions of ethical responsibility is through "community-based service-learning studios."

This idea of a community-based process with a focus on service has an implicit emphasis on engagement, listening, and the prioritization of stakeholders needs. As a concept, this is a powerful one because it focuses on process rather than outcome, skills rather than knowledge, and collaboration in lieu of authorship – all of which are applicable to virtually all project types and, perhaps more importantly, are scalable. As professionals, we are often asked, "What type of architecture do you practise – commercial, residential, civic, etc.?" And in turn, we tend to categorize ourselves by *what* we do, rather than *how* we do it. It is in fact the *how* that provides that framework to better understand the social, cultural, historical, environmental, and spiritual context of the built environment. Barrie's chapter reminds us that it is in our roles as *listener and synthesizer of information* that we as a profession can better understand and address the needs of the communities we serve. It is through this active engagement that, as professionals, we are able to frame a physical solution that responds to the unique social and cultural context of each built project.

chapter nine

Indigenous Leadership and Governance, and Reconciliation

DEBORAH McGREGOR, LORRILEE McGREGOR, CINDY PELTIER,
AND SUSAN MANITOWABI

I. Introduction

The need for reconciliation is an urgent and pressing concern that is long overdue and has the potential to provoke the paradigm shift needed to address contestation within educational contexts.

– S. Styres, Reconciliaction (2020)

Much attention has been paid to reconciliation between Indigenous and non-Indigenous peoples in Canada since the conclusion of Canada's Truth and Reconciliation Commission (TRC) in 2015. The release of the TRC's findings launched a new era in Indigenous–state relationships in Canada and set the tone for the desired future of such relationships. As a result, there has been widespread mobilization of "reconciliation initiatives" across segments of Canadian society, including the academy. Still, it remains contested as to what the ideal path to securing Indigenous justice should be. It is our assertion that state-sanctioned conceptions of reconciliation, as taken up by Canadian institutions (including the academy), have a long way to go to achieving real impact on the lived reality of Indigenous peoples. Moreover, it is these Indigenous understandings of reconciliation that should be receiving greater consideration, rather than less, arising from the peoples who have suffered and, as the news headlines demonstrate, who continue to suffer from historical and ongoing colonization (Richardson & Crawford, 2020a, 2020b).

The TRC contains recommendations that seek to deconstruct the colonial relationship between Indigenous peoples and the Canadian state and its institutions. It can be argued that the TRC Final Report and its Calls to Action (CTA) (TRC, 2015a) have initiated a more frenzied response by post-secondary institutions than any other publicly funded commission or enquiry Canada has ever seen (Daigle, 2019; Gaudry & Lorenz, 2018; Hewitt, 2019; Styres, 2020). This is not to deny that many post-secondary institutions in Canada have implemented Indigenous courses, programs, and services over the past few decades, but what is different about the TRC is the widespread public attention given to it and its far-reaching implications, particularly in education and health.

Our contribution examines how the TRC has served as catalyst for increased efforts to address Indigenous realities in the academy. On the basis of our own experience as university administrators or with administration, we evaluate the impact of TRC's CTA in the efficacy of our work. In health, education, law, justice, and social work, a number of CTA called upon cultural competency training for people working with Indigenous peoples. TRC also made specific recommendations on the content areas to be addressed including, but not limited to the history and legacy of residential schools, United Nations Declaration on the Rights of Indigenous Peoples, treaties, Aboriginal rights, Indigenous law, Aboriginal–Crown relations, and Indigenous teachings and practices. It is not enough to simply learn content areas; interpersonal and skill-based training is required so that knowledge can be acted upon. As such, the TRC also called for skills-based training, including intercultural competency, conflict resolution, human rights, and anti-racism. See TRC's (2015a) "Calls to Action" for a fulsome description of all the areas where competency is required.

Individuals, agencies, and institutions that interact with Indigenous peoples, including the academy, should be knowledgeable about Indigenous health, justice, and education challenges, among other areas. There are no more excuses for ongoing ignorance. In addition to the CTA's calls for knowledgeable, culturally competent citizens in Canada, the TRC laid out 10 principles in particular to guide reconciliation (see TRC 2015b). We focus on principles 4, 7, and 8:

(4) Reconciliation requires constructive action on addressing the ongoing legacies of colonialism that have had destructive impacts on Aboriginal peoples' education, cultures and languages, health, child welfare, the administration of justice, and economic opportunities and prosperity.

(7) The perspectives and understandings of Aboriginal Elders and Traditional Knowledge Keepers of the ethics, concepts, and practices of reconciliation are vital to long-term reconciliation.

(8) Supporting Aboriginal peoples' cultural revitalization and integrating Indigenous knowledge systems, oral histories, laws, protocols, and connections to the land in the reconciliation process are essential. (pp. 3–4)

We base the assessment of our experiences on the CTAs and principles outlined above. The question is no longer *why* educational transformation is required but rather *how* we deliver on these principles ethically, respectfully, and with integrity. There is much truth yet to be told; the experiences of Indigenous scholars within the academy have a critical role to play in revealing the deeply problematic relationships between Indigenous peoples and the Canadian government/state. Furthermore, in this contribution, we also point out the deeply problematic relationships between academic institutions and Indigenous peoples, internal and external to the university. As such, we share stories of our own experience as Indigenous scholars and women working as educators and administrators in spaces that reveal that particular kinds of stories are still being told about Indigenous peoples by so-called Indigenous experts and commentators.

In keeping with the TRC principles outlined above, our contribution focuses on stories as "means to draw insights and possibilities to Indigenous experience and knowledge" (Smith, 2019, p. xi). The collective storytelling in this contribution constitutes a theoretical, methodological and pedagogical realm termed Storywork, a term coined by Sto:lo scholar Joanne Archibald. Storywork, she writes, "harmonizes the often fraught and contested experience of operating between the super-privileged spaces of higher education and the fourth world suffering of Indigenous Peoples and their communities" (Archibald et al., 2019, p. 201). In this chapter, through storywork, we "express encounters with oppressive systems as storied experiences" (p. 12).

As such, in this contribution, four Anishinaabe women, leaders in administration and education, reflect on the actual impact of "reconciliation" initiatives in their university, program, and initiatives. As Indigenous scholars, we thus have a responsibility to tell the truth on our terms. We must *reset* the narrative. Storytelling-based research, especially when university (institutionally) produced, carries much more weight in legal, policy, and educational circles than our families and relatives sharing their stories with us at the kitchen table or in the bush. We may listen, record, write, analyse, and publish those same stories in our scholarship and, all of sudden, they carry more weight. A "storytelling methodology" carries with it much responsibility and knowledge of storytelling protocols that should not be taken lightly. It is not enough to just tell the truth; it matters *what* truth is told, *how* it is told, and *who* tells it (Lambert, 2014).

Telling our stories to the academy brings with it risks as well as opportunities. Our stories can be used against us; they can heal, and they can harm. Storytelling is not to be taken lightly. It must be approached with the same high ethical and moral standards followed by our ancestors.

This means not just pointing out everything that is wrong – that can go on forever. Rather, we must be rigorous in our reflections and self-examination, while basing our alternative set of ethical principles guided by the TRC. Indigenous scholarship that draws upon stories as sources of knowledge has already begun to develop, and even though it may not have been explicitly motivated by the TRC, it does provide a path towards *truth* and reconciliation. Whatever their inspiration, teaching and scholarship is required that supports the principles laid out in the TRC's CTAs, principles, and UNDRIP.

II. Positionality: Accountability of Contributors

It is an increasingly common protocol and expectation that we locate ourselves to enable accountability (Doerfler et al., 2013;

Windchief & San Pedro, 2019). More importantly, as Dr. Peltier shares below, "As Nishinaabe-kwe, I believe it is important to introduce myself in Nishnaabemwin as a measure of respect to all my relations." As scholars, we can identify ourselves through our stories, but also carry responsibility for doing so. As Indigenous scholar Lori Lambert observes, "Hearing the story means having a relationship with the story and teller and knowing there is value to the story" (Lambert, 2014, p. 32). We ask in this contribution, "Are people ready to hear our stories or truths?" Sometimes people do want to listen to alternative stories or truths, but they can be hard to hear, and many view them as threatening to what is accepted as the "truth" told by "experts" (mostly non-Indigenous) about Indigenous experience in the academy. Yet this is slowly changing as Indigenous scholars begin to assert their voices (Daigle, 2019; Hewitt, 2019; Hunt, 2014; McGregor, 2019; Todd, 2018;).

Aanii.Boozhoo (Greeting)

Deborah McGregor ndizhnizkaaz (my name). Wiigwaakingaa n'doonjibaa (where I am from). I am Anishinabe from Whitefish River First Nation and I am associate professor and Canada Research Chair in Indigenous Environmental Justice at York University. I have been teaching for three decades on Indigenous knowledge systems, Indigenous environmental governance, and Indigenous research methodologies. I have lived in Toronto for decades and my life's work is to ensure a sustainable future. I have served in an administrative position, as former director for the then Centre for Aboriginal Initiatives at the University of Toronto.

Boozhoo nwiijkiwenydig giinwaa mnik bezndaageyeg (hello, my friends, those of you who are listening). Msko biidaabano kwe ndizhnikaaz (my spirit name is Red Dawn Woman), Nme ndoodem (my clan is Sturgeon), Wiikwemkoong miinwaa Nbisiing ndoonjba (I come from Wiikwemkoong and Nbisiing). My name is Cindy Peltier, and I am associate professor and chair in Indigenous Education, and recently served as the associate dean of arts and science at Nipissing University. Prior to taking on an academic position, I held administrative and leadership roles in the education and health sectors in First Nation schools and organizations. I have developed and taught new undergraduate courses in Indigenous health and wellness in the Faculty of Arts and Science in Native (now Indigenous) Studies, redesigned elective courses called

Understanding Indigenous Pedagogies and Indigenous Education in Canada for the Schulich School of Education, and a developed a new course in Indigenous research within the Faculty of Graduate Studies.

Susan Manitowabi ndiznikaaz (my name is Susan Manitowabi), Jidmoonh-kwe Anishinaabe noozwin (my Anishinaabe name is Squirrel-woman), Wigwaskinaga minwaa N'Swakamok ndoonjiibaa (I come from Whitefish River First Nation and live in Sudbury), Mkwa ndodem (I am from the Bear clan). I am the interim associate vice president – Indigenous and Academic Programs (AVPIAP) at Laurentian University. In my time at Laurentian University, I have had several roles: chair of the Native Human Services Program (now the School of Indigenous Relations, founding director of the School of Indigenous Relations, faculty member in the SIR, and now the AVPIAP (interim).

Lorrilee McGregor n'diznakaaz. Wagaskinaga n'donjaba. Mukwa dodem. Anishinaabe n'daaw. As Anishinaabe, we are taught to introduce ourselves in our language and to identify who we are related to. My mother, Marion, was born in Kaboni, one of the settlements in Wiik-wemkoong, and my father, Murray-baa, who is now in the spirit world, was born in Wagaskinaga. Prior to my current faculty appointment at the Northern Ontario School of Medicine, I worked as a research consultant for First Nations and Indigenous organizations. I was also a sessional instructor at the University of Sudbury and taught courses in the Indigenous Studies program.

We focus on why the truth still matters and a path forward can yield positive outcomes if we care to learn from our experiences. Our stories in some ways formed a type of talking circle, in which we related our experience in response to prompts relevant to this volume on ethical leadership. We reflected upon three themes:

- What opportunities has TRC created for Indigenous peoples in your university or academic unit? Did the TRC make a difference? If so, how? What does "reconciliation" mean?
- What has your experience as a university administrator been like? Were you able to advance Indigenous initiatives? If so, what, how, when? How did it go?
- Recommendations for an ethical path forward.

III. Theory: "More of the Same" or "the Add On" Approach to "Indigenous" Initiatives

In the spring of 2019, *Academic Matters*, a journal of higher education, published a special issue, *Decolonizing the University in an Era of Truth and Reconciliation* (OCUFA, 2019). Editor-in-Chief Ben Lewis stated, "The TRC's purpose was to document the truth – a goal aligned with the core mission of the University" (p. 2). He added, "Decolonization at all levels of our education system is crucial…. Many universities have taken up the TRC's Calls to Action and made public commitments to Indigenization and reconciliation" (p. 2). However, "there is real concern these initiatives do not reach the foundations of the academy. The past year has seen several resignations of Indigenous academic leaders who argue that university governing bodies are not committed to the work required for reconciliation and decolonization" (p. 2).

In "Reframing Reconciliation: A Move towards Conciliation in Academia," Indigenous legal scholar Ashley Courchene observes, "Reconciliation in Academia is Dead" as injustices persist in almost every aspect of Indigenous lives. She points out that "many post-secondary initiatives ring hollow with Indigenous faculty members and students" (OCUFA, 2019, p. 22). She states that, as Indigenous academics, we need to shift our thinking to "conciliation," seeking solutions to the pervasive injustices that continue to characterize Indigenous-non-Indigenous relations, particularly with the state. Relationships, Courchene writes, remain as poor between Indigenous and non-Indigenous peoples after the release of the TRC report as before. The point of "reconciliation," she argues, is to focus the discussion on "conciliation of poor Indigenous-Canadian relations" (p. 23).

Indigenous scholars have pointed out that the dominant research narrative espoused by universities and other research institutions is built upon centuries of imperial and colonial research wherein Indigenous peoples are seen as somehow deficient, damaged, and "in need of intervention" (RCAP, 1996; Smith, 2012). Indigenous peoples are a "problem to be solved" by others who are far more "developed," "evolved," "enlightened," "unbiased," and "expert" (TRC 2015b). Such a narrative has supported many non-Indigenous people's careers in the academy (Mosby, 2013). Worse is the fact that these perceptions are so institutionally embedded that they are rarely questioned (Kuokkanen, 2007; Mihesuah & Cavender Wilson, 2004).

Adam Gaudry and Danielle Lorenz (2018) conducted empirical research to determine the effectiveness of Indigenization, reconciliation, and decolonization in universities in Canada. They noted in their research that there has been a "discursive shift" but little actual transformation. In her research on Reconcili*action*, Sandra Styres (2020) found that

> despite institutional intentionality in addressing the TRC and its Calls to Action, Indigenous faculty, students and institutional actors continue to see little movement towards transformative critical social action in reconciliatory efforts. Their experiences within the universities continue to be traumatizing, harmful and marked in contestation with daily struggles to carve out spaces to be. (p. 167)

These startling findings are supported by our experiences, shared below.

IV. The Stories

Dr. Cindy Peltier shares insights based on her experience as an administrator while pre-tenure in several positions at her university:

> Most Indigenous scholars have agreed that the work of reconciliation involves both Indigenous and non-Indigenous Canadians. Moreover, Indigenous peoples should not shoulder this work. I can say, from experience, that these are ideals, at best. In my experience, most of this work does fall to Indigenous peoples and a handful of dedicated allied scholars. Most non-Indigenous faculty and administrators tend to shy away from this work because of fear – fear of ignorance (e.g., I don't know anything about Indigenous peoples), fear of criticism (e.g., I don't want to be

perceived as misappropriating Indigenous culture), or fear of being perceived as holding racist ideas (e.g., I might say the wrong thing). There are certainly other reasons, but they remain unvoiced, at least to my face, (e.g., I'm not interested, or I don't see how this applies to my work). This lack of engagement has manifested in a host of service responsibilities. I have been a guest speaker across the university (multiple times in multiple classes); hosted professional development workshops for Education and Nursing; sat on organizing and hiring committees for Indigenous initiatives; brokered relationships between elders, knowledge keepers and my non-Indigenous colleagues; served on academic senate. What I would later learn, through the tenure and promotion process involving evaluation of my file by other Indigenous scholars, was that I was engaging in far too much service for a new faculty member. This lends credence to the idea that Indigenous peoples, especially in smaller institutions, shoulder much of the Indigenization and reconciliation work.

I would say that reconciliation involves a deeper commitment – an absence of excuses for the lack of engagement. For example, non-Indigenous peoples can turn their deficit into a strength: "I may not know anything about Indigenous peoples now, but I am committed to learning more by reading, visiting, and engaging in respectful, reciprocal relationships." I have consistently worked to develop respectful relationships with colleagues, students, and community partners. At its most challenging times, reconciliation has involved the ability to mediate and resolve conflicts to restore relationships and resolve issues. At the best of times, relationship building has resulted in learning opportunities for students and faculty with whom I am connected. For example, in my teaching, I have been able to offer both community-based and land-based experiential learning opportunities for my students in all of my courses because of my relationships with community partners – where reciprocity has been central to this work.

Professor Susan Manitowabi shares in her role as interim associate vice president – Indigenous and Academic Programs (AVPIAP) at Laurentian University:

At our institution, a lot of time and effort went into a task force to discuss the Calls to Action coming from the Truth and Reconciliation

Commission. This task force comprised members from all sectors across the university – faculty, staff, administration, support personnel, and students. What struck me was the number of individuals who seemingly were genuinely concerned about responding to the TRC Calls to Action. To me, this was hopeful that Indigenous voices would be heard and acted upon. The task force met four times between September 2018 and May 2019 to engage in dialogue and discussion and determine priorities for action. Ten recommendations for action were identified through this process. The final report from this task force came out in November 2020. It remains to be seen whether the recommendations will be turned into actions. It is my hope that real action is taken and that all the effort put into this task force does not fall by the wayside like so many other reports, such as the Royal Commission on Aboriginal Peoples. I sincerely hope that the work of reconciliation does not fall only to Indigenous people.

There was one new position created at my university in response to the TRC. A project manager was hired to develop strategic plan outcomes and implement recommendations of the Laurentian University Truth and Reconciliation Task Force. If "making a difference" means getting new positions, then yes, the TRC did make a difference. However, the funding needed to carry out the strategic plan and recommendations must be sought from outside the university. I would hardly consider this "making a difference," if Indigenous people need to be constantly looking for additional means to fund such initiatives.

The position of AVPIAP did not come about as a result of the TRC. It already existed at the time of the TRC. In 2006, the inaugural director of Academic Native Affairs was created, later evolving into an associate vice-president, Indigenous Programs in 2009, and then to associate vice-president, Academic and Indigenous Programs in 2011. This position came about as a result of advocacy of the Laurentian University Native Education Council.

Professor Lorrilee McGregor writes of her experience in the newly created medical school:

The formation of the Northern Ontario School of Medicine (NOSM) in 2005 was possible because of the political support of Indigenous leaders in northern Ontario. The school and its wider campus are located on the traditional territory of the Anishinaabek and the Mushkegowuk. One of the school's founding principles is to be "socially accountable" to the people of northern Ontario, which includes a significant number of Indigenous people (approximately 13% of the population in Ontario).[1] Prior to my arrival at NOSM, students had already been learning about the intergenerational impacts of residential schools throughout their first and second years of in-class learning. In fact, prior to being hired there, I gave guest lectures on residential schools. NOSM is also the only medical school in the world that requires students to complete a four-week immersion in an Indigenous community where they learn about the local culture and community-based health service delivery. Many students have reported that this placement is a transformative experience.

Since the school's inception, guidance on Indigenous health issues has been provided to the dean by the Indigenous Reference Group (IRG) whose members are appointed from political territorial organizations. As time went on, members of the IRG became frustrated by the inability to have input into the curriculum as well as other structural issues. In response to this internal turmoil and partly because of the TRC, an external expert panel was tasked with examining the relationship between NOSM and Indigenous peoples and communities. The panel report identified 10 key themes and made 44 recommendations aimed at strengthening the relationship between NOSM and Indigenous communities. At around the same time that this review was occurring, the faculty position I have now posted. The posting specifically asked for "Indigenous lived experience," among other qualifications, because there is so much Indigenous content in the curriculum that an Indigenous insider's perspective was needed for curriculum renewal.

In terms of administrative leadership, we reflected upon our experience as university administrators. Dr. Peltier writes,

Seeking assistance from others, I initiated and chaired an Indigenization steering committee. I invited 15 members, including administrators, faculty, students, elders, and Indigenous community members to engage in this work. Although meetings were well attended and it

218 Deborah McGregor et al.

appeared that there was commitment, we spent months coming up with the terms of reference and outlining a purpose for this committee. This signalled to me that the university did not have a vision for how to define or implement Indigenization. In response, I provided a prospectus for the committee to consider. It originated in a concept described by Nishinaabe elders as braiding – a metaphor for envisioning Indigenization. Braiding for Indigenization involved interlacing three strands to produce strength that would not be possible with any single strand. The three strands included (1) support for teaching, learning, and research (i.e., providing faculty professional development opportunities to assist in Indigenization of teaching, learning, and research practices); (2) Indigenizing the academic environment (i.e., increasing Indigenous presence of elders, knowledge keepers, and other community partners); and (3) personal commitments to reconciliation (i.e., a willingness to address one's attitudes and biases). I often felt I was proposing ideas for the way forward, but Indigenization efforts remained stagnant.

At first, I coordinated, chaired, recorded minutes, invited elders, and provided refreshments for all meetings. When this became too onerous, my colleagues noticed and offered to help. The Office of Indigenous Initiatives offered support in the form of coordination of meetings and minute taking. We ultimately decided that this administrative, university-wide committee would aim to explore best practices and potential challenges in the five broad goals of Indigenization. The Office of the President assumed responsibility for the committee, where the committee would provide reports to the offices of the president; the provost and vice-president, Academic and Research; Senate; and the Nipissing University Indigenous Council on Education.

At one of our final meetings, the Indigenization Steering Committee resolved to refine a vision statement and overall objectives for Nipissing University's Indigenization strategy. We requested financial assistance to engage an external agency to facilitate five proposed roundtable discussions, but this never materialized. The Indigenization Steering Committee has been on hiatus since I assumed the role of associate dean of arts and science. Since then, there has been little discussion about resuming this work, although the university has committed to equity, diversity, and inclusion. In a recent statement, Nipissing confirmed its commitment to a new direction.

At Nipissing, we recognize the importance of acknowledging our shortcomings in the area of equity, diversity and inclusion and more importantly, our responsibility to take concrete action in order to create a respectful, diverse and inclusive culture where our students, staff and faculty can thrive.... Nipissing University is seeking a consultant to conduct a university-wide equity and stakeholder audit. This audit will form the foundation for a more thorough consultation process and development of a detailed action plan.[2]

While I do not mean to seem unsupportive of other "racialized" groups, I wonder what this means for decolonization of the institutional practices and for Indigenization broadly. I do not want to see the TRC's Calls for Action and other potential changes for Indigenous peoples subsumed or lost under other broader calls of "racialized" groups, as I believe our needs and calls are different.

Professor Manitowabi has served in multiple administrative leadership roles at her university and reflects on her experience:

Two major issues that I currently deal with are racism and discrimination, and retention of faculty. Even though the university where I work has done well to attract Indigenous faculty members, it is difficult to retain them. Many Indigenous faculty are early in their careers and see this university as a great starting point. It has been my observation that larger, more well-established institutions can offer more incentives for these junior faculty; at least that is the narrative that I hear from various levels within the institution. I think that one of the reasons these Indigenous faculty members are attracted elsewhere is that there isn't a great deal of support for them here at this institution. For example, no one likes to speak about racism or discrimination, and definitely no one intends to wake up in the morning and say, "Today, I am going to be racist." Yet there are numerous incidences in which others (faculty, staff, and administration) make comments without considering the implication that they have on Indigenous faculty. In general, people don't often know what to do with such comments so, in the end, nothing is done. Some institutions institute cultural competency training workshops for staff, faculty, and administration. This certainly is a move in a positive direction.

Most cultural competency training sessions highlight important contributions of Indigenous people to society in an effort to uplift Indigenous peoples. The hope is that this will build respect for Indigenous peoples and that they are viewed just as important as others in society. This is a good starting point. I think that this does not go far enough. For meaningful change to occur, there needs to be a paradigm shift. People need to go out of their comfort zones and critically reflect on how their actions and/or inactions perpetuate the current situation. By doing this, they can bring the unconscious into conscious awareness and perhaps then they can identify steps within themselves that can lead to create a space of safety and mutual respect.

Professor Lorrilee McGregor, as a tenure track faculty member, who has been spared administration, reflects on how important it is to have the right leadership:

Our new dean, Dr. Sarita Verma, began her tenure in 2019 and renewed the school's focus on northern Ontario and social accountability. In response to the expert panel report, Dr. Verma has supported the formation of an Academic Indigenous Health Education Committee, which will provide recommendations on curricular changes. We now have an associate dean of equity and inclusion that has been filled by Dr. Joseph Leblanc from Wiikwemkoong Unceded Territory. The dean often invites senior Indigenous staff and Indigenous faculty for advice, which I provide; however, this commitment affects the amount of time that I can devote to teaching or my research program.

The Faculty Association has also been very supportive of me as the first full-time Indigenous faculty member at NOSM. They have consulted with me on Indigenous faculty appointments, and they have supported my attendance at the CAUT Aboriginal Academic Conference. The Faculty Association has also adopted the CAUT Policy Statement on Indigenizing the Academy, which they do practise.

The experiences share a defining characteristic when inroads have been made: advocacy and inclusion of Indigenous people beyond the academy. Such inclusive initiatives may consist of political leadership, much like they did in 1972, with the first

self-determination policy, *Indian Control of Indian Education*. Indigenous advisory groups are critical in advancing reconciliation and reconcili*action* efforts and will be the key to transformation. Colonialism and racism remain firmly entrenched in the academy. As Styres (2020) shows, "An analysis of the data revealed that for Indigenous participants, structural racism was visibly operant within the structures of the university" (p. 163). Similar to the experience shared in this chapter, Styres adds,

> Structural racism was also found in institutions that are only interested in reconciliatory efforts that feel good, are not too inconvenient or do not reallocate resources. It was also found within policies and practices that simultaneously acknowledge and erase Indigenous knowledges and perspectives. (p. 164)

Despite the challenges to achieve equity and justice in the academy, Indigenous scholars agree that education remains a critical site for reconciliation. How then can ethical leadership be achieved?

V. An Ethical Path Forward

In this era of truth and reconciliation, bridging gaps in knowledge and planting seeds for future growth, academic institutions across Turtle Island are looking to transform scholarship, unsettle the foundations (structures, practices, and policies), and commit to reconciliation. To do this work in a good way, 10 suggestions are offered.

1 Develop clear ideas of what the terms "Indigenization," "decolonization," and "reconciliation" mean for your institution. These are contested terms.
2 Remember to involve meaningful representation from Indigenous communities in your efforts to Indigenize, decolonize, and reconcile with Indigenous peoples. Indigenous communities beyond the academy are powerful

and should be provided opportunities for decision making within the academy.

3 Committing to Indigenization, decolonization, and reconciliation means taking up the work at many levels. The work should not fall solely on the shoulders of Indigenous scholars.

4 When the "politics of the day" force institutions in other directions, remember your commitments to Indigenous peoples. Do not begin the work if you cannot commit to seeing it through.

5 Remember reciprocity – relationships involve give and take. If you have asks of Indigenous communities, remember that you have a responsibility to give back. For example, if you are afforded learning or research opportunities in these communities, think about what you can offer in return.

6 Rather than thinking of ways to decolonize the entire university (this is overwhelming, because the foundations of this institution were built on Western thought), start with allowing Indigenous ways of being and doing to lead the way in practice. Think about where there is capacity for this and set it up for success.

7 Engagement with Indigenous peoples within and external to the academy should respect and adhere to Indigenous protocols and practices.

8 Ensure that Indigenous governance and administration in the university are led by Indigenous people and financially supported to succeed. Support must be ongoing, not a "one off."

9 Ensure that institutional actors receive knowledge and skills-based training as called for the TRC.

10 Resist the urge to lump Indigenization, decolonization, and reconciliation or the TRC's Calls to Action in with equity, diversity, and inclusion efforts. Indigenous peoples have a different history of colonization, and the TRC's Calls to Action were based on this history.

VI. Conclusion: Generating Ethical Relations

Indigenous faculty are expected to educate students, staff, and the administration about Indigenous life in addition to our very heavy course load and research projects. We're expected to do the heavy lifting and they just sit back and listen. People have to do their own work and examine their own biases and prejudices. It's not my job to change your mind or to reconcile with you. You have to do the work to change your own mind.

– L. McGregor

The TRC generated a narrative that puts responsibility for change squarely on the shoulders of all Canadians and universities that maintain the colonial, one-sided relationship, for their role in telling particular kinds of stories about Indigenous peoples. Universities do indeed stand on Indigenous lands and benefit from the exploitation of those lands, and their associated knowledge, as publicly funded institutions. The benefits of reconciliation have not been reciprocal, and the power dynamics must be transformed to reflect a balance in the relationship – a core reconciliation principle. This chapter reveals that Indigenous faculty still shoulder an unfair burden of realizing reconciliation in their universities. Indigenous scholars in administrative positions still face the same burdens as they did as new faculty (and likely as graduate students).

The "truth" can be scary. It is hard for many, for example, to face the fact that they live on stolen land, or worse, that their land was stolen. The truth can also fuel guilt and unleash grief, perhaps causing even more trauma and hurt. However, *there is an ethical requirement to not cause further hurt and trauma – in other words, to stop the harm.* The truth can also change the story being told about Indigenous peoples, as we tell our own stories, on our own terms, in our own ways.

There are no excuses for the wilful ignorance about the plight of Indigenous peoples within and external to the academy. There have been numerous public commissions and inquiries, including the recent National Inquiry into Missing and Murdered Indigenous

Women and Girls and the resulting Calls to Justice. Hundreds of recommendations have been made. It is time for reconcili*action*.

NOTES

1 These statistics are from the NE LHIN and NW LHIN (Ontario Association of Children's Aid Societies, n.d.).
2 For more information, see Nipissing University (2021).

REFERENCES

Archibald, J.A., Lee-Morgan, J., & De Santolo, J. (Eds.). (2019). *Decolonizing research: Indigenous storywork as methodology.* Zed Books.

Daigle, M. (2019). Tracing the terrain of Indigenous food *sovereignties. The Journal of Peasant Studies, 46*(2), 297–315. https://doi.org/10.1080 /03066150.2017.1324423

Doerfler, J., Niigaanwewidam Sinclair, J., & Kiiwetinepinesiik Stark, H. (Eds.). (2013). *Centering Anishinaabeg studies: Understanding the world through stories.* University of Manitoba Press.

Gaudry, A., & Lorenz, D. (2018). Indigenization as inclusion, reconciliation, and decolonization: Navigating the different visions for Indigenizing the Canadian academy. *AlterNative: An International Journal of Indigenous Peoples, 14*(3), 218–27. https://doi.org/10.1177/1177180118785382

Hewitt, J. (2019). Land acknowledgment, scripting and Julius Caesar. *The Supreme Court Law Review: Osgoode's Annual Constitutional Cases Conference, 88*(1). https://digitalcommons.osgoode.yorku.ca/sclr/vol88 /iss1/2

Hunt, S. (2014). Ontologies of Indigeneity: The politics of embodying a concept. *Cultural Geographies, 21*(1), 27–32. https://doi.org/10.1177 /1474474013500226

Kuokkanen, R.J. (2007). *Reshaping the university: Responsibility, Indigenous epistemes, and the logic of the gift.* University of British Columbia Press. https://www.ubcpress.ca/asset/9128/1/9780774813563.pdf

Lambert, L. (2014). *Research for Indigenous survival: Indigenous research methodologies in the behavioral sciences.* Salish Kootenai College Press.

McGregor, D. (2019). Truth be told: Redefining relationships through Indigenous research. In K. Drake & B. Gunn (Eds.), *Renewing relationships: Indigenous peoples and Canada* (pp. 9–36). Wiyasiwewin Mikiwahp Native Law Centre, University of Saskatchewan.

Mihesuah, D.A., & Cavender Wilson, A. (2004). *Indigenizing the academy: Transforming scholarship and empowering communities.* University of Nebraska Press.

Mosby, I. (2013). Administering colonial science: Nutrition research and human biomedical experimentation in Aboriginal communities and residential schools, 1942–1952. *Histoire sociale / Social History, 46*(1), 145–72. https://doi.org/10.1353/his.2013.0015

Nipissing University. (2021, 20 January). *Update on equity, diversity and inclusion at Nipissing University.* https://www.nipissingu.ca/news/2021/update-equity-diversity-and-inclusion-nipissing-university

Ontario Association of Children's Aid Societies. (n.d.). *About Northern, rural and remote communities.* https://oacas.libguides.com/c.php?g=710398&p=5063055

Ontario Confederation of University Faculty Associations (OCUFA). (2019). Decolonizing the university in an era of truth and reconciliation [Special issue]. *Academic Matters.* https://academicmatters.ca/print-issues/decolonizing-the-university-in-an-era-of-truth-and-reconciliation/

Richardson, L., & Crawford, A. (2020a). COVID-19 and the decolonization of Indigenous public health. *CMAJ, 192*(38), E1098–100. https://doi.org/10.1503/cmaj.200852

Richardson, L., & Crawford, A. (2020b). How Indigenous communities in Canada organized an exemplary public health response to COVID. *Scientific American.* https://www.scientificamerican.com/article/how-indigenous-communities-in-canada-organized-an-exemplary-public-health-response-to-covid/

Royal Commission on Aboriginal Peoples (RCAP). (1996). *People to people, nation to nation: Highlights from the report of the Royal Commission on Aboriginal Peoples.* Minister of Supply and Services. https://www.rcaanc-cirnac.gc.ca/eng/1100100014597/1572547985018

Smith, L.T. (2012). *Decolonizing methodologies: Research and Indigenous peoples.* Otago University Press.

Smith, L.T. (2019). Foreword. In J.A. Archibald, J. Lee-Morgan, & J. De Santolo (Eds.), *Decolonizing research: Indigenous storywork as methodology* (pp. xi–xii). Zed Books.

Styres, S. (2020). Reconcili*action*: Reconciling contestation in the academy. *Power and Education, 12*(2), 157–72. https://doi.org/10.1177/1757743820916845

Todd, Z. (2018). Métis storytelling across time and space: Situating the personal and academic self between homelands. In J. Christensen, C. Cox,

& L. Szabo-Jones (Eds.), *Activating the heart: Storytelling, knowledge sharing and relationship* (pp. 153–70). Wilfrid Laurier University Press.

Truth and Reconciliation Commission of Canada (TRC). (2015a). *Truth and Reconciliation Commission of Canada: Calls to action.* https://ehprnh2mwo3.exactdn.com/wp-content/uploads/2021/01/Calls_to_Action_English2.pdf

Truth and Reconciliation Commission of Canada (TRC). (2015b). *What we have learned: Principles of truth and reconciliation. Report of the Truth and Reconciliation Commission.* https://publications.gc.ca/collections/collection_2015/trc/IR4-6-2015-eng.pdf

Windchief, S., & San Pedro, T. (Eds.). (2019). *Applying Indigenous research methods: Storying with peoples and communities.* Routledge.

"Indigenous Leadership and Governance, and Reconciliation"

ANNE KOVEN AND STEPHANIE SEYMOUR

The authors make a strong case and extend a compelling invitation to understand and add capaciously to their insights and scholarship. We wish to comment on the possibility of extending their learning and advice to the forestry sector. Forestry is a science, an art, a discipline, a professional practice, and a business that operates, for the most part, on Indigenous land, for which Indigenous people have rights and where northern and remote Indigenous communities live. Importantly, forest land is mostly Crown land (or, as the authors point out, stolen Indigenous land. from the perspective of decolonization), and consequently is the landscape – literally and figuratively – upon which deconstructing the colonial relationship between Indigenous peoples and the Canadian state needs to be successful.

Is there evidence of "reconciliation initiatives" among forest scientists, academics, foresters, and industry?

Professional foresters, such as the Ontario Professional Foresters Association, are making some inroads into educating and requiring licensed foresters to be competent in Indigenous culture and history. These steps are in line with the observation that Indigenous peoples should not unfairly carry the burden of reconciliation, and that government and industry have a duty to undertake actions of reconciliation.

The forest industry continues to wrestle with Indigenous rights and the role of Indigenous enterprises. There might be agreement that Indigenous communities living in the forest in which the industry operates are fairly entitled to share economic benefits through training, employment, and resource payments. Newer licensing arrangements require Indigenous involvement, but progress is slow. One innovative case is Indigenous and local participation in the Nawiinginokiima

Forest Management Corporation in Northwestern Ontario, which is building capacity within communities to manage their forests. (For more, see Ontario, 2023). Through the telling of their own stories, the authors implore you to reflect on your own experiences within your roles. At the intersection of forestry and academia, we ask ourselves, What tools are we providing the next generation of forest professionals to undertake effective actions towards reconciliation? Are we planting the seeds for successful relationships between practitioners in the forest sector and Indigenous people and communities? Forestry and academia evolve. Has the forest industry and the way we educate foresters changed to reflect the present and future challenges? Most importantly, when deciding on and implementing change, who is at the table? Are Indigenous voices present, as they should be?

REFERENCE

Ontario. (2023). *Nawiinginokiima Forest Management Corporation*. https://www.pas.gov.on.ca/Home/Agency/366

PART FOUR

The Ethics of Expression

chapter ten

Guiding Creativity and Controversy: A Faith-Based University Experience

J. HARRY FERNHOUT

I. Faith-Based Universities in the Academy

Anyone who has enjoyed significant engagement in a university, whether as a professor, administrator, student, or board member, knows that it is a special kind of place. A university, particularly one steeped in the liberal arts and sciences, is a space where people come together to think, enquire, imagine, teach, learn, theorize, debate, and critique. Contention for ideas is the stock in trade of universities. Besides their role in teaching new generations of students, this is how universities serve society as a whole – sparking the never-ending search for knowledge by fostering a space for creativity and imagination, a place to challenge established ideas and point to fresh paths of understanding. To remain vibrant and healthy, society needs people who critically reflect on "normalcy" and who explore the frontiers of knowledge and challenge thinking dulled by custom and convention. Universities are a primary setting for such reflection and exploration. This is the vocation of a university, and as such it is also the vocation of a faith-based university.[1] For most my academic career I was privileged to serve in leadership positions in two faith-based institutions: first as president of a graduate institute of philosophy in Toronto and later as president of a liberal arts and sciences university in Edmonton. The reflections in this chapter are based on my experience in these contexts.

A university's vocation is precious and fragile, and it needs to be stewarded, because challenging "normalcy" and proposing new perspectives and understandings often generate discomfort and anxiety, especially outside the academy itself. Historically, the principle of academic freedom developed as way of delineating the space for creativity, exploration, and the pursuit of truth that is essential to the university's role in society. Universities Canada's statement on academic freedom expresses this well: "Academic freedom does not exist for its own sake, but rather for important social purposes. Academic freedom is essential to the role of universities in a democratic society. Universities are committed to the pursuit of truth and its communication to others, including students and the broader community" (Universities Canada, 2011, para. 7). In short, academic freedom is essential to the vocation of a university, and as such it is also essential to the vocation of a faith-based university.

Some contend that "academic freedom" and "faith-based university" are mutually exclusive. A few years ago, the Canadian Association of University Teachers (CAUT) investigated several Canadian faith-based universities to determine whether they denied academic freedom by imposing a "faith test" on their faculty. This matter hardly required "investigation"; the institutions in question all made their statements of faith public on their websites and in their hiring policies. Notably, all the targeted institutions were full members of Universities Canada and subscribed to its statement on academic freedom.

CAUT's understanding of academic freedom focuses almost entirely on the freedom of an *individual* professor to teach, undertake research, and publish ideas and findings without institutional interference and without "prescribed doctrine." By contrast, Universities Canada's statement, while affirming individual professors' freedom, includes an institutional dimension: "Academic freedom must be based on institutional integrity, rigorous standards for enquiry and institutional autonomy, which allows universities to set their research and educational priorities" (Universities Canada, 2011, para. 6). This emphasis recognizes that society extends to its universities, not just to individual professors, the privilege and expectation to engage in the search for knowledge without inappropriate outside interference, whether political or religious. Seen in this light, academic freedom is a multidimensional construct, and all universities have identities and missions that provide the context for individual faculty members' exercise of academic freedom. A multidimensional approach, holding individual and institutional components in a creative balance (and tension), creates space for faith-based institutions to articulate a specific mission and simultaneously to practise a genuine specie of academic freedom.[2]

There are, in fact, some advantages to conducting the academic search for truth in a faith-based context. A shared world view or plausibility structure may function, on the inside, as an academic asset rather than a liability, as an intellectual resource rather than a restriction. The shared perspective may raise issues and suggest interpretations that individual scholars in a "multi-university" might overlook or discount. Working together from intellectual common ground fosters interdisciplinarity among the faculty. Faculty members join such a community of learning voluntarily; a faith-based university is an elective association of scholars working within a tradition of enquiry that they believe provides a valuable resource in tracking their search for truth. In this way, a faith-based university can contribute in unique ways to the mosaic of intellectual activity in higher education as a whole.[3]

II. Circles of Responsibility and Accountability

All universities exist in a web of social relationships, or circles of responsibility and accountability. Some involve relationships within the institution itself: responsibilities for and accountability to faculty, students, and non-academic staff. Universities also have complex relationships with other academic institutions. Accountability to regulatory agencies (such as accreditation bodies) and provincial governments require substantial time, energy, and resources. Then there are granting agencies as well as corporate and individual donors to consider. Alumni form an important university constituency. And, of course, universities have a responsibility and accountability to society as a whole; public confidence in the importance and value of institutions of higher education is essential to their well-being.

A faith-based university shares in these same circles of responsibility and accountability with one important addition: a constituency that supports its academic mission spiritually and, usually, financially. In some instances, this constituency takes the form of a particular institutional church or denominational tradition. My own experience is with institutions that are not owned by or affiliated with a particular church denomination. Rather, the legal, moral, and spiritual owners are a body of (mostly non-academic) people who band together in a non-profit association to create and maintain an institution with a particular faith-inspired identity and mission in higher education. The members of the association elect a board of governors to oversee the business affairs of the university and to appoint a president and senior leaders. As in most universities, governance is bicameral; the board has an arm's-length relationship to a senate (consisting of both internal and external academics and the president), which handles academic matters such as program approval and evaluation, recommendations on faculty appointment and advancement, strategic research plans, etc.

This institutional relationship to a largely non-academic constituency adds an interesting, sometimes challenging circle of accountability and responsibility to the life of a faith-based university. While it shares, with all universities, a responsibility/accountability to society as a whole, a faith-based university practises this responsibility and accountability simultaneously in and through its responsibility and accountability to its spiritual, moral, and legal owners. This relationship requires continual cultivation to ensure that it flourishes as an organic, mutual relationship of service; it cannot be allowed to wither into a one-way link of financial support for the university. When it works well, this relationship serves as a continual reminder that a faith-based university is an expression of a wider faith community that it is called to serve within the framework of its service to society as a whole.

An important challenge for all university leaders is to ensure that the institution functions effectively in its circles of responsibility and accountability. But the potential for tension and controversy within or between these different circles is always a significant possibility. When tension and controversy occur, university leaders must rise to the occasion to deal with and guide these critical challenges. The added circle of responsibility and accountability in faith-based universities can be instructive in this regard; accountability and responsibility to the circle of spiritual, moral, and legal owners accentuates certain features of dealing with controversy, and can, I believe, shed helpful light on this topic for university leaders in general.

III. Creativity, Contention, and Controversy

As already noted, the vocation of a university is to facilitate the never-ending search for knowledge by fostering a space for creativity and imagination, a place to challenge established ideas and point to fresh paths of understanding through teaching and research. In a healthy academic environment, there is a predisposition to creativity and change. Creativity goes hand-in-hand with *contention* (contending for new ideas and interpretations) and *controversy* (disagreement over ideas and interpretations). A university, if it is doing what it should be, is by nature a bit of an unruly place. A university environment can be unsettling because it challenges familiar understandings of the world.

This is where a faith-based university's circle of responsibility and accountability to a non-academic spiritual and moral constituency often comes into play. This relationship is built on and maintained by the partners' mutual enthusiasm for the mission of the university and the constituency's trust in those appointed to carry out that mission. Such enthusiasm and trust are inextricably linked not only to spiritual and moral support for the mission, but also to financial support, because faith-based universities are generally much less reliant on public funding than mainstream universities. This funding factor complicates the relationship and, consequently, also complicates the role of university leaders and faculty members in guiding the university's academic vocation.

In the academic environment, unsettling ideas typically elicit a response such as "That's interesting; let's reflect on it." But what is *interestingly* unsettling in the academy can be *alarmingly* unsettling in its non-academic constituencies. When ideas and proposals (and their possible implications) fall outside people's "normal," they may respond with alarm because the new ideas represent intimidating territory. This "alarmingly unsettled" response can be accentuated if a faith-based university's non-academic constituency tends to be conservative theologically and in its general orientation to new issues. Segments of the non-academic constituency, like some segments of society at large, may tend to view change with scepticism. In ideal circumstances, this predisposition to "conserve" acts as a healthy check and balance on the academic predisposition to change. But when stretched too far, a non-academic community's predisposition to conserve can become a reaction that freezes discussion. The university's disposition to creativity in teaching and research is then regarded with suspicion.[4]

As a rule, academic issues that are specific to a discipline are not very unsettling outside of the academy (with the exception, in some quarters, of issues such as human origins). In their own disciplinary contexts, the creativity exercised by faculty is often too technical or specialized to generate a reaction in the non-academic constituency. Generally speaking, the closer the work of university faculty gets to the life-world of the non-academic constituency, the more potentially unsettling it can become. For example, critical consideration of environmental issues in a social context that relies on fossil fuel extraction will inevitably generate lively debate. The flashpoints for reactions that freeze discussion are most often social-moral issues with which the broader culture is also engaged. Such issues may or may not lie within a particular professor's specific field of expertise, but they are nonetheless issues on which professors are expected to make contributions as thought leaders in society. Alternately, a professor may on occasion publicly address a controversial issue (through a speech or publication) as a concerned citizen or member of a faith community. While not acting in their academic capacity as such, these engagements will still have reverberations for the university. In these various instances, the difference in tolerance levels for unsettling debate within the university and outside it can be volatile. While this is true of university contexts in general, the added circle of responsibility and accountability in faith-based universities makes them more susceptible to this dynamic.

In this context, it is the responsibility of university presidents and other senior leaders, along with the board of governors, to cultivate understanding of and enthusiasm for the academic calling of the university and its faculty. Presidents need to be cheerleaders for the mission and the vital importance of the academic freedom of the institution and its academic staff. In a faith-based university, this includes encouraging, in the support constituency, a spirit that welcomes exploration and tolerates differences of opinion. The message from university leaders should be that toleration of differences is not incompatible with strong convictions. Rather, toleration is an expression of humility; it indicates that we hold our ideas and interpretations with openness, recognizing that we may not have the whole truth on the matter at hand and that we may, in fact, be wrong. Tolerance means putting up with the ideas of those with whom we differ because we may have more to learn.[5]

Of course, it is vital that university leaders and boards take up this challenge, not only in times of crisis, but also (and especially) when there is no immediate controversy on the horizon. The aim of such advocacy is to build a relationship of trust that can withstand stormy weather, should it arise. Building this trust requires a high level of personal interaction with key leaders in the university's non-academic circles, such that the president and other university leaders are seen as trusted spokespersons for the institution.

To use an analogy, a university president is like a conductor of an orchestra playing musical selections in which dissonance plays a key role in making the harmony come alive. Presidents and other university leaders need to cultivate an appreciation for dissonance. A university's gift for dissonance can add verve to the life of its circles of accountability and responsibility. A faith-based university's support constituency should be encouraged to expect some dissonance from its academic partners. One task of presidents and boards is to be conscious of how much constructive dissonance the university's circles of responsibility and accountability can absorb while still maintaining essential harmony.

Presidents and other institutional leaders must play a similar role within the university itself. In relation to the board, this task involves creating an understanding of the difference between issues that are central to the university's core identity and the much broader range of issues that are fair game for exploration and debate by the university community. On the other hand, in relation to the faculty and staff, the president and institutional leaders must foster appreciation for, rather than distrust of, the institution's non-academic circles of engagement. Faculty should be encouraged to regard their teaching, research, writing, and speaking as service to the university's support community and to society as a whole. This includes recognizing that what is "interestingly unsettling" to them may be "alarmingly unsettling" outside their academic context. A healthy relationship between the university and its circles of accountability and responsibility requires mutual respect. Where such respect exists, faculty can exercise wise judgment on the timing, place, context, and audience of their contributions. University leaders and academic staff need to do their utmost to avoid double standards on what views are deemed to be acceptable internally while public sharing of these views is avoided or prohibited. Double standards are incompatible with intellectual honesty and the university's integrity in relation to its communities of support. In short, a key task of the university and its faculty is to exercise freedom in a manner that reflects and celebrates the university's identity, manifests a spirit of community and love, and thereby generates confidence in the university's commitment to its mission.

When creativity erupts into controversy, university leaders and the board of governors play a crucial role in guiding the situation. This is the time for presidents and board chairs to reiterate their commitment to the task of the university and its faculty, and to call for trust and patience. It is not the time for defensiveness or a rush to judgment. University leaders and boards should do their utmost to avoid aligning themselves with one side of an issue but should instead ensure that professor(s) involved receive the benefit of due process and fair assessment. In particular, the board should resist undue pressure from constituents calmly and consistently. The board should avoid trying to solve a problem by adopting an institutional position on any issue that is not at the core of institutional identity. Taking formal positions seldom settles a matter, can have damaging effects inside and outside of the university, and can be extremely difficult to undo. Due process also means that the president, working with the board chair, steers the course through the process and acts as the sole institutional spokesperson about it.

In the challenging circumstances of controversy, it is particularly important that university leaders continue to embody the institution's attitudinal commitments. If those commitments involve "love, joy, peace, forbearance, kindness, goodness, faithfulness, gentleness and self-control"[6] and a strong sense of community, then these should be evident particularly when difficulties arise. In short, what is required is what Richard Mouw (1992, p. 6) calls "convicted civility" by all involved.[7]

IV. Types of Controversy

Creative controversy, as has been outlined above, is the healthy energy related to the pursuit of knowledge that is part and parcel of the academic vocation. Such controversy is unsettling but also stimulating. It challenges and encourages people to reflectively reconsider an issue or concern. Many people in society, including members of a faith-based university's non-academic constituency, understand and, in fact, expect such stimulation and challenge from universities. Creative controversy does not undermine trust but reflects the constructive functioning of academic freedom. At its best, it is characterized by honest dialogue in which all parties are open to learning from each other.

Negative controversy lacks the above-described characteristics but creates polarization and a breakdown of trust. It can be generated and amplified in several ways. For example, a professor or an institution may exercise poor judgment in communicating about an academic or other issue with the result that members of the support community are alarmed rather than stimulated and challenged. Alternatively, a professor or an institution may approach an issue in a manner that segments of the support constituency judge to be at odds with the institution's faith identity. In other words, there may be a difference of opinion on whether the issue in question is central or peripheral to the institution's identity. Negative controversy erodes the relationship between the university and its support community by undermining trust. When a negative controversy erupts, it is exceedingly difficult to transform it into a creative one.

An *intolerable absence of controversy* occurs when a university and its academic staff fail to exercise their calling to provide creative, stimulating leadership, perhaps out of a desire to play safe. One way in which this may come to the fore is through faculty self-censorship. Faculty members may not share their creative thinking, because they do not want to deal with colleagues who disagree, negative student opinions, or blowback from the non-academic community. Or worse, university leadership may discourage creative thinking because it is disruptive. In a faith-based university, this represents a failure to serve the support constituency and society at large in the unique way that such universities can. A long-term, healthy relationship of trust and enthusiasm cannot be sustained on this basis. At some point, when members of the support constituency confront important life issues, they will ask why the university is not providing leadership and will look for inspiration elsewhere.

A matter that is perhaps more existential in faith-based universities than mainstream universities is whether it is ever legitimate to speak of *intolerable creative controversy*. This would be associated with certain flashpoint (often moral) issues that, at face value, are legitimately the subject of creative engagement by the university. A professor or the university may not deem their views on the issue (or the institution's way of addressing it) to be at odds with the institution's faith basis, but the issue itself is so sensitive in academic or nonacademic circles that efforts to address it will inevitably result in negative controversy. Despite concerted efforts to act wisely, the negative controversy would then be so acute as to place the institution at risk because the trust of the support community would be irreparably harmed.

Because of their relationship to a special circle of accountability and responsibility, faith-based universities run the risk of implicitly treating some issues as "intolerably creative," without open consideration. Countering this requires strong institutional leadership to avoid placing the institution in a "double standards" dilemma. It remains an open question as to whether treating something as "intolerable creative controversy" is ever legitimate. At a minimum, any decision to refrain from addressing a certain topic should be for a specified limited time and should not be experienced by the faculty as coming from the top down. Rather, any such a decision should result from an open process (particularly among the board and faculty) and should be revisited regularly. Such deliberation should give due consideration to the impact on the perception of the university's commitment to academic freedom in the wider academic world. And any such decision should not be kept from the support constituency but should be shared wisely to prepare the ground for future engagement with the matter.

V. An Illustration: Omar Khadr and The King's University

In late October 2010, Canadian Omar Khadr was on trial in a US military tribunal in Guantanamo Bay, Cuba. He stood accused of the murder of US soldier Christopher Speer in a firefight in Afghanistan in 2002 when he was 15 years old. Convinced that circumstances in the tribunal were stacked against him, Khadr made a plea deal. In the context of his sentencing, he was asked what he hoped to do when his sentence was completed. The next day, the front page of the *Edmonton Sun*, over a dark courtroom sketch, announced, "Khadr Dreams of E-town: Convicted Terrorist Wants to Apply to City's King's University" (*Edmonton Sun*, 2010).

To say that Omar Khadr was a controversial figure in Canada in 2010 is a vast understatement. Two books circulating at the time illustrate the polarization of Canadian opinion (Levant, 2011; Shepherd, 2008). Khadr was seen as either a child soldier under international law, a victim of circumstance, injustice, and torture who should be brought home for a fair trial and rehabilitation, or as the hardened, indoctrinated son of Canada's first family of terror who deserved to be punished for his heinous war crimes. Khadr's situation was a regular topic in Question Period in the House of Commons, and the government of the day took a hard line against his repatriation.

That Khadr, a devout Muslim, would express a desire to enrol in a small Christian university a world away from Guantanamo Bay is perhaps the stuff of divine humour. The King's University's engagement with the Khadr story began two years earlier with a guest lecture by his Canadian lawyer, Dennis Edney, who told Khadr's story at an all-campus Interdisciplinary Studies conference. He declared Khadr's situation to be hopeless. Edney's account galvanized some faculty members and students, particularly English professor Arlette Zinck. As Zinck put it, a Christian university whose mission statement includes inspiring and equipping learners to "bring renewal and reconciliation to every walk of life" cannot accept the notion of "hopeless." Zinck, some of her colleagues, and a group of students began to research Khadr's story, held awareness-raising events, and attempted to engage politicians and the public. One of their more mundane activities turned out to be most significant; Zinck and some students wrote cards and letters to Khadr, delivered to Guantanamo by Edney. This correspondence led an informal learning process as Zinck encouraged Khadr to use his time in solitary detention to read books and write reports for her. This very human contact in a situation of extreme isolation inspired Khadr's expressed hope to one day attend King's. After Khadr's conviction, the US military asked Zinck to design and carry out an educational program for him while in US custody. Zinck enlisted colleagues from King's and other universities in this project, which continued when Khadr was transferred to prisons in Canada, until his release in 2015.[8]

VI. The King's University's Response

The university's engagement with the Khadr story was the most divisive and challenging controversy I confronted in my tenure as president of King's and, in fact, in my entire career. There were times when it would have been convenient to declare this an "intolerable creative controversy." This high-profile story repeatedly placed the university in an uncomfortable media spotlight. King's very directly experienced the polarization about Khadr that existed in Canadian society at large. People with no prior association with King's called to give the president a piece of their mind. Some people felt King's involvement was an opportunistic attempt to attract attention at Khadr's expense. Expressions of support from some quarters were outweighed by suggestions of what might happen if Khadr ever set foot on King's campus. On two occasions, I delivered hate mail directed at Zinck to the Edmonton police. Similar, but much less vehement, divisions emerged in the King's support constituency. Some donors withdrew their support while others expressed concerns about sending their sons and daughters to an institution where they might encounter a convicted terrorist. Internally, while most faculty and students were sympathetic to Khadr's situation, others were quietly or vocally opposed to any institutional involvement.

King's engagement with Khadr's story illustrates aspects of dealing with controversy in an academic context. For one thing, it demonstrates the complex character of controversies. Was this an issue that arose directly out of the academic work of faculty members, or did the involvement of faculty and students fall outside their academic responsibilities? Was Arlette Zinck involved primarily as an English professor or as a concerned citizen? Was this a creative controversy, a negative controversy, or an intolerable creative controversy, as described above? The answer is, "All of the above." It was a mixed situation from the beginning. Life is mixed and complicated, and so are controversies.

From the beginning, a key question posed in various quarters was, Why is King's, a Christian institution, concerning itself with the divisive story of someone detained in a foreign prison and accused of a war crime? The key element in King's response was that this engagement was our educational responsibility. While Khadr's story was not a curricular topic as such, it had been placed before the student body in a (required) Interdisciplinary Studies conference. Members of the faculty felt that it was morally irresponsible to confront students with a desperate story and leave them with a sense that the situation was "hopeless." Professor Zinck and others responded by encouraging students to learn as much as possible about Khadr's situation by researching the story and drawing their own conclusions.

The university's leadership team concluded that it was important to foster this climate of exploration and debate; this, it seemed to us, was implicit in the institutional mission to equip students to be agents of reconciliation and renewal in society. At the same time, we tried to steer clear of aligning the institution either for or against Khadr; this was not the institution's role, regardless of our personal inclinations. It was understood that when faculty and student engagement led to public advocacy, they were not acting in the first instance as representative of the institution. Maintaining these fine distinctions was difficult, but making them was nevertheless important to maintain a focus on the university's proper role.[9]

The vital role that university leaders and the board of governors play in advocating for the task of the university and its faculty emerged clearly in this experience. When King's engagement began, the leadership team was blessed with a considerable reservoir of trust internally, with the board of governors, and in the support constituency. That trust was sorely needed over the several years in which the story played out. As president, I was called upon to explain and advocate for King's engagement in many contexts. Internally, we held town hall–style conversations with faculty and students to explain our support for the engagement efforts on the one hand and our institutional non-alignment on the other. I assured everyone that the university had space for dissenting opinions and asked for respectful and charitable disagreement and debate. King's also held town hall meetings in communities around Alberta to tell our story, to remind people of the task of a university, to ask for patience and, above all, continued trust in the integrity of our mission. Visits with individual donors followed a similar pattern. Periodic letters and articles were sent to the university's supporters. And, of course, there were many media interviews and letters to the editor to try to stay on top of the issue.

A few months into the controversy, I made my role much more difficult by an unguarded comment that appeared to align the university on one side of the debate. In an informal conversation, some participants made suggestions about generous steps they would take if and when Khadr were ever released and moved to Edmonton. Somewhat tongue-in-cheek, I responded that King's should perhaps provide similar generosity by giving Khadr a break on tuition. This comment was announced publicly at a large awareness-raising event as a commitment to provide Khadr with free tuition. Not surprisingly, this became part of media stories about the event and generated a strong public reaction, particularly among donors who had no interest in seeing their support used in this way. Damage control to assure the constituency and the general public that King's had not made a formal commitment along these lines had only mixed results. The "commitment" was repeated in media stories for years, and even made its way into a legal filing in the military tribunal in Guantanamo. This inadvertent failure to maintain the distinction between advocacy and the proper role of the university to foster creative debate made life immeasurably more difficult. It underscored the importance of remaining vigilant on the unique role of a university and its president at all times.

As the developments in the Khadr case unfolded, King's made an effort to collaborate with other partners to educate students and the public and, frankly, to distribute the load of institutional engagement. Initially, other universities were reticent to become involved. Students had greater success in engaging their peers in events at the University of Alberta and MacEwan University. Over time, King's developed a very constructive collaboration with the Centre for Religion and Public Life at the University of Alberta to host a series of well-attended lectures that provided important learning on, for example, the legal status of the US military tribunal in which Khadr was tried.

A remarkable feature of the Khadr controversy at King's was that – with some notable exceptions – it was characterized by what Zinck later called "intelligent charity," a phrase she borrowed from Christian literary scholar Alan Jacobs. The phrase describes the kind of *thoughtful engagement* that seeks to know fully, and to respond with wisdom and care for all concerned. The phrase is rooted in the core conviction that animates most world faiths, the golden rule that requires that we consider deeply and from a variety of points of view, then assess our action based *on how we ourselves would like to be treated*. (Zinck, 2016)

This disposition enabled participants in debates and advocacy to give differing points of view charitable consideration instead of reacting defensively or angrily.

VII. Sequel

Arlette Zinck and her team continued Omar Khadr's educational program while he was incarcerated in Canada, first in maximum- and later in medium-security prisons.[10] In May 2015, Khadr was released on bail. When asked what he would like to say to Prime Minister Stephen Harper, Khadr responded, "I'm going to have to disappoint him; I'm a better person than he thinks I am" (CTV News, 2015). That September, Khadr enrolled in courses at King's. Seven years after his story was first told from the same stage, Khadr was interviewed at the university's fall all-campus Interdisciplinary Studies conference. He spoke of how hope embodied in his faith had carried him through his dark story. Hopeless turned to hope: a fitting end to a remarkable story.

NOTES

1 While "faith-based university" is the common term for the kind of institution I have in mind, I use this designation with reservations. The term "faith-*based*" suggests a static duality: a faith foundation on which a university edifice is constructed with little dynamic interaction between the two. In my view, a "faith-based" university should be one is one in which the interplay of "faith" and "university" is constant and ongoing in every dimension of its institutional life. "Faith-*transparent* university" would be a better designation. In the postmodern era it is broadly

accepted that all knowing is a human practice that starts somewhere and is contextualized in a world view of some kind. A distinguishing feature of a "faith-transparent university" is that it declares its beliefs upfront. If such an institution meets generally accepted academic standards, it should be seen as a worthy participant in the academic mosaic.

It is also important to note that "faith" in the current context refers to the Christian faith. "Faith-based" universities in Canada all have some sort of Christian identity. However, a university "based" in another world religion would likely share many of the features and dynamics of institutions addressed in this chapter.

2 An often-overlooked dimension of academic freedom is students' freedom enquiry. Students are entitled to a fair and broad representation of their subject of study. Evaluation of student work must respect their creative freedom and consider the academic quality of their work rather than their agreement with their professors' views.

3 On a practical level, scholars in faith-based universities may have the additional asset of connections with networks of organizations engaged with the role of faith/religion in public life (politics, education) or social movements focused on, for example, justice or climate change.

4 This dynamic is not unique to faith-based universities. Similar issues arise, for example, when a public university offers an honorary doctorate to someone whose public profile is at odds with major elements of the university's constituency.

5 In a Christian faith-based context, leaders can appeal to the conviction that what we know, we know in part. In the words of the apostle Paul, "Now I know in part; then I shall know in full, as I am fully known" (I Corinthians 3:12).

6 These are the fruits of the Spirit listed by St. Paul (Galatians 5:22–3).

7 For a fuller discussion of the role of presidents, faculties, and boards in these matters, see Diekema (2000).

8 The story of the engagement of The King's University and Arlette Zinck with Omar Khadr has been told in the *Chronicle of Higher Education* (Wilheim, 2014) and *University Affairs* (Mouallem, 2016), as well as many other media.

9 An example of how this nuanced stance (encouraging exploration but not aligning the institution) played out had to do with faculty research/scholarship expectations. The King's University employed Boyer's multidimensional model of scholarship (Boyer, 1990). Professor Zinck was encouraged to consider her engagement with students and the public as *scholarship of application* (one of Boyer's four dimensions of

scholarship). In this way the institution acknowledged her work as part of her scholarly expectations while maintaining that she did not represent an institutional position in this work.

10 The educational program for Khadr eventually blossomed into the Ephesus Project, a program through which accredited King's University courses in physics, mathematics, English, history, philosophy, and theology are offered to inmates in Canadian prisons in cooperation with Book Clubs for Inmates, a Canadian charity whose mission is to encourage literacy to enable prisoners to develop empathy, listening skills, and self-awareness.

REFERENCES

Boyer, E. (1990). *Scholarship reconsidered: Priorities of the professoriate*. Carnegie Foundation for the Advancement of Teaching.

CTV News. (2015, 7 May). Khadr: "See who I am as a person, not as a name." https://www.ctvnews.ca/canada/khadr-see-who-i-am-as-a-person -not-as-a-name-1.2363711

Diekema, A. (2000). *Academic freedom and Christian scholarship*. Eerdmans.

Edmonton Sun. (2010, 19 October). Khadr dreams of e-town: Convicted terrorist wants to apply to city's King's University.

Levant, E. (2011). *The enemy within: Terror, lies and the whitewashing of Omar Khadr*. McClelland & Stewart.

Mouallem, O. (2016, 7 September). *Welcoming Omar Khadr to The King's University*. University Affairs. https://www.universityaffairs.ca /features/feature-article/welcoming-omar-khadr-kings-university/

Mouw, R.J. (1992). *Uncommon decency: Christian civility in an uncivil world*. InterVarsity Press.

Shepherd, M. (2008). *Guantanamo's child: The untold story of Omar Khadr*. Wiley.

Universities Canada. (2011, 25 October). *Statement on academic freedom*. https://www.univcan.ca/media-room/media-releases/statement-on -academic-freedom/

Wilheim, I. (2014, 28 April). The professor and the prisoner. *Chronicle of Higher Education*. https://www.chronicle.com/article/the-professor -and-the-prisoner/

Zinck, A. (2016, 31 March). *The engaged university and the responsibility of its educators*. McMaster University Seminar Series on Higher Education: Practice, Policy and Public Life, McMaster University, Hamilton, ON, Canada.

"Guiding Creativity and Controversy: A Faith-Based University Experience"

NADA CONIĆ
Spiritual Counsellor

As someone who leads spiritual retreats and hopes to heal theological divides, I approached Dr. Fernhout's article with prejudices against the fundamentalist, authoritarian, and theocratic tendencies of many "faith-based" schools. It was not until I read the name "Omar Khadr" that I realized that Dr. Fernhout was part of the story that moved me to tears of gratitude and pride when I first watched it play out on the news and again as he retold it.

His theme is a challenge to all people of hope: how to manage tension and conflict in the communal search for truth and betterment. University was where I discovered that "criticism," "argument," "challenge," and "disagreement" could be desirable and valuable. It was a revelation, and an alternative to silent acquiescence and mental dimming. Risking conflict is necessary if one is "to think, inquire, imagine, teach, learn, and theorize." But there must be rules of engagement and a common purpose that will create a context of civility and trust. Every human association must manage the tension between creativity and conformity, freedom and authority, diversity and unity, curiosity, and fear. The natural variations within a given religion or society are at least as great as the differences between them – unless artificially suppressed.

What Dr. Fernhout offers is an academic model in which freedom of enquiry and conscience is not curtailed by an uncomprehending external authority. Instead, it is sustained and guided from within a faith community spanning students, teachers, and supporters, all committed to loving engagement with the world.

Dr. Zinck and her students reached out to Omar Khadr in accord with the school's mission to "bring renewal and reconciliation to every walk of life." This mission reaches beyond the purely scholarly or the narrowly sectarian: it summons the whole person and community of faith to achieve creative resolutions to controversy and damaging division.

chapter eleven

University Governance and Campus Speech

L.W. SUMNER

A university department has invited a controversial academic speaker to deliver a series of three lectures. A group of left-wing students considers some of the speaker's writings, especially his analysis of the causes of Black urban poverty, to be racist. At the first event, the speaker is harassed by a few members of the audience but is able to deliver his lecture. At the second, some students take over the platform in order to prevent the lecture from proceeding. As a result, the second and third lectures are cancelled.

Sound familiar? Instances of disruption, disinvitation, or "no-platforming" of invited speakers have recently become commonplace on university campuses, especially in the United States.[1] But the foregoing event was not recent, and it occurred in Canada. The speaker in question was the well-known conservative sociologist Edward Banfield, the host of the planned lecture series was the Department of Political Economy at the University of Toronto, and the date was March 1974 (Friedland, 2013, pp. 539–41). At the time, the university was heavily criticized for its handling of the affair, especially for its failure to ensure that the remaining lectures could go forward without disruption. University administrators continue to face criticism for the ways in which they choose to intervene, or not to intervene, in speaking events held on their campuses. Clearly the fact that these problems are not new has not made them any easier to solve.

In its broadest form, the question we have before us is this: When university administrators learn of a planned speaking event on campus that appears likely to be contentious or problematic, how should they respond? What would ethical leadership look like in these circumstances? In this form, however, the question is too broad. As one way of narrowing it, I will specify that "university administrators" are here to be understood as those with the ultimate responsibility for overseeing such events (usually the academic vice-president). Similar questions may apply to more junior levels of administration (deans, directors, department chairs, etc.), but I will confine my attention to the desk where the buck stops.

We also need a more focused understanding of the ways in which campus speech might be "contentious or problematic." At one time, obscenity might have been an issue (imagine that the campus film society announces a screening of *Deep Throat*), but those issues have latterly receded from view. The dominating concern today is hate speech, understood broadly as any form of expression that is intended to arouse hatred or contempt towards members of a particular social group. I will follow that trend, so that our question now becomes: When top university administrators have reason to believe that a planned speaking event on campus may feature hate speech (at least in the eyes of some), how should they respond?

In what follows, I will address that question (or at least some aspects of it) as it arises for Canadian universities. With that setting in mind, some legal context is important. In Canada, unlike the United States, hate speech is regulated by criminal law. Section 319(2) of the *Criminal Code* (Canada, 1985) prohibits "communicating statements, other than in private conversation" that "wilfully promote hatred against any identifiable group."[2] For the purpose of this section, an "identifiable group" is defined as "any section of the public distinguished by colour, race, religion, national or ethnic origin, age, sex, sexual orientation, gender identity or expression, or mental or physical disability" (s. 318(4)). It is worth noting that in order to secure a conviction for promoting hatred, it is both necessary and sufficient to establish that the speaker *intended* that effect, but need not actually have *achieved* it.

The law of the land applies everywhere, including on university campuses. So if campus speakers are unwise enough to engage in

hate speech, within the meaning of the statute, they expose themselves to the possibility of a charge and of prosecution. In this
event, there is no role for university administrators; enforcement
of the criminal law is a police matter. (Actually, there may be a role
for administrators, but I will return to that later.)

Furthermore, administrators would be unwise to take pre-
emptive action – even action that falls short of cancelling the event –
in anticipation that an invited speaker might cross the line. In
March 2010, the American right-wing commentator Ann Coulter
was scheduled to give a talk at the University of Ottawa. Prior to
the event, the university's academic vice-president sent Coulter a
warning, cautioning her to watch her words lest she face criminal
charges for promoting hatred. Coulter subsequently cancelled the
event, not strictly because of the warning, but because sponsors
feared that demonstrations outside the venue might turn violent.
In a subsequent interview, Coulter did not neglect the opportunity
to mock the university: "It's at the absolute bush league, bottom
of the barrel schools that you get the worst treatment and still I've
never seen this before. I'm guessing the scores to get into the University of Ottawa are not very challenging" (Chase, 2010, paras.
6–7).

The legal restrictions of hate speech are, however, only part
of the story and ultimately not a very important part. As I have
said, when those restrictions are transgressed in campus speech,
university administrators have little to do except let the law take
its course. The more serious and difficult question concerns campus speech that is hateful without rising to the level of a criminal
offence. Freedom of expression enjoys constitutional protection
under section 2(b) of the *Charter of Rights and Freedoms*. In order not
to offend the *Charter*, the bar for a successful prosecution for hate
promotion has been set very high, by providing speakers with a
formidable array of defences. Besides the obvious defence of truth,
a speaker's statements are also immunized against prosecution if
they "were relevant to any subject of public interest, the discussion
of which was for the public benefit, and if on reasonable grounds
he believed them to be true" (Canada, 1985, s. 319(3)).[3] That is a
loophole that only the most extreme, or obtuse, speaker could fail

to take advantage of. (Perhaps the University of Ottawa administration should also have informed Coulter of that fact.)

The implication of all this for university administrators is that
campus speech may be hateful without being unlawful. The
waters are further muddied by the fact that the key components of
the hate speech law are themselves vague and contentious; what
may appear to some as an attempt to arouse hatred will look to
others as honest and tough-minded political commentary. As an
example, let's use Israeli Apartheid Week (IAW), a series of lectures and rallies that is held annually on some Canadian campuses.
The avowed aim of its organizers is to "educate people about the
nature of Israel as an apartheid system" and to build support for a
global Boycott, Divestment, and Sanction campaign against Israel
(Israeli Apartheid Week, n.d.). So far, it seems to fit comfortably
within the bounds of political speech critical of Israel, and neither
the organizers nor the speakers have ever been charged with promoting hatred. However, many of these events have been accused
by observers, Jewish and non-Jewish alike, of being anti-Semitic.[4]
Since the law of the land is not in play here, the burden of deciding
whether to respond to Israeli Apartheid Week, and if so in what
way, falls squarely on the shoulders of university administrators.

Campus events featuring right-wing provocateurs like Ann
Coulter are likely to fall in the same grey area. Coulter, who has
argued that American immigration policies amount to the geno-
cide of white people (Wikipedia, 2020), is fully capable of incendi-
ary remarks calculated to offend some racial or religious or ethnic
constituency on campus. But what she has to say is also unlikely to
rise to the level of a criminal offence, even if she is not tutored on
Canadian law in advance of her appearance.

What is the appropriate response by the university administration in advance of such events? Would there ever be grounds for
intervening to cancel any of them? I want to think about this question in the following way.[5] The jurisdiction of university administrators over speaking events ends at the boundaries of their
campus. It would be equally open to some off-campus group to
stage Israeli Apartheid Week, or to invite Coulter to speak, at a
venue elsewhere in the community. In that case, municipal officials

would face the same decision whether to allow the event to proceed. We can then ask whether the factors to be taken into account
in making this decision are the same on- and off-campus. Do university administrators have more reason to intervene in a situation
like this, or less? Should the bounds of free speech be narrower on
campus, or broader? (Or, perhaps, just the same.)

There are arguments to be made for each option, arguments
that speak to the special nature and mission of the university. The
strongest case in favour of a very broad free speech zone on campus invokes the traditional idea of the university as a domain with
a distinctive commitment to open and free enquiry. As the University of Toronto Governing Council (1992, p. 2) puts it,

> [T]he essential purpose of the University is to engage in the pursuit
> of truth, the advancement of learning and the dissemination of knowl-
> edge. To achieve this purpose, all members of the University must have
> as a prerequisite freedom of speech and expression, which means the
> right to examine, question, investigate, speculate, and comment on any
> issue without reference to prescribed doctrine.[6]

It seems to follow from this conception of the university's mission
that speakers should be free to express, and audiences should be
free to hear, all opinions on matters of public interest, however odi-
ous or offensive to some those opinions might be. The University
of Toronto draws this very conclusion: "The University must allow
the fullest range of debate. It should not limit that debate by pre-
ordaining conclusions or punishing or inhibiting the reasonable
exercise of free speech" (p. 2).

The University of Chicago has taken a very similar position in a
widely influential statement of principle:

> Because the University is committed to free and open inquiry in all mat-
> ters, it guarantees all members of the University community the broad-
> est possible latitude to speak, write, listen, challenge, and learn.... [I]t
> is not the proper role of the University to attempt to shield individuals
> from ideas and opinions they find unwelcome, disagreeable, or even
> deeply offensive.... [T]he University's fundamental commitment is to

the principle that debate or deliberation may not be suppressed because the ideas put forth are thought by some or even by most members of the University community to be offensive, unwise, immoral, or wrong-headed. It is for the individual members of the University community, not for the University as an institution, to make those judgments for themselves, and to act on those judgments not by seeking to suppress speech, but by openly and vigorously contesting the ideas that they oppose. (Committee on Freedom of Expression, 2015, p. 2)

These "Chicago Principles" have subsequently been adopted or endorsed at more than 70 post-secondary institutions across the United States.

On this view of the university's purpose, its administrators should be particularly reluctant to shut down campus speech, possibly more reluctant than their counterpart municipal authorities, who lack the same sense of mission. In that case, the bounds of free expression must not be narrower on campus than they are in the non-academic world, and arguably should be wider.

Arguments for the contrary view, however, are also rooted in a conception of the peculiar nature of the university. I will consider four of them.

I. The Argument from Academic Freedom

One version of this argument has been articulated and defended in a recent article by Robert Mark Simpson (2020). As he conceives of it, academic freedom resembles free speech in guaranteeing a wide-ranging liberty of expression and enquiry, but differs from it by applying strictly within the special scholarly domains of teaching and research.[7] Within these domains, Simpson argues, it is accompanied by the expectation that scholarly work is properly "subject to quality controls on the basis of general professional standards of accuracy and coherence" (p. 291), controls for which, he suggests, there is no real analogue in non-scholarly on-campus speaking activities. Simpson's argumentative target is this misalignment between academic freedom and campus speech; the standards of the former, he argues, should be applied to the latter:

[S]peech expressing ill-informed or badly reasoned ideas need not receive any special protection in universities, except if it falls under the protection of academic freedom, for example, if it occurs as part of the university's formal teaching and research activities. Free speech is a fundamental liberty in social intercourse per se, but it is not a mandatory commitment for the university. Thus, we can at least sometimes exclude or marginalize speakers and ideas that fall short of the intellectual standards which define academia and conduce to its core epistemic aims. (p. 316)

It follows from Simpson's analysis that speech that might be properly allowed in the wider community may properly be disallowed on campus. Simpson proposes that speaking invitations by campus groups be vetted, not by university administrators, but by faculty experts in the appropriate field. (This vetting would apply to *all* campus speakers, not just those thought likely to promote hatred.) "And where the considered judgment of the institution's academic experts is that an invited speaker's work manifestly fails to attain to the kind of intellectual standards that further its epistemic mission, then, other things being equal, that institution should refrain from offering a platform to that speaker" (p. 317).

I leave to others to imagine how well a system requiring speaker invitations by student groups to be approved by faculty experts might work out in practice. There is, it seems to me, a much deeper problem with Simpson's analysis and proposal. Let's return to his starting point, the topic of academic freedom. According to the Canadian Association of University Teachers Council (2018, s. 2),

Academic freedom includes the right, without restriction by prescribed doctrine, to freedom to teach and discuss; freedom to carry out research and disseminate and publish the results thereof; freedom to produce and perform creative works; freedom to engage in service; freedom to express one's opinion about the institution, its administration, and the system in which one works; freedom to acquire, preserve, and provide access to documentary material in all formats; and freedom to participate in professional and representative academic bodies. Academic freedom always entails freedom from institutional censorship.

Notable by its absence from this statement is any reference to the *quality* of the work that academics are to be free to engage in; they are equally free to carry out their teaching and research, without institutional interference, whether they do it well or badly. Of course, they are expected by the university to do it well, and the quality of their performance is constantly being assessed for purposes such as tenure, promotion, and remuneration. But these assessments are a matter not of academic freedom but of academic or professional standards. If faculty members are denied tenure or promotion on the basis of negative assessments of the quality of their teaching or research, this outcome is not a restriction of their academic freedom but a judgment of their failure to live up to professional expectations.[8]

Simpson constantly conflates the two, to the detriment of his argument. That argument actually has little to do with academic freedom and rests instead on the premise that the standards that are appropriate in classroom teaching, in research seminars, in professional conferences and workshops, and in the preparation of scholarly work for publication should also be applied outside these contexts to all other activities on campus.[9] Any invited speaker whose credentials fail to meet these standards may properly be denied a campus platform. That high bar will suffice to exclude Ann Coulter, and possibly also some of the presenters at Israeli Apartheid Week, as well as a host of other non-academic speakers who may not hold advanced degrees or qualify as experts in their field. However, these invited speakers are not engaged in any of the aforementioned scholarly activities, nor are they contending for tenure, promotion, or a salary increase; instead, they have been solicited because they have been deemed to have something worthwhile to say on some matter of public interest. Despite their lack of academic credentials, there may still be much to learn from them.

II. The Argument from Civility

Simpson also makes the related point that discourse in scholarly settings – in classrooms, research seminars, etc. – is expected to be civil. (Anyone who has attended many academic presentations knows that they are not always civil.) Uncivil discourse can lead to the distress of targeted audience members, which Simpson (2020) suggests

> is out of place on the campus common, for much the same reason that it is out of place in the seminar room itself. It is a kind of distress which is not integral to the targeted individual's learning experience, and which can greatly detract from it. (p. 300)

This is now a rather different ground for regulating campus speech. Speakers need not be experts, and need not measure up to lofty academic standards, and may in principle espouse any opinions they like, as long as they do so in a civil manner. Ann Coulter and Israeli Apartheid Week will still not make the cut, but now for a different reason.

Since we all think civility a good thing, this is an appealing idea. However, those who contend that the university may rightly suppress uncivil speech must face the question how this might be accomplished. Incivility admits of many gradations, from the merely ill-mannered to the scurrilous and abusive. Where is the line to be drawn at what is acceptable on campus, and who is to draw it? Most university administrators seem to show little relish for serving as the arbiters of civility. The University of Toronto Governing Council states that "although no member of the University should use language or indulge in behaviour intended to demean others…, the values of mutual respect and civility may, on occasion, be superseded by the need to protect lawful freedom of speech" (p. 2). The University of Chicago takes an even stronger stand:

> Although the University greatly values civility, and although all members of the University community share in the responsibility for maintaining a climate of mutual respect, concerns about civility and mutual respect can never be used as a justification for closing off discussion of ideas, however offensive or disagreeable those ideas may be to some members of our community. (Committee on Freedom of Expression, 2015, p. 2)

Simpson's appeal to civility serves to remind us that we need to distinguish two different kinds of restraint on speech. Content restrictions stipulate certain ideas or opinions that may not be expressed by any speaker on any occasion.[10] Holocaust denial might serve as a case in point. Context restrictions, by contrast, will permit the expression of these ideas or opinions, but not at the wrong time, or in the wrong place, or in the wrong manner. John Stuart Mill, who rejected content restrictions on speech, was alive to this distinction. The opinion that corn dealers are starvers of the poor, he says, may be freely circulated through the press but may not be delivered to an angry mob assembled in front of the corn dealer's house (Mill, 2003, p. 121). Civility constraints are context restrictions on campus speech: you may express hateful views, but only in language that is subtle and coded, rather than forceful and blunt. For the most part, the hate promotion section of the *Criminal Code* imposes a content restriction: you may not use language that wilfully promotes hatred against an identifiable group (unless you are saved by one of the available defences). However, it also contains a context restriction: you are not liable if you use that language "in private conversation." There is a strong case to be made that university administrators should not be in the business of imposing content restrictions on campus speech. Time, place, and manner restrictions, however, may be another matter.

The "Chicago Principles" stipulate that "the University may reasonably regulate the time, place, and manner of expression to ensure that it does not disrupt the ordinary activities of the University" (Committee on Freedom of Expression, 2015, p. 2). The University of Toronto Governing Council (1992)'s *Statement on Freedom of Speech* is more specific:

> Of necessity, there are limits to the right of free speech, for example, when members of the University use speech as a direct attack that has the effect of preventing the lawful exercise of speech by members or invited guests, or interfering with the exercise of authorized University business, the University may intervene. (p. 2)

It follows from this statement that, in the Banfield affair, the university would have been justified in suppressing the speech (and conduct) of the protesting students in order to permit Banfield's lectures to proceed. In fact, we can say something stronger: acting in this way would have been not merely permissible, but obligatory. To this point, we have been tacitly assuming that the duties of university administrators vis-à-vis campus speech are entirely negative: duties not to intervene, for instance, by cancelling or shutting down speaking engagements. But much more germane are positive duties to facilitate or enable speech events, by not permitting others to shut them down. This was the signal failing of the University of Toronto administration in 1974: it should have taken steps to ensure that Banfield's two remaining lectures could be delivered at a time and in a place where they could be protected from intervention by protestors, if necessary, by the use of campus, or even municipal, police. The protesting students were entitled to advocate their point of view, but not in such a way as to suppress Banfield's speech.

The university may therefore be permitted, or even required, to intervene when campus speech becomes sufficiently unruly or disruptive. But this does not give it a licence to screen all speaking events for possible incivility. It is not Israeli Apartheid Week or a talk by Ann Coulter that is likely to have the effect of "preventing the lawful exercise of speech," but rather the reactions of their opponents.

III. The Argument from Student Protection

Simpson's appeal to civility noted the distress that uncivil speech can cause to "targeted audience members." However, this point could be broadened to apply to hate speech in general. There is no reasonable doubt that racist, sexist, or homophobic discourse can hurt its intended targets. The university already has the responsibility to protect vulnerable students, as much as it can, against such threats as racist bullying and sexual harassment. It would therefore be but a short step to argue that it should also take steps to protect them from the hurt that can be inflicted by insults or abuse.

However, I am sceptical that universities have this in loco parentis function of sheltering their students against the pernicious effects of hate. For one thing, the very idea of making the campus a "safe space" in this respect seems quixotic. In the age of social media, hate speech is pervasive; it does not respect campus boundaries and students cannot be insulated against it. Unlike other vectors on which hatred can spread unchecked, scheduled on-campus speaking events have the great advantage of being optional and easily avoided; if you don't want to listen to Ann Coulter fulminate about Mexicans or Muslims, then you need only give her talk a miss. In any case, if the university does indeed have this protective responsibility towards its students, then there is a more constructive way for it to fulfil it than by preventing them from hearing controversial speakers. One function the university clearly does have is to teach students to think critically, to demand evidence for opinions, to challenge outlandish assertions, and to see through lies, distortions, and misrepresentations. If it has done its job, then it will have equipped them to fight back against hateful speech with the weapons of facts and logic. University administrators who consider no-platforming speakers show no confidence in the ability of their students to call out hateful rhetoric for what it is. If anything, students should be less in need of protection against the hurtful effects of extreme speech than members of the broader community who have not had the same educational advantages.

IV. The Argument from Legitimization

This argument is often put in the following form: when a university hosts an event like Israeli Apartheid Week, or a speaker like Coulter, it implicitly legitimizes the opinions that will thereby be espoused. Universities, it will be said, are prestigious institutions, and so their prestige will rub off on their invited speakers. Neil Levy puts this point nicely, in a slightly more technical way. Levy distinguishes between two kinds of evidence for a speaker's opinions: *first-order* evidence, which consists in the arguments for and against those opinions, and *higher-order* evidence, which bears on determining whether the speaker's opinions deserve to be taken seriously.

An invitation to speak at a university campus, a prestigious event or to write an opinion piece for a newspaper provides (*prima facie*) higher-order evidence. It is evidence that the speaker is credible; that she has an opinion deserving a respectful hearing. It typically certifies expertise, and expertise is higher-order evidence that the person's opinion should be given particular weight. (Levy, 2019, para. 5)

There is clearly something to this argument. When an academic unit in a university (a faculty, department, centre, etc.), or a group of faculty members in such a unit, issues an invitation to a visiting speaker, they are indeed implying that this person has the appropriate credentials to contribute something worthwhile on the announced topic. After all, the members of the unit in question have the expertise to determine who is, and who is not, worth listening to, and they have no interest in wasting their time, and their colleagues' time, on second-raters or charlatans. So, such an invitation does constitute higher-order evidence of credibility. Having been an invited speaker at the highly rated Department of X at the internationally renowned University of Y can add lustre to any curriculum vitae. In the case of these invitations, however, it is hard to imagine university administrators having grounds to overrule the academic judgments of their colleagues.

The point, however, does not generalize to other campus speaking events, especially invitations by student groups. They may well lack the expertise to distinguish wheat from chaff, or may decide to invite speakers, like Coulter, just because they are provocative, or have celebrity status, or are likely to fill the hall. A speaking invitation from a student group will often not constitute higher-order evidence of expertise or credibility, in which case university administrators have no more reason to no-platform a campus speaker than do their municipal counterparts. We are reminded here again of Simpson's distinction between the more scholarly domains of the university and the rest of the campus: the conventions and assumptions that apply to the former may have no purchase in the latter.[11]

Levy's point, however, does apply particularly forcefully to one category of speaker invitations: those issued by the university itself. In inviting someone to address commencement, for instance, the university administration is clearly certifying this person as having the requisite knowledge or experience to deliver a message it would benefit the graduating students to hear. It is therefore very important for university administrators to vet proposed commencement speakers carefully, so as to avoid those with a history of espousing views that are demeaning or blatantly unscientific. As some universities have discovered to their regret, the cost of not doing their homework can be high.[12]

To recapitulate, the question I have been addressing is whether the bounds of free speech should be broader or narrower on campus than in the outside world. Broader limits are supported by the mission of the university to promote and protect free enquiry. Four arguments were then canvassed on the other side of the question: that campus speech should be held to the high standards of scholarly discourse, that uncivil speech should be discouraged or suppressed, that students deserve special protection from hate, and that university platforms can confer legitimacy on speakers with hateful or otherwise objectionable messages. My conclusion is that none of these latter arguments succeed, thus that the bounds of free speech on the university campus should be at least as broad as – and arguably should be broader than – they are elsewhere in the community.

This result is good news for university administrators. As far as the regulation of campus speech is concerned, what ethical governance will demand of them will nearly always be: absolutely nothing. They will have reason to become actively involved only in order to ensure that a speaking event proceeds safely, or when it threatens to disrupt the functioning of the university, or when it is itself threatened with disruption by protesting groups. In those instances, the justification for intervention will be to protect and facilitate speech, not to shut it down.

ACKNOWLEDGMENTS

I am grateful to Tom Hurka, Cheryl Misak, and Kent McNeil for very valuable comments on an earlier draft of this chapter.

NOTES

1 The Foundation for Individual Rights and Expression (FIRE, n.d.) has catalogued over 400 "disinvitation attempts," about half of them successful, at American universities since 2000.

2 This is the provision that was upheld as constitutional by the Supreme Court of Canada (1990).

3 In addition to these defences, prosecution for hate promotion also requires the consent of the provincial attorney general or minister of justice. Partly for this reason, Ernst Zündel, the notorious Holocaust denier, was never prosecuted in Canada for promoting hatred.

4 See, for example, the 2012 statement by Jason Kenney, minister of citizenship, immigration, and multiculturalism (Kenney, 2012).

5 I owe this way of thinking about it to Michael Marrus.

6 The University of Toronto's position here is not anomalous. Very similar statements can be found at most Canadian post-secondary institutions.

7 Simpson often gives the impression that academic freedom belongs exclusively to university faculty, in their professional pursuits. But surely it applies equally to students in their scholarly activities. The salient distinction is between teaching and research, on the one hand, and the manifold other activities, including speaking activities, that can occur on university campuses.

8 Of course, the former can be, and undoubtedly has been, disguised as the latter. Nonetheless, they are fundamentally different.

9 "The picture that I am recommending is one in which the communicative climate of the campus at large is characterized by similar kinds of rigor, thoughtfulness, and deference to academic expertise to those of the lecture theater or faculty research seminar" (Simpson, 2020, p. 299).

10 Simpson (2020, pp. 292–4) further muddies the waters by conflating content restrictions with the application of professional standards to scholarly work.

11 Of course, Coulter will record the fact that she spoke at *the university*, not that she was hosted there by some fringe campus group. So, a little of the prestige of the institution will inevitably rub off on her. This unfortunate reality is not, at least by itself, sufficient justification for denying her a campus platform.

12 In 2009 Ben Stein, the actor and game show host, was invited to deliver a commencement address at the University of Vermont. It then came to light that Stein was an enthusiastic denier of evolution and advocate of intelligent design creationism. After a letter-writing campaign to protest

the invitation, including such prominent figures as Richard Dawkins, Stein agreed to withdraw from the talk. See Chronicle of Higher Education (2009).

REFERENCES

Canada. (1985). *Criminal Code*, RSC 1985, c C-46.

Canadian Association of University Teachers Council. (2018, November). *Academic freedom: CAUT policy statement*. Academic freedom. https://www.caut.ca/about-us/caut-policy/lists/caut-policy-statements/policy-statement-on-academic-freedom

Chase, S. (2010, 23 March). Ann Coulter's speech in Ottawa cancelled. *The Globe & Mail*. https://www.theglobeandmail.com/news/politics/ann-coulters-speech-in-ottawa-cancelled/article4352616/

Chronicle of Higher Education. (2009, 3 February). *Ben Stein backs out of commencement gig at Vermont over views on evolution*. https://www.chronicle.com/article/ben-stein-backs-out-of-commencement-gig-at-vermont-over-views-on-evolution/

Committee on Freedom of Expression. (2015, January). *Report of the Committee on Freedom of Expression*. University of Chicago. https://provost.uchicago.edu/sites/default/files/documents/reports/FOECommitteeReport.pdf

Foundation for Individual Rights and Expression. (n.d.). *Disinvitation database*. Retrieved 12 October 2020 from https://www.thefire.org/research/disinvitation-database/

Friedland, M.L. (2013). *The University of Toronto: A history*. University of Toronto Press.

Israeli Apartheid Week. (n.d.). *About Israeli Apartheid Week*. https://web.archive.org/web/20090224200120/http://apartheidweek.org/en/about

Kenney, J. (2012, 6 March). *Statement by Minister Jason Kenney condemning "Israel Apartheid Week."* CJPAC. https://www.canada.ca/en/news/archive/2012/03/minister-kenney-issues-statement-israeli-apartheid-week-.html

Levy, N. (2019, 4 March). *Why no-platforming is sometimes a justifiable position*. Aeon. https://aeon.co/ideas/why-no-platforming-is-sometimes-a-justifiable-position

Mill, J.S. (2003). *On liberty* (D. Bromwich & G. Kateb, Eds.). Yale University Press. (Original work published 1859)

Simpson, R.M. (2020, April). The relation between academic freedom and free speech. *Ethics, 130*(3), 287–319. https://doi.org/10.1086/707211

Supreme Court of Canada. (1990). *R v Keegstra,* [1990] 3 SCR 697.

University of Toronto Governing Council. (1992, 28 May). Statement on freedom of speech. University of Toronto. https://governingcouncil .utoronto.ca/sites/default/files/2020-03/Freedom%20of%20 Speech%2C%20Statement%20on%20Protection%20of%20.pdf

Ann Coulter: Immigration. (2020, 21 September). In *Wikipedia.* https:// en.wikipedia.org/w/index.php?title=Ann_Coulter&oldid=979500527 #Immigration

"University Governance and Campus Speech"

CHRISTOPHER A. OLLSON
Environmental Health Scientist and Consultant

Professor Sumner provides a strong argument for the freedom of invited speakers to express their views, regardless of how abhorrent or factually incorrect they may be, on campus without intervention from upper administration. Similar challenges arise off-campus during the permitting of controversial major infrastructure projects. Whether it is the extraction of the Alberta oil sands, construction of municipal waste incinerators, or development of renewable energy projects, all have their detractors. This may manifest itself in organized opposition amongst those who wish to make their views known. Society provides them formal recourse to offer written and/or oral testimony to the appropriate government permitting authority.

Often, opposition groups do not believe that their voices have been heard in the formal process and turn to social media to organize protest campaigns and express their views. Emotions run high in the quest to sway public opinion. There should be no question in a democracy that lawful expression of such opposing views should be encouraged and even welcomed by project proponents.

Nevertheless, as a society, should we draw a line in the sand at posts that aggressively single out and personally attack an individual involved in such a project? These postings can be far from civil and may be offensive, or even hurtful, to the targeted individual. Similar to on-campus speech, unlawful demonstrations or illegal threats made against individuals are the purview of the police. However distasteful, sadly we must stomach even the most objectionable postings by those hiding behind the anonymity of the internet.

PART FIVE

The Art of Leadership

chapter twelve

Spaces of Virtue in Universities

BRUCE B. JANZ

Can the university be a space of virtue? What would that even mean? Who gets to define it? In the liberal West, we tend to think that virtue is something that is said only of individuals, and spaces are virtuous just because they are constituted by individual actions. And so it makes little sense to talk about a space of virtue: we as individuals are virtuous or not, and the spaces we inhabit, such as universities, are just the result of the decisions made by individuals.

This picture of the relationship between space and virtue is, I want to claim, a limited and ultimately unhelpful way to think about the nature of virtue or, for that matter, the nature of the university. In what follows, I want to rethink the space of the university as a space of possible virtue.

What is driving this investigation? As is often the case, there is a "Hmm, that's weird" moment for me, a moment when things do not add up, when what you expect to happen isn't happening or when something is happening that shouldn't be. For me, as a former department chair and a current co-director of a digital humanities centre, it is the recognition of the gap (indeed, sometimes the gulf) between the ways we conceptualize the structure of the university and the rhetoric around that, and the *actual experience* of faculty, staff, and administrators within those structures. (We will leave students for another discussion, although that is also an interesting one).

The gap comes in the space between the effort put in by administrators to create structures within universities to promote their missions and excel at their core strategic plans, and the information available about the experience of faculty and others within those structures. One might think that the more a university rises in prominence and excels at its mission, the more faculty would be satisfied in their jobs. Anecdotally, though, I have found this to not be the case, and there is data to back up my perception. Faculty disaffection, low morale, and burnout is widespread. This has been measured in numerous studies (see, for instance, Hall et al., 2019; Sabagh et al., 2018; Zábrodská et al., 2018). Most administrators can probably point to examples of faculty who disengage, fail to live up to potential, or even leave academia entirely or transfer to another university.

Environmental factors in faculty and administrative dissatisfaction are certainly acknowledged in these studies. We recognize that bullying and mobbing, for instance, can happen in workplaces, not just in classrooms. (For mobbing in universities see Harper, 2013; Keim & McDermott, 2010; and more generally see Duffy & Sperry, 2014). We recognize that there are problematic structures for people in specific groups or classes, relating to issues such as gender, race, age, and disability. And we recognize that there can be toxic environments (Pfeffer, 2018).

All of these recognitions, though, tend to be understood in individualist terms, probably because those are the terms that most readily suggest actionable solutions. We have someone to blame or hold responsible. The workplace is toxic, we think, because of *this* particular person, and dealing with that specific person offers a path to fixing the problem. Or, in the case of phenomena like burnout, the problem might implicitly be the faculty member himself or herself. Burnout is again an individual failing, a person's inability to balance demands and work within an existing system.

In other cases, a faculty member might be labelled a malcontent or a complainer – again, reflecting an individual's inability to fit into a structure. Or there might not be a specific problem but the chance or anticipation of one, and so campus compliance policies and rules are developed, and faculty are asked to take training and sign off on documents that assure the university that they understand what is expected of them, what their legal and community obligations are, and that they promise to abide by the rules. In this case, there might not be any specific individual who is unable to adjust to a system, but the idea that such individuals are the main source of problems is enough justification to set up such a juridical structure.

What these disparate examples have in common is the idea that what is to be managed is individual action, and that problems among members of the university come out of things that individuals do to each other. This then assumes that the space of virtue is the space of individual behaviour. It is a space of moral rectitude, but also a space in which flourishing is in the hands of individual decisions and action. People can fail each other, of course, but there is still someone to blame if that happens, and a direct path to fixing the problem. Identify who messed up, correct the situation, and all should be well.

And yet, all is often not well. I continue to be struck by both my anecdotal experience and the many studies about faculty satisfaction, some of which were mentioned earlier, which conclude that faculty are not, in fact, satisfied. This seems like more than just a widespread failure of individual virtue. This seems instead like failure at a different register.

If this space of virtue is not just the sum total of the actions of individuals, what is it? At the very least, I think that we can put virtue in the context of two other concepts that move us away from this individualist thinking. First, there is the nature of knowledge about and in the university. A space of virtue emerges in the context of what we know, what we should and can know, what we don't know or choose to ignore, and what our responsibilities are towards creating, narrating, and preserving knowledge. Second, there is the nature of the social organizations, institutions, or structures in which meaningful individual action takes place. This includes both formal ones such as government, the media, the university, and informal ones, such as our political or religious opinions that create communities of affinity and care.

Virtue in these terms is far more interesting, in my opinion, than the rehearsal of ethical theories, or the consideration of the most extreme thought experiments we can imagine. Virtue is not just ethics but ethos, the characteristic ways or spirit of a culture. This does not mean that ethos is nothing but a culturally contingent or relativist inventory of activities, but it is instead a culturally embedded set of practices such that even the abstract rules that we think are central to an ethical system make sense only within the context of human lived experience.

It is fine to have a rule that there should be no murder, or that there should only be truth-telling, but ethos is the space in which we figure out just what that means, how we define our actions in terms of these abstractions, how we articulate our ethical ideas to each other and persuade each other to join us, and so forth. So the question is, How do we live well (however we define that), as individuals and as groups, given that every action happens within the context of other actions by individuals and groups, and have ambiguity and interpretation at every level which comes from limited or partial knowledge and contextual (especially institutional, organizational, or structural) factors? Virtue in the university is about more than how individuals act in this space, or even about how the leaders of the institution speak on its behalf. The question of virtue must include the question of how we produce knowledge, what counts as knowledge, how it is evaluated and incentivized and rewarded, as well as the nature of the social organization in which these questions arise, including the models and metaphors we use to understand and act within the organization.

So, then, what is virtue in the university? It is not achieved by simply abiding by the rules of the compliance office, or the dictates of policy documents decided on by upper administration. Does it not just happen when the university has a shared vision or statement of purpose, and everyone works towards its success? Is it not just all the actions of individuals within a space, added up? I think it is more than that. But what more?

We can perhaps see it most clearly if we think about the tensions that make virtue difficult to achieve in the university, and that make it difficult to see the space of thought and practice in the university as a space where virtue can flourish, at least in the contemporary world. Virtue, I want to maintain (and this is in line with the classic Greek sense of the term), is the space of the possible. It focuses on what could be done and what should be done, rather than simply on what should not be done. The virtuous life is the life lived to the fullest, the life that makes its mark by realizing in oneself and the world the latent potentialities, bringing them into actuality. Virtue in its classical sense is a space of excellence of any sort, or perhaps more precisely, of all sorts working together.

It might seem as if this has no necessary moral core to it – one could be an excellent criminal, after all. But that is not virtue, because it does not allow flourishing in all areas. Virtue is the actualization of potentialities that build networks and connections, that enable more creativity rather than less to take place, that protect and preserve while allowing to grow and flourish. The criminal might be excellent at being a criminal but, in pursuing criminality, he or she is cut off from many other opportunities for excellence since society will not tolerate criminality. One cannot be an excellent criminal and an excellent church leader (for instance) unless either the criminality is well hidden, or it is not regarded as criminality by those who support this person in that church.

As it stands, this is an abstract definition. It needs to be so, though, because when it comes to virtue, there are no rules. This does not mean that rules are not useful or necessary, but that they are subordinate to virtue. A rule in itself tells us little about virtue, and does not in itself produce it, but virtue might tell us a great deal about rules. As well, virtue is not reducible to values. It is tempting, when asked what constitutes virtue, to list some commendable qualities – integrity, honesty, industriousness, and so forth. The kind of virtue in a space of virtue takes these as epiphenomena, that is, as by-products of activity in the space, not as the cause of the space. There can be good people, exhibiting qualities that we value and admire, and together their action could produce a non-virtuous, even a stultifying space. There is no direct path from individual qualities to the space of virtue, but the space of virtue does help to define and exemplify those qualities. This is certainly true of the university – everyone might have these values, and yet the space of virtue could still be deeply compromised.

This is relevant to the university because of the tensions I just mentioned. A university is a space of thought and practice. Some universities are very large and complex, but even the small ones are connected to each other in innumerable ways and therefore their models replicate broadly, whether they be best practices for research or neoliberal forms of governance that dilute faculty input and move them towards being more like employees. They are spaces of virtue, that is, spaces in which virtue might be realized. However, they can also be spaces in which specific desired outcomes end up taking precedence over the pursuit of virtue and, when that happens, the creativity of virtue can become subordinated to the predictability and programmability of structures in a large institution.

This tension, I want to argue, is pervasive across universities and has a unique character because of what universities have historically been and what they are expected to be now. Historically (by which I mean over the last couple of hundred years), they have been sites of knowledge creation. That creation came from those trained in disciplinary methods and questions. Those methods and questions suggested or required structures to maintain and scaffold their activity. As a result, departments developed and, from there, administrative structures evolved as the logic of knowledge creation and dissemination expanded. In some cases, those administrative structures emerged because of tensions or problems in the scaffolding of knowledge creation. So, for instance, as various sciences required more equipment and more complex procedures, more administration was required to make these things possible. There have been lab assistants as far back as there have been labs, but the proliferation of support and administrative staff came with changes in what was required to produce and certify knowledge. (e.g., institutional review boards, grant oversight, etc.) We could tell a similar story about how teaching works in a large-scale setting.

This is not the only source of the evolution of staffing and administration, though. As universities are seen as producing public goods, oversight by state entities and accrediting agencies also produces tensions in the process of knowledge creation and dissemination that must be resolved, in this case through the credentialing of people within the university and the incentivizing and shaping of the kinds of research that is done. Granting agencies play a large role in this as well – research is tailored to the terms of the money available, which is often but not always shaped by academic priorities. And so again, administration rises to meet the practical challenges of these external requirements. More structures and policies emerge.

The point of this familiar story is to recognize the direction of the flow within the classic university structure – as knowledge is created and disseminated, structures in the form of administration and staff emerge to make it possible to create that knowledge within the social world.

But once those structures are created, they have a force of their own. Every administrator who is there to serve, that is, who is there to facilitate the creation and dissemination of knowledge, must do so in a rational and equitable manner. That requires policies, procedures, rules, and in some cases, just a set of best practices that might not be written down at all, but that come to be accepted, the "way things are done around here."

There is one other aspect to sketch out before we can start to understand the situation that faculty, staff, and administrators find themselves in within the space of virtue in a university, and that is university culture. Sometimes, "culture" is used by marketers to try to present an attractive and compelling image of the university to prospective students, parents, supporters, and legislators. It's a fun school, a social place as well as an academic one, a place with school spirit. At other times, culture is invoked when something goes wrong. When my university had a scandal over some state funds used inappropriately for a new building (as it happens, the building in which my humanities centre resides), and the legislature rapped the knuckles of upper administrators, the common response was that there was a problematic culture within the institution. That would be fixed, legislators were promised, by the administrators who had not already been fired. We would fix the culture in which it seemed OK to play fast and loose with state funds in order to build a much-needed academic building. Culture, then, is seen as a force that makes individuals do (in this case) the wrong thing, and fixing the culture will fix the people's actions.

Something seems a bit off with these uses of "culture," particularly to anyone who studies culture in any detail. In the marketing uses of culture, it seems more like a narrative we use and control about the institution, to achieve desired ends. In its use as an excuse for bad behaviour, it seems like a way of distributing blame widely but shallowly, that is, suggesting that the institution itself has a problem, not any individual (or at least, not very much). "Culture" used in these ways is a counterpart to the individual, a way of giving a reason that individuals do what they do. At worst, this version of culture just distributes blame for problems without actually getting to structural questions that might be more important.

Culture is, of course, much more than this for an anthropologist or cultural studies scholar, or anyone else who studies some aspect of cultural production such as texts, historical artefacts, art, or language. The intuition to look towards institutional culture is a good one, but using it in these ways vastly oversimplifies what that culture might be. It also suggests, in that oversimplification, that it can be controlled. Indeed, we see this kind of talk regularly, when diversity and equity offices on campuses talk about changing the culture to be more equitable and combat racism and sexism, or information technology offices talk about changing the campus culture to promote information security, or when compliance offices talk about changing the culture to get people to fall in line with institutional policies and rules (or to shield the university from legal liability), or when administrations set up a new set of rules and procedures to deal with a pandemic.

So, if culture is more than what can be marketed, controlled, or legislated, what is it? And how, in the university, does it help us think through what virtue might look like? It will help to sketch out what culture actually looks like in the university, and why both faculty and administrators might need to care about something more than the superficial version that often gets circulated.

University structures are not a single thing. They are, rather, multiple networks that interact in a variety of ways. If we look at the life of any one faculty member, we can identify structures outside the university that intersect with and complicate the space of virtue. That faculty member might be part of a department network, a university one, a professional and/or disciplinary one, a community, an industry, and multiple government networks, not to mention numerous private networks, and all these will have practices, imperatives, opportunities, and restrictions. Sometimes these diverse networks sync with each other seamlessly, but more often there is friction between them, or at least they are not isomorphic. And, importantly, there can also be autopoiesis when these networks interact with each other – emergent properties or effects that are not predictable from the properties of the networks themselves or the actors within them. We might think of these as unintended consequences, but that suggests that we should simply do a better job of anticipating consequences in order to rule out unintended ones. In fact, it is impossible to do so. Every set of complex networks has emergent properties alongside planned or programmed ones. Every network mutates because each has its own feedback and correction or change mechanisms.

This clearly draws on cybernetic theory and network theory and, as such, might seem abstract, but in fact it has significance for life within the university, as experienced by faculty, administrator, staff, and student alike. A model of the university that has multiple networks that have emergent properties stands in contrast to other often invoked or assumed models of the university, including a religious or monastic model, a paternalistic model, a business model, a corporate model (not the same as a business model), a factory model, and others. The university bears resemblance to all of these at times, but it is not any of them, at least not exclusively.

A managerial university attempts to simplify this complicated picture. Administrators are put in place and paid the highest salaries in the university to produce certain outcomes. Many no doubt believe that they are promoting virtue within the university. To the extent that a single model is assumed, though, this will be almost impossible to do. A managed university will achieve productivity but will struggle with creativity. It will tend to identify its core strengths or high-impact areas and focus on them, not realizing that isolating these things might undermine their strength by removing an emergent property of the complex space.

This emergent network analysis, though, is only part of the picture. If there were nothing but networks producing emergent properties, it would be hard to see what kind of agency any specific person might have. And it likely feels that way to a lot of people who have been in the university for a long time. The structures can seem rigid, the bureaucracies unyielding, the incentive structures perverse (rewarding the ambitious rather than the skilled), and the values conflicted. It can be difficult to describe the culture, if we think about culture as more than just values and attitudes people might hold and include shared and assumed products and practices, and in particular focus on how creativity happens. Every culture is a living thing, changing itself from what it is to what it might be, and the same is true of the university. It seems complicated, and it is, but more important than that, it is complex.

It is worth distinguishing between complexity and complicatedness. If something is complicated, that means that there are many steps necessary to achieving a desired outcome. A difficult recipe is complicated. Building a space shuttle is complicated. The difficulty of the steps might be in the fact that they are numerous, or hard to understand, or hard to implement, or have very little room for error. Complexity is something different. A system is complex when, even though components have relatively simple rules or procedures, results occur that are not predictable just by understanding the rules. Ants are complex in this sense – there is no leader giving order to achieve a complicated outcome, but rather many ants, operating on relatively simple rules, end up building bridges out of their bodies and many other complex formations. Murmurations of starlings are complex formations that emerge from relatively simple rules about flight, proximity to other birds, reactions to predators, and so forth. Economies, genomes, weather patterns, neural connections – these are all complex in this sense. The university, I am arguing here, may be complicated, but more importantly it is complex, and that complexity has been overlooked and, in fact, ignoring it stands in the way of the space of virtue that I imagine. We cannot be fully creative members of the community under the conditions of the amelioration of complicatedness, but we can be in the spaces that complexity affords.

The managerial university does not in fact simplify or stream-
line complexity, for the simple reason that that cannot be done. It
does, though, attempt to simplify complicatedness, through clear
rules and procedures. Of course, it does not always succeed (each
intervention has new unintended results), but the point is that
complexity is something else entirely, and it is key to understanding one major reason why it is so difficult to achieve a space of
virtue in a complex organization like a university. If there were an
algorithm for it, a set of instructions that allowed us to harness and
control a complicated reality, then university faculty and administrators (who often are faculty also) would be the first to do that.
But the problem of the university being complicated, while this is
surely the case, is different from the problem of complexity within
the university.

The point here is that greater control does not produce greater
virtue. So, what to do in order to remove blocks to a complex space
of virtue? Here are a few of many possible suggestions.

Appoint a chief systems officer, or at least assign someone who
understands how complex systems work to oversee the interre-
lationships and interfaces between systems in the university and
beyond. For instance, when a new system-wide software system
is rolled out, what implications does it have for other systems? Is
there a way of streamlining multiple systems so that, for example,
one need only put in some information once instead of multiple
times? Is there a way of seeing a new digital tool as having costs,
usually on users downstream, and not just opportunities to produce data about something? How can we identify the places where
systems either work against each other or could operate in a virtuous circle, enhancing each other? Do we see data as proprietary to
the office that produced it, or is it part of the university, usable by
others in ways not foreseen by those who gathered it in the first
place?

It is important to not think of this person as an efficiency expert.
The goal is not efficiency but virtue. A drive for efficiency tends to
find ways to get more output while having less input in a system.
Many members of the university at all levels already feel as if that
search has reached a breaking point. Faculty report working 60- and

70-hour weeks regularly, or more (and for many, this is even worse during the COVID-19 pandemic). Very few can do more than they are doing. But that is a different question from one about how disparate systems work together, or don't, and what the emergent properties are of having systems interacting with each other.

One thing that a person like this would need to do would be to produce an economic model of the university. This is not a fiscal model, which every university has, but a much rarer thing. In an economic model, the university would be seen as a set of exchanges and networks. It would be understood as a place of incentives for activities (which of course it already is), but those incentives would not always be monetary. There would be an understanding of externalities, and risk, and demand curves. There would be a clear understanding of common-pool resources and "owned" resources, and how they relate to each other. It would understand pricing and value within its own set of exchanges, not simply as a function of things like cost to the student or revenues accrued from various sources.

A former dean I knew once described the economic model of his own upper administration as close to a Soviet-style economy, with its central planning and control over the economy but at the same time with the illusion of incentivizing desirable activity. He was not far off – but what does that economic model say about what is possible and what is not possible in the university? There must be some centralization in any university structure, but how is it handled? What are the unintended consequences of the incentives currently in place?

So, someone looking at systems would be able to describe these things and leverage virtuous feedback loops instead of allowing destructive consequences to emerge. This is obviously a very difficult job, and one that would face significant resistance among some offices and some faculty within an institution. None of us want to hear that what we are doing is resulting in problems elsewhere in the university. None want to hear that we are producing perverse incentives or negative feedback loops. But not knowing that means that these things just continue, and the possibility of a space of virtue becomes more remote.

Incentivize inaction and negative action. Every office on campus is charged with doing something, and that usually means adding a new procedure, a new program, a new piece of software, or something else. That office cannot be judged as successful if it doesn't do that. But what if the right answer in some cases is to do nothing? What if, in fact, the right answer is to take away programs, simplify structures? That is not always the right thing to do, but in my experience in universities, it is almost never done. Progress always means adding more, and adding more comes with costs. Those costs might be to other offices, now given a seemingly small job, which in fact might not be so small, and might be uncompensated labour, and might snowball with all the other small jobs from all the other offices and become untenable.

One implication of incentivizing inaction is making space for the right kinds of failure. This is failure that comes with trying something new, the failure that comes when we recognize that the future is largely unknown and unknowable, and all we can do is try. Most current reward structures in the university do not recognize the value of failure, understanding it as a kind of lack of progress, and an indication that the individual who failed is in some way deficient or not up to the task of operating in the modern university. Many units within the university remain indefinitely in more or less the same form they have always had, and changing them can seem like failure. Without failure, though, we do not have a space of virtue, just a space of production.

Recognize "women's work." This is not literally just work that women do, although that too needs to be recognized. I mean by this the work that is undervalued, that is necessary for the networks and activities of the university to exist at all, but that are not incentivized or are recognized as minimally valuable in promotion and merit documents. Tenure-track faculty have only two promotions they can look forward to in their entire career – from assistant to associate and from associate to full professor – making the professoriate almost unique among professions. It also means that recognition and incentives are going to look different from other professions. Many other incentives in the contemporary university are in fact just more labour – applications for competitive awards, for instance, which just pit faculty against each other rather than recognizing contributions in themselves.

Listen to, and beyond, faculty and administration complaints. This is difficult, mostly because the ones most in need of listening to are often the ones least likely to say anything about their experience. Surveys of faculty satisfaction such as COACHE[1] do not make it more likely that they will be heard, because many have already checked out or decided that the best they can do is look out for their own interests. Exit interviews, when they are done, are also unreliable. There is no requirement of honesty or participation for any of these and, if there were such a requirement, that too would skew responses.

And yet, there are faculty who will give up tenure to go to a "lesser" school. There are faculty and administrators who will retire early, others who will request only online teaching, and yet others will disengage with their colleagues and become ghosts. Some will lash out and be labelled as malcontents, others will manipulate behind the scenes. Some of this will be explainable by the jockeying that happens in a space of scarce resources, but not all are explainable that way. "Listening beyond" the complaints means listening not just to the explicit message, but to the space of action that makes this action rational for the person. No one comes to work at a university in order to be mediocre, but some end up that way. Why does that happen, and how can those who might have the ability to change things identify what happened to change a pursuit of excellence into a struggle to stay afloat? I once heard a provost, a Black woman, talk about going to the Black faculty and staff association and asking a simple question: Are you thriving or are you surviving? And the response was unanimous – they were all just surviving. Were all these people just not up to the task of the modern university? Of course not. This is not a space of excellence for those people, and it will not be changed by having sensitivity and inclusion training. Something more fundamental is wrong with a system that produces these results – not just for Black faculty, but for everyone, faculty, staff, and administration alike.

Get past the model of paternalism. There are many possible models for relationships within the university, but one very common one is for relationships of power and status to be mapped onto parent–child relationships. This is perhaps most commonly felt between faculty and administrators, when faculty feel as if they are treated like brilliant, talented, but ungrateful and self-absorbed children and administrators are longsuffering providers and the moral compass of the institution. This relationship is not limited to faculty-administrators, though – it is also felt between lower-level and upper-level administrators. It is reinforced when the president of the institution is treated as a "first family," when information is doled out in overly soothing fashion designed to get everyone to not worry and trust "mom and dad" to make the big decisions, and when trust itself is assumed and expected rather than earned.

The problems with paternalism are numerous and well known but, for our purposes, the key issue is that this model oversimplifies the complex systems relations within the university. The family model is a poor one for a complex institution. The president of Netflix, Reed Hastings, and business professor Erin Meyer recognize this in *No Rules Rules* (Hastings & Meyer, 2020). They describe the culture at Netflix as one that rejects the family metaphor in favour of the team metaphor. In a team, you get the best player for a position you can, and then you trust that person's ability and professionalism to produce something good. The model does not completely apply to the university (for one thing, universities can't trade players and get rid of underperformers, nor should they), but in fact, there is already a rigorous hiring process and trial period in the form of a tenure-track review process, and so some of these elements already exist. What does not exist very often, though, is commensurate trust in the abilities of faculty to do the right thing and to create something new, except in the limited scope of their own research. Culture is discussed at universities without ever speaking with cultural studies scholars. Ethics can be discussed without ever talking to philosophers, communication can be discussed without talking to communications department experts, and so forth. And the regime of regulation at most universities communicates that people are not, in fact, trusted at all.

Create a space within your own sphere of influence where you can do all this, even if you cannot affect the larger forces themselves. These ideas might seem interesting as they stand, but the reality of university life will lead many to think that they are untenable in the current situation. And this is correct if we imagine that we are going to change the entire university. But the recognition of complexity does not require that. It is possible to carve out spaces of virtue within a larger structure. Sometimes a department chair can do some of the things I suggest within a department. Sometimes deans or administrators in charge of an office on campus can try to create these conditions in their own area. The point is that the fact that we are all parts of multiple networks does not mean that we are without agency, even when the forces from the outside that constrain action are intense. Every administrator is in a liminal position, the point between their own area and the other forces (other offices, other administrators, the state, accreditors, etc.) that seek to mould what happens within the university. Every position of authority is also one of representation, and an opportunity to both represent the goals of the institution to their people and represent the virtue of their people (and the barriers to that virtue) to the institution and beyond.

This is clearly at best a schematic overview of some issues. A space of virtue is possible, but it will not happen if we simply focus on individual behaviour, as important as that might be. We are all multiples, we all are different versions of ourselves in different spaces, and we all act on the basis of what our spaces afford. The question is how we can we focus on the university as something other than the sum of individual actions, as a space in which unanticipated and emergent properties come from the interaction of the various networks within and outside of the university. How can we move from thinking about virtue in the university as holding and performing personal values, and see it instead as the collective creation of a space that makes some kinds of activity more likely and other kinds less likely, incentivizing and rewarding some things and downplaying others?

NOTE

1 The Collaborative on Academic Careers in Higher Education (2023) is a
   set of surveys used by over 300 institutions to study faculty satisfaction,
   during their employment and at their exit. Data from all surveys provides
   benchmarks and comparisons for data collected in specific institutions.

REFERENCES

Collaborative on Academic Careers in Higher Education (COACHE). (2023).
   *A research-practice partnership and network of peer institutions dedicated
   to improving outcomes in faculty recruitment, development, and retention.*
   Harvard University. https://coache.gse.harvard.edu/
Duffy, M., & Sperry, L. (2014). *Overcoming mobbing: A recovery guide for
   workplace aggression and bullying.* Oxford University Press.
Hall, N.C., Lee, S.Y., & Rahimi, S. (2019). Self-efficacy, procrastination,
   and burnout in postsecondary faculty: An international longitudinal
   analysis. *PLoS ONE, 14*(12), e0226716. https://doi.org/10.1371/journal
   .pone.0226716
Harper, J. (2013). *Mobbed!: What to do when they really are out to get you.*
   Backdoor Press.
Hastings, R., & Meyer, E. (2020). *No rules rules: Netflix and the culture of
   reinvention.* Penguin Press.
Keim, J., & McDermott, J.C. (2010). Mobbing: Workplace violence in the
   academy. *The Educational Forum, 74*(2), 167–73. https://doi.org/10.1080
   /00131721003608505
Pfeffer, J. (2018). *Dying for a paycheck.* HarperCollins.
Sabagh, Z., Hall, N.C., & Saroyan, A. (2018). Antecedents, correlates and
   consequences of faculty burnout. *Educational Research, 60*(2), 131–56.
   https://doi.org/10.1080/00131881.2018.1461573
Zábrodská, K., Mudrák, J., Šolcová, I., Květon, P., Blatný, M., & Machovcová,
   K. (2018). Burnout among university faculty: The central role of work–
   family conflict. *Educational Psychology, 38*(6), 800–19. https://doi.org
   /10.1080/01443410.2017.1340590

"Spaces of Virtue in Universities"

INDIRA V. SAMARASEKERA
Director of Magna International, TC Energy, and Stelco,
Advisor for Bennett Jones

Virtue stands for moral excellence – an opportune theme deserving reinvigoration in universities, corporations, governments, and charitable organizations. The erosion of trust in these institutions can be linked to a decline in virtuous behaviour ranging from truthfulness to justice, courage to magnanimity, and magnificence to ambition, which are among the twelve virtues defined by Aristotle.

Moral decline in the pillars of society is being linked to growing inequality, slow progress in addressing social justice, the rise of misinformation, diminishing social mobility, increased stress and mental health issues, and inadequate response to existential threats such as climate change and cyber-attacks. The far-reaching consequence of inattention to these concerns will be a loss of freedom, an increase in corruption, a deterioration in democracy, and a rise in authoritarianism as witnessed around the world.

Bruce Jantz reminds us that the imperative of addressing virtue does not lie in extolling its value but in creating the space for virtue through governance and the structures of administration, so it is a lived experience for individuals in an organization and in society. This is no easy task, given the complexity of modern institutions, conflicting demands from constituents, and rise in communication technologies, which render it more difficult to build consensus. Never has moral leadership that raises our collective aspirations for virtue been more important than it is today. A recommitment to building spaces of virtue in society will revive the social compact essential for a thriving democracy, renew our trust in institutions, improving the quality of life for current and future generations.

chapter thirteen

The Art of Having the Right Thing Happen

ROBERT MUGERAUER

In 1637, Baltasar Gracián, a Spanish Jesuit, wrote *The Art of Worldly Wisdom* (1991), a practical guide to personal and professional success. He offers wonderfully subtle advice, in part covering what might be considered a sensible cultivation of context-appropriate behaviour in often treacherous, political-courtly situations. His maxims include: "Avoid becoming disliked" (maxim 119), "Cultivate relationships with those who can teach you" (11), "Know how to wait" (55), "Get to know what is needed in different occupations" (104), and "Know how to say 'no'" (70). He finally proposes the goal not of gaining power in itself but of working to perfect ourselves, thus "being able to do more good" (102). He suggests that one should "Be a person of Integrity" (29), "Let your behavior be fine and noble" (88), and the final maxim, "In one word, be a saint" (300).

However, his ideas and language are slippery, requiring the reader to seriously ponder whether the advice comes as acceptable, or as engendering a cynical, at times perhaps unethical attitude. For example, in maxim 77 he says, "Be all things to all people. Notice people's moods and adapt yourself to each, genial or serious as the case may be. Follow their lead, glossing over the changes as cunningly as possible." That advice certainly can be taken in multiple ways. Similarly ambiguous is the maxim "Make use of your enemies" (84). Morally questionable examples include, "Find out each person's thumbscrew" (26), and "Know how to put ills off on another" (149).

Overall, Gracián does not pause at ethical boundaries that would interfere with his strategies, nor, for example, does he stop short of deceit. His engaging work really does challenge the reader to think carefully all along, which is what I also hope from my readers. This chapter may have little of Graciá's linguistic grace or intricacy, but it does intend to provide a few experientially tested insights that allow us to engage in positive, collegial activity, including leadership in an ethically robust manner.

The best compliment I ever received as an administrator came at the University of Washington, after my tenure as dean of the college of architecture and urban planning (2000–6). The head of our college's IT department randomly said one day, "I'm amazed at your management style. You never tell people what to do but, in the end, things always turn out to be the way you wanted." I had never analysed how I worked, nor had any idea that I had this kind of recognizable profile. But that comment 15 years ago has since generated enough reflection to make it worthwhile for me to take up the presumptuous task of writing on this subject matter.

In this chapter, I argue that leadership is less a science or a craft than it is an "art" of understanding how to comport oneself, not by exercising brute power or subterfuge, but by acting ethically oneself, and by manifesting such character to the collegial parties directly involved, as well as to the overall academic community in and beyond one's own institution. When I reflect upon concrete moments of my administrative terms as dean or provost, I hope that concrete personal examples may help to illustrate to the reader how leadership is, indeed, such an art – one involving sound praxis emerging from good judgment gained through lived experience.

I should add that leadership as an art is also necessarily driven by a strong sense of morality – not in the sense that one follows a set of prescribed rules or principles (though one might occasionally legitimately do so). Rather, as the classic hermeneutic theorist Hans-Georg Gadamer (1975) understood, such moral knowledge "is concerned with right living in general" (p. 296). The ethics and art of leadership are guided by what both Aristotle (1994) and Gadamer called *phronesis* – a practical knowledge "directed towards the concrete situation" (p. 21). In Gadamer's own words,

Although the practice of this virtue [*phronesis*] means that one distinguishes what should be done from what should not, it is not simply practical shrewdness and general cleverness. The distinction between what should and should not be done includes the distinction between the proper and the improper and thus presumes a moral attitude, which it continues to develop. (p. 22)

The moral knowledge that emerges is different from that of a craftsman who has learned his or her trade: "What is right, for example, cannot be fully determined independently of the situation that requires a right action from me, whereas the eidos of what a craftsman desires to make is fully determined by the use for which it is intended" (Gadamer 1975, p. 283). As noted by Stefanovic (2000),

[T]here is a fundamental moment of discernment in the moral decision-making process that distinguishes it from the idealized version of technical knowledge… [T]he former involves not only a manipulation of explicit facts, but a unique seeing and attunement to the moral imperative. (p. 126).

In short, the art of moral leadership involves experience, critical interpretation of the concrete situation at hand, sound judgment, and the full inclusion of reason, emotions, memory, imagination, attuned sensibilities, and indeed the wisdom achieved through making occasional mistakes.

So, what lessons emerge when I survey my own experience of leadership? In this chapter, I imagine what advice I might share with someone beginning the administrative journey. The linear order and headings required for organization, of course, do not reflect the order of discovery, but may make for a more coherent presentation in a polished essay. In many ways, this advice manifests complexity theory, where each element co-constitutes and modulates the others and, in this regard, I encourage readers to browse from one idea to another, moving ahead as seems interesting.[1] The art of having the right thing happen is not just complicated, it is complex, requiring each of us to address wicked, dynamic problems that reflect the mystery of lived experience itself.

I. Make Prevailing Conditions Explicit, Working Out the Lay of the Land

Simple as it seems, we usually become so involved in what is going on around us that we remain unaware of what we always, already pre-reflectively experience and take for granted in our lives. The fact is, however, that our pre-reflective experience guides what we consciously do. When I first moved to Texas from the Midwest in 1967, letting my life-long, short haircut give way to a curly, hippy-fied exuberance, I set out to explore what was for me the exotic atmosphere of Austin. Following Wisconsin habits, when I was walking around on a hot August day, the taverns on East Sixth Street beckoned. I heard conjunto music coming from one such venue, so started to enter. My pre-reflective awareness was on duty: as soon as I opened the door to the cool dark interior of what I expected to be a familiar kind of place, I ended up hurriedly closing the door and backing out. There had been "no thinking" to that point.

Once outside it was not hard to figure out that "this was not a place for me to be." What had registered, and became obvious with a few minutes' distance, was that the bar had a half dozen Chicano patrons, all of whom, along with the bartender, looked at me in surprise, the puzzlement clear: "What in the world are you doing here? Who in the world are you?" There was not any hostile expression or deep ethical dynamic here. It was simply that a kind of Sartrean "gaze" objectified me, distanced me out of the lifeworld going on there (Sartre, 1953, pp. 340ff). Similar ventures into country and western bars resulted in the same clear understanding, "I don't belong here," though usually this was emphasized by the bartender asking, in response to my long hippy-length hair, "Can I help you, ma'am?!"

That we always do operate out of such pre-reflective understanding is lost on us when we believe we are in a comfortable atmosphere, as certainly is the case when operating as a dean or provost in a college or university after 15 years of academic life. The first "wake-up" lesson, then, is to attend to the pre-conceptual, pre-verbalized experience we have of even familiar situations. Do not become self-consciously timid but recognize that, in the midst of academic life underway, even if it occurs where you have been for years, it is important to continuously assess what is going on. If you are new to your administrative site, you will have to put the pieces together and, unavoidably, will say and do things that are problematic "because you didn't know better." How could you have known that two of your department chairs have been feuding for years over a given office space? You simply intended to be agreeable when one of them asked if he could put a new faculty member into it.

In addition to being alert as you go along, I find it is important to learn enough of the basics. I suggest finding a couple of colleagues to draw you a map of the lay of the land. Literally ask them to draw you a map. Lay out who aligns with whom, over what issues and in what circumstances. Of course, such an early understanding may need substantial adjustment as you go along, ranging from reinterpreting who really is doing what, to assessing the trustworthiness of your guides to the original mapping.

The necessary mode of participation is not in the least passive; on the contrary, you need to be keenly alert, actively working out not just the basic alignments, but those that do not appear unless prodded, albeit unintentionally, by your well-intended words and deeds.

II. Dealing with Factions

As the *Federalist Papers*[2] ratifying the US Constitution point out, there always will be factions. There will always be tensions, even quarrels, among community members, often between individuals but also between subgroups. These will never disappear into a harmony of cosmic "oneness" amongst faculty and staff. A leader's job will include reducing friction among the factions, but not the naive or endless effort of eliminating them. The more that kind of friction happens, the more opportunities there are for differences to emerge, including novel alignments among parties that otherwise disagree on other matters. As with the founders of the US system of governance, the major administrative task is to allow what is going to happen to happen, but to keep it in appropriate bounds.

Hence, our universities' seemingly cumbersome system of checks and balances: formalized levels of authority, differing academic positions within departments and, certainly, among departments, tenure rights, and so on. The continual challenge is to try to understand what is at stake for the different parties. Recognizing that one may encounter colleagues who are unmovably, prima facie unreasonable, an administrative leader needs to try to figure out what most deeply matters to different stakeholders. It is important to try to find the "green fuse that drives the flower" (see Thomas, 1952).

In many ways, being an administrator is to serve as ball bearing. No matter what level the position, one will always be in between: as a chair, one is between faculty and a dean, or if a dean, then between one's college and other colleges within the university or between one's college and the provost. If one is a provost, one is between the academic realm and other parts of the system, often affected by external pressures. As a ball bearing, the function is to allow multiple connected forces to move smoothly, without grinding on one another. If the situation overall is one of being responsible for keeping things going as they have been, there may still be problems, again involving old and new antagonisms, desires that spring eternal, and costs to each party. Or, when change is at hand, a leader will encounter a tangle of forces from within their sphere, from above in higher administrative or other power sources often from outside academia. Of course, ball bearings take a lot of heat and may well burn out – about which more is below, remembering that this chapter is about leading parts of an institution, not about one's own career or specifically personal interests.

III. Listening and Incremental "Pre-negotiation"

All of this indicates the importance of trying to be a listener par excellence. To be trusted, it is important that one has a personal view and be honest about it. It is also helpful to colleagues, especially new ones, to know what a leader's inclination or position is at any given point. This message can be presented clearly and simply – while conveying just as clearly that one is open to modifying one's views. It is important to avoid giving false hope or misleading impressions about a realistic situation (some ideas are simply not acceptable), but one should not crush hopes that can be legitimately left open. The task here is to listen, to try to hear, really hear, what each person or party wants, what each can live with, what would increase conflict. Listen, discuss, and consider alternatives prior to and outside of scheduled meetings or voting situations. In other words, with one or more parties to be satisfied gently, work through what can be negotiated to an agreeable position, and only then move ahead.

Importantly, this approach of listening is never mere ritual. One of my early PhD students, Val Silvey, drew from Habermas's communication theory to prepare her dissertation on the policies and decision making of the Texas Water Commission, which oversaw water management across the state. Her most intriguing initial finding was that little of significance emerged at any of the mandated public meetings held around the state. Decisions were often made by commission members in advance of any public meeting, resulting in an empty ritual of stakeholder consultation, which was to include input not only from citizens but from the wide variety of local administrators who had an interest in the matters at hand. Ultimately, in such cases, the broader community was neither legitimately heard nor acknowledged. Such an approach is both exclusionary and unethical.

Similar processes often emerge at zoning commission meetings when architects seek variances for their clients' projects. Two of my students reported in their graduate theses how common it was for development plan presentations to have already been informally approved by commission members, prior to formal consultations with the public. In effect, input from these hearings was simply recorded, then largely ignored.

In contrast, I counsel to genuinely involve all relevant parties in respectful participation. Not only is it important to be transparent and inclusive in formal public consultations but in addition, it may be useful to consider alternatives and compromises with all stakeholders informally prior to any formal ratification of a decision. Gradually and gently, one can then pre-negotiate what can be formally presented and agreed upon. Often, through genuine dialogue, even the most potentially aggravated participants may themselves bring forward an acceptable plan. Certainly, there can remain much to debate during the formal meeting, but it can be less confrontational once key issues have been discussed informally in advance. In that way, the formal meeting can often proceed with no major harm or loss of face to anyone.

IV. Project Ahead, Especially "Problems Ahoy"

A most important skill that administrators must refine is the ability to look forward to future possible outcomes and the unfolding consequences of a particular course of action. This strategy is essential if one is to be truly prepared to deal with what emerges.

Personally, I operate by first asking myself with any new project, "What are the pitfalls? What are the possible downsides?" Sometimes people misunderstand this approach, taking it to mean that I have a negative attitude. Not so. It is a matter of realism. Unanticipated consequences always threaten what we do, even if we are well-intended. A related ethical charge, as in medicine, is "do no harm." The principle of non-maleficence always should take priority before that of beneficence.

It is useful to begin by considering, Who is likely to object? From inside? From "above" in the administrative hierarchy? From outside (in such a vast, unpredictable realm)? Be ready to consider whether those likely to object (1) may not understand the issues at hand (either innocently or perversely refusing to do so); (2) may experience a new fear; (3) may be re-agitated in regard to an old disagreement; or (4) may stand in substantial disagreement.

As an example of an especially frustrating university "standoff," consider the issue of the admissions process. I have long held that a range of information is necessary for decisions about program applicants: grade point average, GRE (Graduate Record Examination) scores, letters of recommendation, statement of intent, and so on. While aware of the shortcomings of standardized tests such as the GREs, I believe that it does matter whether someone scores in the range of, say, the 80th percentile rather than the 15th.

However, there has been a general trend to take GREs less seriously as indicators of possible success, with many schools altogether dropping them as central factors of the admissions process. Many believe that such testing methods remain insensitive to the diversity of legitimate ways of knowing across cross-cultural and racial divides. Consequently, one might imagine a dean objecting to the use of GREs, believing them to be discriminatory and, therefore, of decreasing importance in peer institutions. Extensive debates could be expected to ensue, with a wild tangle of differing views, academic and extra-academic social interpretations, and pragmatic considerations.

How to resolve such problems? No matter where one stands on this issue, rather than being confrontational with committee members, once again one must be reminded to maintain respectful dialogue and listen to who wants or needs what. To do so, it is important to be in touch, listen, listen, listen, then listen some more, talk informally all along, not just when a touchy issue emerges within the formal structure of the admissions process. The conversations that happen behind the scenes can help to ensure a respectful resolution amongst different viewpoints.

V. Think Backward, from the Goal Back Through Each Step Needed to Get There

As the complement to projecting ahead, I practise and recommend thinking backward, from the goal, were it to be accomplished, and how one might get there. What actually has to come about? Of course, there are a great many possible alternatives, so one must articulate and work through multiple possible scenarios. It is important to establish which specific steps are necessary, even if not individually sufficient, to accomplish one's goal. If a decision requires broad, though not unanimous, agreement, it is still important that all parties assess the matter at hand and be given the opportunity to express a basic position. For that to happen, everyone needs to have and comprehend the facts of the matter, express reasons for support or disagreement, and be satisfied that principles and particular issues are met (or at least not threatened).

VI. Do as Much as Possible Outside (and Prior to) Formal Structures

There is danger to having the formal meeting be the only site where views are expressed and debated. That situation normally involves "winners" and "losers," from which no good is likely to come. Not wishing to lose face, participants may become unnecessarily, even uncharacteristically, hostile. Once again, the answer is lots and lots of listening, talking, listening outside of regular meetings, preferably in the least formal format. It might be best to avoiding summoning people to the provost's or dean's office – that already sets up an uneven power situation. There is often little need to show that one has power. My advice to those who wish to influence a decision is: roam around, talk to people in the hallways, coffee shop, while encountering each other crossing campus, dropping by their office, casually asking, "Do you have a minute to talk about…?"

VII. Create Opening – Make Room

Often, to maintain positive forms of dialogue, one must remove blockades. There are all sorts, everywhere. They might involve turf defence, personal career ambitions, need to be absent at a supposedly crucial time but not wanting to make a public announcement about it, a prior experience when an initiative was undertaken but ended disastrously...

An opening for dialogue can often be made quietly. In any case, it is important that a decision maker be in full command of the complex of legal specifics, such as university rules and regulations, which are all too seldom read or understood. One needs to aspire to have a better command of the details and processes than others. And then, of course, even major processes such as tenure require judgment calls and interpretation of general guidelines. In some cases, practices do not conform to the regulations. What are these practices and is it worth the social stress of correcting them?

The same applies to budget planning. Often, there are constraints and obstacles that may not be immediately evident. Have funds been "hidden," tucked away by predecessors? Is there unspent money in benefits because more affiliate faculty or part-time instructors, who receive less benefits than tenure-track faculty, have been hired? Or might it be the other way around, that the benefits budget is underfunded and will need adjustment? What is the flexibility for expenditure? Whose permissions are required to implement or change an allocation in different categories of resources, including varying endowments?

Identifying what kind of assumptions lie behind such decisions and how one makes room for different sets of practices allows for a possible opening to allow alternative budget strategies and scenarios.

Another example relates to one of my charges as a new dean of architecture and planning at Washington, when I was to establish a college-wide PhD program. While no funding was available, the program was felt by many to be a high priority for the university. To be genuinely interdisciplinary, I convened a year's worth of discussions, in which all faculty were invited to explicitly state what areas of research they wanted to pursue. From an initial 30 interests originally expressed, we collectively settled on three "tracks" broad enough to include most everything, but focal enough to gain graduate school and state higher education approval: history, theory, and representation; sustainable built and natural environments; and the digital-computational sphere.

How to deliver the program without adequate funding? Departments promised to provide one faculty member to teach new required core courses and to allocate TA positions to support the program. As the pieces were slowly put in place, the question of base funding continued to loom. By sheer luck, the college received two generous endowments with the wonderful specification of "for use at the dean's discretion." I met with department chairs and we came to an agreement that I would dedicate these funds to the PhD program, allowing for three first-year fellowships to be matched by graduate school tuition waivers, TA positions, and faculty research funding. The program continues to operate in this way 20 years later. We made room for the program by means of many discussions that opened up these new program possibilities. We had prepared and were ready to act when the unanticipated gifts arrived.

Opening up space for change reminds us that what Heidegger calls existential possibilities are what matter.[3] As we make choices in life, some options are closed off – not everything remains possible. So, in addition to creating new programs, sometimes it becomes necessary to close some down to make room for other possibilities. Earlier in my career, I had to make a difficult decision (in consultation with all department chairs) to eliminate a gerontology unit in the course of dramatic budget cuts. A faculty member and staff person lost their positions. It was a sad moment for all, and there were hard feelings towards me for making that final decision. Some community members would not forgive me. In this case, this painful action helped open the way to the next step of balancing salary expenses on the way to the goal of keeping the university solvent.

One last point here: it is important to take the insights gained by ecosystem management, complexity, and self-organization theory, in making room for future developments. Often, when pressed to "act now," we use what we understand to guide decision making in a narrowly linear way. For example, we chose to eliminate mosquitoes with DDT, on the basis of our knowledge at the time;

however, that resulted in the silent spring of changed relationships among predators and prey, with severe damage to both wildlife and ecosystems. Similarly, we earlier chose to prevent forest fires to preserve them in climax condition, leading to dangerous accumulation of undergrowth and fires of unheard of magnitudes. Eventually, we learned that the dynamic of healthy forests requires periodic burning to enrich the soil, make room for new growth, and more.

The overall lesson: act incrementally, acknowledging complexity. When we make a strategic change, we should give phenomena enough time to unfold in a new way so that we can see what actual outcomes emerge. Here the short and long temporal cycles need to be more completely understood, as explained by panarchy theory.[4] The same is true of academic institutions: What if we have a seemingly large number of senior, tenured faculty who are expensive and hold slots that might be well filled by new junior hires? Do we offer attractive early retirement incentives? How does that affect the dedication of energy by faculty who just recently have been promoted to (full) professor? Will they feel endangered, feel they are measured by their "cost" versus someone else who is "less expensive"? What of the good work and dedication of those senior faculty who do not want to retire early and be put "out of the way"? Does the stock market and thus the value of their retirement funds provide the most important measure for decision making? Or do expertise and dedication need to be acknowledged and rewarded?

The answer: Go slowly, act incrementally. Allow time for changes. Act in a way that one is still able to stop or even reverse decisions based on the perceived outcomes.

VIII. Gather Supporters and Gain Good Will

Clearly, operating with multiple possible courses of action at any given time is not something that one can do by oneself. One needs supporters. This does not mean having a block of people "on your side." Rather it means that, especially before big decisions need to be made, there needs to be a record of positive interactions. One must be trusted on the basis of what one does as one goes along, not the week before a question is called. What could be more obvious, but not at all so easy to do every day: treat all colleagues decently, fairly. Ideally, one needs to be trusted even when one has to say "no." Continually, make clear what needs to be done, neither hiding your preference or position, nor pushing it. Indicate what an incremental decision means: "We'll try it, see how that goes, then reassess options."

In working to retain support, again it is essential to be attuned to subtle differences amongst stakeholders. Because no one is likely to support you no matter what, stay sensitive to the multiple, often shifting interests and views of those whose help you need. Here, a good deal of help can come with a wise use of intermediaries.

A dean needs a department chair who knows and can negotiate differences between factions in her unit; a provost needs multiple division-chairs, department chairs, and other central administrators to help. Normally these others are involved in a tangle of problems at any stage, so it is reasonable to seek their counsel and ask for their help. What do they see, what do they predict? For example, while serving as a provost at another school, I found that the director of personnel usually was struggling with the same complaints and impasses as had come forward to me. Together we often were able to figure out how to forestall or even remedy violations involving equal opportunity laws, pay disputes, and contract difficulties.

Reciprocally, if possible and acceptable, help others who request or require assistance. Practise generosity whenever possible. I did not need Gracián to tell me, "Be the bearers of Praise" (188). Early on in my tenure as dean, realizing that I received news of a faculty member's tenure and promotion before it was formally announced, I spontaneously would take a bottle of champagne and a handful of cups to my colleague's classroom and make the announcement. The surprise was always a hit, with major cheering from the class. Faculty members regularly commented on this initiative years later as one of the happy moments of campus life. Why are such (or similar, non-alcoholic!) gestures not common?

IX. Hard Things

With respect to people and money, hard things will happen. They will have to happen, with you as the focally responsible party. As noted earlier, one cannot reasonably expect that everyone will be happy when major change occurs. Still, the idea is to negotiate towards acceptance, if not agreement. Allow people to be angry, to you directly as well as in meetings, in a socially acceptable, non-disruptive manner.

I had been told that my president and provost felt that high on the agenda for me when I became dean of architecture and planning in 2000 was the task of dealing with the persistent, notorious tensions among our departments. In my first meeting with the department chairs, the antagonism was evident, as one chair slammed down his materials, uttered some not-very-nice words, and stormed out. It took my full six years of tenure as dean to help to resolve the situation, but it did happen. This was the result of many small steps: avoiding the hiring of uncooperative chairs, finding creative interdisciplinary projects in which different departmental faculty and students could work fruitfully together, strategic increases in salaries to the most willing to work together, and much more. The key was to support ideas that would maximize cooperation.

Hundreds of fires had to be put out along the way, including terminating certain individuals – the most difficult task I have faced. But when it is clear that it does need to be done, stay awake all night, endure the stomachache, the tension as they come into your office. But do it: be clear, firm, and calm.

X. 10. How to Learn and Make Better Judgments – *Phronesis*

Of course, we are obliged to learn to be better administrators – to learn from experience, from what goes right, what wrong. In this regard, I would recommend:

• Monitor yourself.

- Be quick and sincere in apologizing when you have made a mistake.
- Do not force things by evoking your authority. The approach is obnoxious and never works in the long run anyway. Explicitly evoking authority in fact shows weakness and a lack of self-confidence. You can be effective simply by acting normally without insisting that others defer to your power. It is clear to everyone that you have certain powers.

As noted at the start of this chapter, Aristotle's (1994) notion of *phronesis* is distinct from *episteme* – strict scientific knowledge of what cannot be otherwise – and from *doxa*, or mere opinion. *Phronesis* is understanding gained by experience that enables one ethically and socially-politically to act with good judgment when, as almost always is the case, we know neither all the factors involved nor really all the consequences that will follow from our actions (Mugerauer, 2021). *Phronesis*, which usually is translated as "practical judgment" or "experience-based understanding" (or even "practical wisdom"), is primarily a mode of empirical understanding that is gained through thoughtful experience. We think this way when a situation is uncertain because there are so many dynamic variables acting simultaneously on each other and together in the world.

Phronesis (Mugerauer, 2021) enables good decisions in situations when we are uncertain what factors matter and particularly when those factors themselves are unstable. In fact, *phronesis* (Mugerauer, 2021) is quite common in our everyday lives, since normally we do not expect certainty in our changing world. Hence, we reasonably depend on our accumulated life experience where we already have considerable discernment of what has proven to be the case or what successfully works in our life world. From this reflective reservoir of experience, we judge which elements are relevant to the situation at hand and deliberate about what is most appropriate, then choose a course of action.

The cultivation of *phronesis* (Mugerauer, 2021), then, could be seen as a summative directive for ethical leadership in academic governance – a lifelong task. My guiding star, steady in my own experience and thinking, does agree with at least one thing Gracián says: "See to it that things end well" (maxim 66).

NOTES

1 For an elaboration of a complexity ethics see Mugerauer (2020).
2 See "Federalist Papers: Primary Documents in American History" (1787–88).
3 Though not intentional, given my long interest in philosopher Martin Heidegger, many of my comments echo his ideas. What I present here is drawn from how I go about things; but given the correlations I think it worthwhile to refer the reader to Mugerauer (2010).
4 From the large literature on resilience and complexity theory, see, for example, Gunderson and Holling (2002).

REFERENCES

Aristotle. (1994). *Nicomachean ethics* (H. Rackham, Trans.). Harvard University Press.

Federalist Papers: Primary Documents in American History. (1787–88). Library of Congress. https://guides.loc.gov/federalist-papers/full-text

Gadamer, H.-G. (1975). *Truth and method*. The Seabury Press.

Gracián, B. (1991). *The art of worldly wisdom* (J. Jacobs, Trans.). Doubleday.

Gunderson, L., & Holling, C.S. (Eds.). (2002). *Panarchy: Understanding transformations in human and natural systems*. Island Press.

Mugerauer, R. (2010). *Heidegger and homecoming*. University of Toronto Press.

Mugerauer, R. (2020). Towards a complexity ethics: Understanding and action on behalf of life-world well-being. In I.L. Stefanovic (Ed.), *The wonder of water: Lived experience, policy, and practice* (pp. 213–34). University of Toronto Press.

Mugerauer, R. (2021, June). Professional judgement in clinical practice (part 3): A better alternative to strong evidence-based medicine. *Journal of Evaluation in Clinical Practice, 27*(3), 612–23. https://doi.org/10.1111/jep.13512

Sartre, J.-P. (1953). *Being and nothingness*. Washington Square Press.

Stefanovic, I.L. (2000). *Safeguarding our common future: Rethinking sustainable development*. State University of New York Press.

Thomas, D. (1952). The force that through the green fuse drives the flower. Academy of American Poets. https://poets.org/poem/force-through-green-fuse-drives-flower

"The Art of Having the Right Thing Happen"

DAVID MILLER

Managing Director, International Diplomacy and Advocacy, C40 Cities Climate Leadership Group, and Former Mayor of Toronto, Canada

Bob Mugerauer argues, on the basis of his university experience, that leadership is a learned art.

He is, of course, correct.

But the lessons I have taken from leadership roles in politics, non-governmental organizations, and boards are different from those Bob articulates so persuasively in this chapter.

The biggest lesson I have learned is that the leader must have a clarity of purpose grounded in deeply held personal values and those of the institution. My political career, for example, was defined by strong and effective efforts to use the power of government to build a society where no one was left behind. These values came from my upbringing in a small English farming village in the 1960s, where class was clearly defined and clearly unjust – even to the eyes of an eight-year-old boy.

The clarity of purpose must start with the leader's truly held values – but it must be grounded in the values, goals and aspirations of the institution itself. Bob's point about listening is one with which I very much agree: "The task here is to listen, to try to hear, really hear, what each person or party wants, what each can live with, what would increase conflict" (p. 295).

The very best leaders help craft the common sense of purpose aligned with their personal values and with the goals and aspirations of the institution. This starts with listening.

It has an important corollary: the leader must represent and protect that sense of common purpose at all times. This not only means communicating it well – in our day-to-day professional lives. It is easy to forget that we are part of a bigger enterprise unless a leader helps to remind us of our joint sense of purpose and to inspire us when necessary. It also means protecting the institution by making difficult decisions when needed and by taking responsibility for the institution's failures, including the mistakes of others. This is sometimes hard to do but is immensely powerful for the institution. Not only do people know they are protected, they also know the institution is as well, reinforcing the sense of common purpose and, in most cases, the individual's belief in the common project.

It is that belief that is most powerful. And for me, it is what a good leader must deliver – because not only is it essential, it cannot be delivered by anyone else.

REFERENCE

Mugerauer, R. (2023). The art of having the right thing happen. In I.L. Stefanovic (Ed.), *Conversations on ethical leadership: Lessons learned from university governance* (pp. 289–305). University of Toronto Press.

chapter fourteen

Concluding Remarks: Building a University's Sense of Place

INGRID LEMAN STEFANOVIC

Give me a place to stand, and I will move the world.

– Archimedes

There is no creation without place.

– Edward Casey

What defines a *good*, successful, well-functioning university? Clearly, as reflected in the chapters of this book, the answer invites multiple stories and diverse perspectives. But in addition to a variety of discrete avenues to follow, a trace of something else underlies this conversation. More than an inventory of explicit, calculative features, an institution's identity is also defined by more nebulous, intangible elements.

As a philosopher by training, I believe that one of the great moments of modern thought occurs with the realization that human beings are not, as Descartes surmised, simply isolated subjects or solipsistic, thinking *things*, situated in a world of discrete material objects. On the contrary, our interpretation of the world is always fluid: inasmuch as we exist, we exist *somewhere*, in *relation* to others, primordially situated within the context of some place geographically, culturally, temporally, politically, and indeed, ontologically. As geographer Ted Relph (2021) notes, "Place is not some sort of incidental amenity but a vital aspect of how people everywhere relate to the world" (p. 24). Simply put, it is impossible to exist in the absence of place. That acknowledgment is more than just a trivial theoretical statement. Instead, it reflects the cardinal reality of our historically lived, embodied experience of the world and, I suggest, can significantly inform our understanding of what universities should be today and in the future.

University leaders would be wise to acknowledge that an institution's sense of place is difficult to articulate because it is often obscure and oneiric, nowhere but everywhere, compelling yet unspoken. The concept of place has been said to "resist theoretical reductionism," acknowledging the reality that often "the world cannot be understood in solely causal terms" (Janz, 2005, p. 89). Consequently, as noted by eminent place theorist Jeff Malpas (1999), "In many of the most basic respects, our dependence on place is something that always remains implicit or else can only be explicated with great difficulty" (p. 177).

Certainly, as we seek to better clarify and facilitate a productive and meaningful sense of place within our universities, it becomes evident that there is no silver bullet here: "place" is as diverse a notion as the innumerable local places that define it. That said, the place literature is voluminous (Bachelard, 1964; Casey, 1993; Donohoe, 2017; Malpas, 1999; Mugerauer, 1994; Relph, 1976; Seamon, 2018; Seamon & Mugerauer, 1985; Smith, 2001; Stefanovic, 2000; Stefanovic & Scharper, 2012). So, Part One sets the stage by discussing what we mean when we refer to a sense of place that is both virtuous and meaningful. Part Two then extends that conversation to show how important values need to be preserved if university leaders are to identify and productively shape a university's identity and a positive, hopeful, empathetic sense of place.

I. Acknowledging Place

Admittedly, for those new to the topic, conversations about the phenomenon of place may sound vague and even inapt in the context of discussions on responsible university leadership. Nevertheless, without much forethought, each of us becomes deeply aware and distressed when *displacement* occurs and the power of place is disrupted: witness the recent COVID-19 pandemic. Certainly, universities worldwide have been *physically* dislocated as most employees and students moved home. But more than this, as leaders are well aware, the very identity and aspirations of their institutions have been disturbed financially, socially, culturally, pedagogically, and in terms of research and lab protocols.[1] From cancellation of sports and athletic events to worsening student mental health and erosion of trust in reopening protocols, universities have been forced to reorient their priorities at all levels as a result of the pandemic.

Because it is so taken for granted, it is often only when it is lost or disrupted that a former sense of place becomes perceptible, precisely through its absence. Just as our own good health "manifests itself precisely by virtue of escaping our attention," an institution's sense of place is very much taken for granted and consists of more than an inventory of objective, quantifiable characteristics that are present at hand (Gadamer, 1996, p. 96).

Certainly, place does include some physical parameters and is legitimately associated with individual buildings, delineated geographical departmental locations, landscaped walkways, and similar structural realities that materially define our institutions. But even that overall physical design is more than simply an inventory of built structures; instead, it communicates different values. The stone walkways and time-honoured halls of Oxford University deliver a different message about the significance of deep, historical tradition than Arthur Erickson's quintessential modernist design of Simon Fraser University – an institution that, unsurprisingly, given its architecture, prided itself for many years as being Canada's innovative, modern "radical university" (Johnson, 2005; Stefanovic, 2020, p. 126). As Ellen Eve Frank (1979) puts it, "Architecture has a language of sorts" (p. 254). The physical landscape and settings of our institutions often speak to the world views and values that define them.

But beyond the materiality of place, there are also unique departmental cultures, friendships, and other elements of human experience that hold a more ephemeral quality. And these material and oneiric qualities often overlap. In the words of phenomenological geographer David Seamon (2013), "Place is not the material environment distinct from people related to it but, rather, the indivisible, normally unnoticed phenomenon of person-or-people-experiencing-place" (p. 150). Once I inhabit it, my office is no longer simply a geographical location. It becomes *my* place. The classroom becomes *my* classroom when I share time with my students, and it becomes *theirs* when they attend class. And, as Seamon reminds us, the wonder of place is that it is not pre-programmed: there is a serendipitous quality to sometimes unexpected encounters – "meeting an old friend accidentally on the sidewalk; enjoying the extemporaneous performance of an itinerant street musician" – that contribute, "in smaller and larger measure, to the pleasure of being alive" and that define our campuses' sense of place (Seamon, 2018, p. 118). The physical and the experiential are deeply intertwined; they belong together, and, in that respect, the relation becomes more important than what is related (Warren, 1987).

Place theorists emphasize the integral belonging of lived experience to the world within which such experience plays out. In the words of J.E. Malpas (1999), "Place is integral to the very structure and possibility of experience ... understanding the structure and possibility of experience ... is inseparable from an understanding and appreciation of the concept of place" (pp. 32–3).

And of course, as integrally related to place, human experience is intensely *value laden*. There are expectations, sometimes only implicit, about what is appropriate behaviour and what standards *ought* to be followed. Those values are rarely universally applicable or static: as Ed Casey (1993) reminds us, "Time is an extension of the extensiveness of place" (p. 13). As inherently temporal and relational, sense of place is not a quantifiable, bounded entity. Rather, it remains to some extent elusive, vulnerable, and open to change.

Consequently, deciphering and shaping an ethic of place requires more than simply a handbook of written rules but, instead, invites new challenges for university leaders. As Mugerauer pointed out in an earlier chapter, more than simply a learned craft, ethical leadership is itself an art. Much as Plato distinguished between a true statesman and a mere functionary, we can distinguish between the wisdom of responsible leadership and merely bureaucratic regulation. How is the success of a statesman or responsible leader to be measured? Gadamer (1996) explains:

> Plato distinguishes between two different kinds of measure. The first is that which is used when one wants to take a measurement and the procedure is brought to the object from without. The second is the measure which is to be found within the object itself. The Greek expressions here are *metron* for the first sort of measure, and *metrion* for the second. In Germany, we speak of "das Angemessene," of which is appropriate or fitting. What does "appropriate" mean here? Clearly in the present context it refers to that *inner* measure which is proper to a self-sustaining whole. (p. 98)

Gadamer (1996) concludes that "we encounter two different forms of measure, one belonging to the domain of science, the other belonging to the totality of our being-in-the-world" (p. 99). In this regard, university leaders are frequently driven by *metron* – metrics, such as QS rankings, quantifiable student evaluations, budget models, and so on. Each of these tools informs decision making, often legitimately, to a large degree.

Perhaps, though, university leaders should also give more explicit attention to the implicit values and ways in which their institutions breathe and function daily. As French phenomenologist Gaston Bachelard (1960) rightly points out, "The subconscious is ceaselessly murmuring, and it is by listening to these murmurs that one hears the truth" (p. 59). How do we begin to listen for such truth?

Aristotle might have suggested that such leaders should draw from a kind of knowledge that he called *phronesis* – a practical wisdom derived from experience, reflective of a deep capacity for judgment and an ability to apply sound principles towards achieving the good life. While principles must always guide sound reasoning, those principles should be tempered by the conditions of context, lived experience, and place. The big question that leaders might want to ask themselves is, What kind of values are morally appropriate or fitting at one's specific institution in order to support its broader mission and its meaningful sense of place?

II. Valuing the University's Sense of Place

Perhaps it is easiest to define to which kind of place we should *not* aspire. My sense is that evaluating the university solely in terms of calculative measures and reducing it simply to its instrumental value misses the point of higher learning. As a professor and dean, I saw how the sense of place of a university is certainly affected by its quantifiable research accomplishments and stature, its financial viability, and its robust student enrolments. But is there something else to preserve in defining more holistically the value of a particular university?

British sociologist Michael Burawoy (2011) argues that one of the most compelling pressures faced today by the university as an institution is its instrumentalization – specifically, its commodification and regulation (p. 27). Citing drastic reductions in state funding of universities over the last decades, he shows how commercialization mandates, increasing tuitions, online teaching, and reliance upon external donors have shifted the university narrative from one of public education to one that increasingly aspires to the mission of an efficient corporation (p. 29). William S. Hamrick (2002) agrees, going so far as to warn how "much of education has been ruined by giving in to social pressures to treat students as consumers and faculty and staff as salespeople whose main object is to please their customers" (p. 101). (I must say that, in that regard, I always cringed when students themselves described the first days of their academic semesters in terms of "shopping around" for different courses and instructors.)

In addition, Burawoy argues, the "regulation model" of the university ensures that the primary focus is on productivity and accountability. From international ranking systems (such as Times Higher Education) to measurement of faculty research output through peer-reviewed publications, "commodification of knowledge leads to production for the highest bidder" (Burawoy, 2011, p. 31).

Burawoy is not alone in expressing such concerns. British professor Ulf Schmidt recently made the difficult decision to leave his teaching post at the University of Kent in Britain and take his "research millions" to Hamburg, Germany, post-Brexit. In his view, universities in England were becoming "morally bankrupt":

> Young people are told they are "consumers" in a shop where they can choose what and when to learn. They can expect a "service." Some have taken their university to court if their course did not "deliver" promised results. This is no longer a viable, decent learning environment in which students from all walks of life and cultures are supported to achieve their potential. This is not a place in which the next generation of citizens can flourish. The rise in the number of students suffering from mental health issues speaks volumes. A student suicide is "managed" by the media department for fear of bad publicity. What matters are "bums on seats" to keep the ship afloat. (Schmidt, 2020, para. 6)

Burawoy (2011, p. 40) argues that these subtle commodifying changes compromise the integrity of universities as places of critical engagement and deliberative democracy. "The university," he suggests, "should be viewed as a *critical public sphere* in which there is indeed discussion among academics about the nature of the university and its place in society," just as much as "the university has to be at the centre of organizing public discussion about the direction of society" (pp. 40–1). Our commentators show how important this last point can be.

Certainly, while research and teaching are core to the vision of any great university, both are only augmented by the essential kind of rich, spirited, open, free, respectful dialogue that defines a virtuous, informative spirit of place. This fact is expressed so clearly in the chapters in this book written by Wayne Sumner and Harry Fernhout. Both are clear that if universities compromise their support of genuine dialogue, they cease to be authentic places of learning.

That dialogue must also be respectful of diverse voices, from the Indigenous (as noted by Deborah McGregor et al., chapter 9) to other minority groups (see Tricia Glazebrook's chapter 7). Certainly, university leaders have a responsibility "to create that moral space where people will be able to evaluate different suggestions" (Horgan-Jones 2020, para. 7). Commitment to community engagement invites a variety of professional voices (see Thomas Barrie's chapter 8) as integral to an inclusive, discursive sense of place at universities. And it invites a deep sensibility towards environmental care (see Stefanovic and Hausgenecht) and sustainability issues (see Robinson et al., chapter 2), as a healthy planet is the condition of well-being at all levels.

Building a university's constructive sense of place certainly requires that bricks-and-mortar issues, such as adequate resourcing (see Myers, chapter 3), provide a supportive framework for advancing a culture of excellence (see Giardini, chapter 6) and academic integrity (see Thacker, chapter 4). But it also depends on leaders who are attuned to the art of governance (see Mugerauer, chapter 13) and who are willing to prioritize universities as spaces of virtue (see Janz, chapter 12). And of course, in that respect, universities certainly need leaders "who others will follow, not unquestioningly but with confidence and respect" (Lewis, 2007, p. 256).

Finally – and perhaps foremost – building a strong sense of place at our post-secondary institutions requires transforming our relationship with students from a merely transactional one to a bond of respect and primary focus (see King, chapter 5). In the words of the president of Trinity College Dublin,

> Universities are not there merely to produce students who are useful.... They are there to produce citizens who are respectful of the rights of others to participate, and also to be able to participate fully, drawing on a wide range of scholarship. (Horgan-Jones 2020, paras. 2–3)

Moreover, as former dean of Harvard Harry R. Lewis (2007) notes, "Over the decades, I have heard many academic discussions about teaching, about the curriculum, about grading, about athletics, and about responding to student misdeeds. I have almost never heard discussions among professors about making students better people" (p. xv). Lewis feels strongly that the soul of our educational institutions is lost unless we realize that we need to foster among our students a sense of "personal strength, integrity, kindness, cooperation, compassion," teaching them how to become "people of good character" and "how to leave the world a better place than you found it" (p. xiv).

According to some, the recent COVID-19 pandemic provides us with an opportunity to rethink the very humanity of our educational institutions. It is giving us

> an opportunity to make a pivot that we should have made long ago. We have been on a treadmill of short-term fixes, pretending that if we just get the right test, the right incentives, put the right pressure on teachers and students, they will achieve what is good for them, like it or not. But we are realizing what we should have known all along: that you can't widget your way to powerful learning, that relationships are critical for learning, that students' interests need to be stimulated and their selves need to be recognized. (Mehta, 2020, para. 20)

In a post-pandemic world, a number of university leaders are urging us to turn the disruption into an opportunity for change. Certainly, there are some who wonder, "After Coronavirus ... will students come back?" (Hartocollis, 2020). Other sceptics go so far as to argue that online learning is now completely transforming the university as we know it. They claim that, previously, the academy was where one physically went to obtain knowledge, but today, digital instruction has apparently completely changed the flow of information, which is no longer contained within the university's walls.

John Naughton refers to Columbia University scholar Eli Noam's 1995 article that prophesied how technology will bring information to the people, rather than being sought within the walls of the academy. "What then is the role of the university?" Noam asked 25 years ago (cited in Naughton, 2021, para. 3).

> Will the impact of electronics on the university be like that of printing on the medieval cathedral, ending its central role in information transfer? Have we reached the end of the line of a model that goes back to Nineveh, more than 2,500 years ago? (cited in Naughton 2021, para. 3)

Naughton believes that Noam's article was prescient and that, post-pandemic, universities need to "wise up" and acknowledge the power of digital platforms and online learning, while recognizing that college campuses are already a thing of the past.

Entrepreneur Elon Musk voices a similarly sceptical sentiment about the future of universities. According to Musk, college today is "basically for fun and not for learning," given that information is so freely available online and "you can learn anything you want for free" (Aratani, 2020, para. 5). These and other proponents of a changed university environment raise important points. I readily admit that I was involved in launching some of the earliest distance education professional programs at the University of Toronto, back in the early 2000s. Even then, I saw the value of online learning. And certainly today, we have been forced, through the pandemic, to accept distance education as a necessity.

That said, I am persuaded that the university experience has much more to do with educating virtuous citizens than imparting information online. Post-secondary leaders need to be reminded that "when you talk about really engaging, the most important thing is showing up as a human being" (Hurt, 2021, p. 44). Being human means engaging with the world not just visually and aurally but through each of the senses, including touch. Lived experiences of social interaction between students, faculty, staff, and the wider community impart a richness of learning opportunities that are simply unavailable exclusively online. What is, in this concluding chapter, referred to as "sense of place" includes that embodied depth of experience of diverse voices, multidimensional and varied perspectives, and assorted memories that are fed by the daily lived interactions of campus life. More than just being "fun" (and why not include "fun" in that experience?!), university life builds understanding that comes from interacting with and benefiting from the wisdom of exemplary faculty members who are devoted to the kind of pedagogical and research programs that consist of much more than the delivery of discrete bits of information that are available through Google searches.

In that vein, Patricia McGuire (2020), president of Trinity Washington University, challenges us to "reclaim our moral purpose as sources of knowledge, service and even hope" (para. 5). In doing so, let us not forget that recovering a sense of place at our post-secondary institutions demands that we privilege the humanity of our faculty, staff, and students over their utility within competitive rankings. Let us keep front and centre the values that distinguish our universities as evidence-based, truth-seeking, collaborative, dialogical, respectful places of higher learning. Let us build safe spaces, geographically as well as online, that inspire excellence, that celebrate research integrity, that excite and motivate society's quest for meaningful enquiry. And certainly, let us ensure that our institutions retain a measure of positivity and hope among the challenges faced by society, from pandemics to global environmental change. Without a realistic, grounded, but hopeful perspective, the values that sustain a university's deepest sense of place are at risk.

In this vein, I share a story about a staff member who worked at Simon Fraser University, on the top of Burnaby Mountain in British Columbia, a province of Western Canada. One day, as she and her young daughter headed to my colleague's office, they passed up through the mountain roads, covered in rain and thick cloud cover, eventually emerging into the glory of a sunlit campus. Upon arrival, her delighted daughter turned to her and said, "Mom, you work with the angels!" My friend laughingly thought to herself at the time – *and with the demons!*

Over the length of our careers, most of us have encountered people who have exhibited heartless, self-centred, aggressive, even devious behaviour. These experiences have defined occasional tough moments, best put behind us. My final suggestion is that we do not forget to foster universities as places of kindness. Perhaps this sounds unusual to some, particularly as a parting thought. But when I recall my most memorable moments over the last 50 years since first enrolling as a university student myself, they are defined by professors who were empathetic towards their students, by staff members who were warm and collegial, and by colleagues who were respectful and collaborative. Others have felt the same, recognizing how a sense of humanity, kindness, and support at university can define a young person's entire research and career trajectory in unexpectedly significant ways (Seamon, 1987).

I am reminded of a recent study of more than 600 medical students that found that in their first year, those who were selfish and focused simply on their own progress performed better than their colleagues who did not exhibit those qualities. By second year, however, those who were more generous with their time, offering to assist fellow students, had apparently caught up. By third year, this second group had reportedly overtaken their peers, and by their final year, they had significantly higher grades. In fact, "a kinder attitude was a more powerful predictor of school grades than the effect of smoking on lung cancer rates" (Sayed, 2020, para. 18). Clearly, the message here is not that students should exhibit kindness for the utility of higher grades but rather that being virtuous often has its own just rewards.

Perhaps we should all give some thought to creating a sense of place at our own institutions that fosters an ethic of care, empathy, and kindness. In the end, privileging values of collaboration over competition, collective cooperation over egocentric ambition, may be some of the most important initiatives that university leaders should support in creating learning environments that are also, always, places of genuine virtue.

ACKNOWLEDGMENTS

I am grateful to Dr. David Seamon, professor emeritus, University of Kansas, pre-eminent place theorist and editor of the *Environmental and Architectural Phenomenology Newsletter*, for his helpful feedback on this final entry of our volume.

NOTE

1 See the selection of essays on the impact of COVID-19 on university campuses, presented in The Chronicle of Higher Education (2020).

REFERENCES

Aratani, L. (2020, 10 March). Elon Musk says "college is basically for fun and not for learning." *The Guardian*. https://www.theguardian.com /technology/2020/mar/10/elon-musk-college-for-fun-not-learning

Bachelard, G. (1960). *The poetics of reverie: Childhood, language and the cosmos* (D. Russell, Trans.). Beacon Press.

Bachelard, G. (1964). *The poetics of space* (M. Jolas, Trans.). Beacon Press.

Burawoy, M. (2011). Redefining the public university: Global and national contexts. In J, Holmwood (Ed.), *A manifesto for the public university* (pp. 27–41). Bloomsbury.

Casey, E. (1993). *Getting back into place: Toward a renewed understanding of the place-world.* Indiana University Press.

The Chronicle of Higher Education. (2020, 4 March). *Coronavirus hits campus.* https://www.chronicle.com/package/coronavirus-hits-campus/

Donohoe, J. (Ed). (2017). *Place and phenomenology.* Rowman & Littlefield.

Frank, E.E. (1979). *Literary architecture: Essays toward a tradition.* University of California Press.

Gadamer, H.-G. (1996). *The enigma of health.* Stanford University Press.

Hamrick, W.S. (2002). *Kindness and the good society.* State University of New York Press.

Hartocollis, A. (2020, 15 April). After coronavirus, colleges worry: Will students come back? *New York Times.* https://www.nytimes.com/2020/04/15/us/coronavirus-colleges-universities-admissions.html

Horgan-Jones, J. (2020, 2 March). Universities do not exist "to produce students who are useful," president says. *Irish Times.* https://www.irishtimes.com/news/ireland/irish-news/universities-do-not-exist-to-produce-students-who-are-useful-president-says-1.4190859

Hurt, K. (2021, March/April). Ready, set, engage. PM Network. Project Management Institute, 44.

Janz, B.B. (2005). Walls and borders: The range of place. *City & Community,* 4(1), 87–94. https://doi.org/10.1111/j.1535-6841.2005.00104.x

Johnson, H. (2005). *Radical campus: Making Simon Fraser University.* Douglas & McIntyre.

Lewis, H.R. (2007). *Excellence without a soul: Does liberal education have a future?* PublicAffairs Books.

Malpas, J.E. (1999). *Place and experience: A philosophical topography.* Cambridge University Press.

McGuire, P. (2020, 10 April). No more "normal": This crisis demands that colleges step back from self-absorption. In *How will the pandemic change higher education?.* The Chronicle of Higher Education. https://www.chronicle.com/article/how-will-the-pandemic-change-higher-education/

Mehta, J. (2020, 23 December). Make schools more human. *New York Times.* https://www.nytimes.com/2020/12/23/opinion/covid-schools-vaccine.html

Mugerauer, R. (1994). *Interpretations on behalf of place: Environmental displacements and alternative responses*. State University of New York Press.

Naughton, J. (2021, 13 February). Universities need to wise up – or risk being consigned to history. *The Guardian*. https://www.theguardian.com/commentisfree/2021/feb/13/universities-need-to-wise-up-or-risk-being-consigned-to-history

Relph, E. (1976). *Place and placelessness*. Pion.

Relph, E. (2021). The future of place. *Environmental and architectural phenomenology*, 32(1), 17–25.

Sayed, M. (2020, 30 March). *Coronavirus: The good that can come out of an upside-down world*. BBC News. https://www.bbc.com/news/world-us-canada-52094332

Schmidt, U. (2020, 8 September). Higher education in the UK is morally bankrupt. I'm taking my family and my research millions, and I'm off. *The Guardian*. https://www.theguardian.com/education/2020/sep/08/higher-education-in-the-uk-is-morally-bankrupt-im-taking-my-family-and-my-research-millions-and-im-off

Seamon, D. (1987, December). Phenomenology and the Clark experience. *Journal of Environmental Psychology*, 7(4), 367–77. https://doi.org/10.1016/S0272-4944(87)80010-5

Seamon, D. (2013, September). Lived bodies, place and phenomenology: Implications for human rights and environmental justice. *Journal of Human Rights and the Environment*, 4(2), 143–66. https://doi.org/10.4337/jhre.2013.02.02

Seamon, D. (2018). *Life takes place: Phenomenology, lifeworlds, and place making*. Routledge.

Seamon, D., & Mugerauer, R. (1985). *Dwelling, place and environment: Towards a phenomenology of person and world*. Martinus Nijhoff Publishers.

Smith, M. (2001). *An ethics of place: Radical ecology, postmodernity and social theory*. State University of New York Press.

Stefanovic, I.L. (2000). *Safeguarding our common future*. State University of New York Press.

Stefanovic, I.L. (Ed.). (2020). *The wonder of water: Lived experience, policy and practice*. University of Toronto Press.

Stefanovic, I.L., & Scharper, S. (Eds.). (2012). *The natural city: Re-envisioning the built environment*. University of Toronto Press.

Warren, K.J. (1987, Spring). Feminism and ecology: Making connections. *Environmental Ethics*, 9(1), 3–20. https://doi.org/10.5840/enviroethics19879113

Chapter Contributors

Ayako Ariga, MPP, joined the University of Toronto in 2014 and serves as the secretary and project manager of the President's Advisory Committee on the Environment, Climate Change, and Sustainability. In her role, she facilitates the development of sustainability curricular pathways programs and liaises with teaching, research, operations, community partnerships, and communications portfolios.

Thomas Barrie is a professor of architecture at North Carolina State University where he directs the Affordable Housing and Sustainable Communities Initiative. His scholarship focuses on the cultural significance, symbolism, ritual use of the built environment, and he has published and lectured extensively in his subject areas. Professor Barrie is a Fellow of the American Institute of Architects, an ACSA Distinguished Professor, and a member of the NC State Academy of Faculty Engaged in Extension. He is also co-founder and chair of the Architecture, Culture and Spirituality Forum.

Rashad Brugmann is a graduate of the University of Toronto, where he studied civil engineering. While at U of T, Rashad was involved in research to advance academic and institutional sustainability at the university. Rashad works as a building science engineer at RDH Building Science Inc.

Nicolas Côté is a Canadian social anthropologist and consultant. He worked for several years at the University of Toronto to advance social and environmental sustainability in teaching, research, and operations. In anthropology, he specializes in issues of social division and polarization around energy transition challenges.

Dione Dias has been at the University of Toronto for over a decade as a student and staff member. In her time at U of T, she studied environmental studies, environmental geography, and forest conservation. She later worked at the St. George Sustainability Office and is now working with the Committee on the Environment, Climate Change and Sustainability.

J. Harry Fernhout grew up in Thunder Bay, Ontario, the son of immigrant parents. He completed a master of philosophy at the Institute for Christian Studies (ICS) in Toronto in 1975 and a doctorate in philosophy of education at the University of Toronto in 1986. Harry served as president of ICS from 1990 to 2005. He was then appointed as president of The King's University in Edmonton, where he served until his retirement in 2013. Harry and his wife Hilda live in Brampton, Ontario, near nine of their thirteen grandchildren.

Anne Giardini is an executive, lawyer, corporate director, and writer of fiction and non-fiction. She served on the Board of Governors of Simon Fraser University for five years before being serving as SFU's eleventh chancellor from 2014 to 2020.

Tricia Glazebrook is professor of philosophy at Washington State University. She is an ecofeminist and works with women subsistence farmers in Ghana to collect empirical data on the impacts of climate change on agriculture, food security, and nutrition, and to document adaptation strategies. She publishes on climate policy and finance, gender in UNFCCC policy and in Intergovernmental Panel on Climate Change Assessment Reports. She studies the capacity of international climate finance to meet women agriculturalists' needs in Ghana. She also works in Heidegger studies and military ethics.

Simone Hausknecht is a researcher, educator, and learning designer. She is educational developer with the Centre for Educational Excellence at Simon Fraser University. She earned a PhD in education from Simon Fraser University and holds degrees in English, teaching, and health sciences from universities in Australia and Canada. Simone's research is focused on a wide range of topics and areas surrounding education, including interdisciplinary and transdisciplinary practices, educational technology, intergenerational relationships, and community-based research. She served as research assistant to Professor

Ingrid Leman Stefanovic for their SSHRC-funded project, Interpreting Interdisciplinarity: The Case of Environmental Studies.

Meghan Henderson is a researcher and analyst at Environment and Climate Change Canada. She is a graduate of the University of Toronto, where she studied political science and ethics, society, and law. Her research interests lie at the intersection of climate policy, ethics, inequality, and governance.

Bruce B. Janz is professor in the Department of Philosophy and a core faculty member in the Texts and Technology PhD Program, at the University of Central Florida. He is former chair of the Department of Philosophy, and co-director of the Center for Humanities and Digital Research at UCF. He works and publishes in African philosophy, concepts of place and space across multiple disciplines, interdisciplinarity and university culture, digital humanities, hermeneutics and phenomenology, and contemporary culture. He has taught in Canada, the United States, Kenya, and South Africa.

Sarah J. King is director, Environmental and Sustainability Studies at Grand Valley State University, where she also chairs the University Research and Development Committee. She works within a collaborative team of students, faculty, and staff to support the GVSU Sustainable Agriculture Project and was Farm Club advisor for many years. Before coming to GV, she held positions at Queen's University and Wilfrid Laurier University.

Susan Manitowabi is Anishinaabe-kwe from Whitefish River First Nation. She is associate vice president, Indigenous and Academic Programs, and founding director of the School of Indigenous Relations at Laurentian University. She has been a professor in this program since 2003. Her doctoral work focuses on the engagement of the "Raising the Spirit" Mental Wellness Team First Nations with First Nations mental health programs. She is a long-time member of the Manitoulin Anishinaabe Research Review Committee and was a member on the National Council on Ethics in Human Research. Her research interests include: Aboriginal mental health; traditional Aboriginal healing practices; Aboriginal child welfare; Indigenous research; and Aboriginal mental health policy development and community development. Her contributions to on-line learning include the development of a flexible weighting option for online learners as well as open education resource development.

Deborah McGregor, Anishinabe, is associate professor and Canada Research Chair: Indigenous Environmental Justice, at Osgoode Hall Law School and Faculty of Environmental Studies, York University. Professor McGregor's research has focused on Indigenous knowledge systems and their applications in diverse contexts including environmental and water governance, environmental justice, health and environment, climate change, and Indigenous legal traditions. Professor McGregor remains actively involved in a variety of Indigenous communities, serving as an advisor and continuing to engage in community-based research and initiatives. She has been at the forefront of Indigenous environmental justice and Indigenous research theory and practice. Her work has been shared through the IEJ project website https://iejproject.info.yorku.ca/ and UKRI International Collaboration on Indigenous research https://www.indigenous.ncrm.ac.uk/.

Lorrilee McGregor is an Anishinaabe from Whitefish River First Nation on Manitoulin Island. She is an assistant professor at the Northern Ontario School of Medicine at Laurentian University in Sudbury where she teaches about Indigenous peoples' health. Dr. McGregor has focused her research on First Nation community health issues such as mental health and addictions, diabetes, physical activity, and nutrition. She has also worked with First Nation communities and organizations on program evaluation and strategic planning. For the past 18 years, Dr. McGregor has been an active member of the Manitoulin Anishinaabek Research Review Committee, a community research ethics committee, and has served as the chair for most of that time.

Robert Mugerauer (deceased 2022) was professor and dean emeritus at the University of Washington. He served as academic dean and provost at St. Edward's University in Austin, Texas from 1979 to 1985, then as dean of the College of Architecture and Urban Planning at the University of Washington from 2000 to 2006. His research applied continental thought and dynamic complexity theory to decision making and issues of health and well-being. His most recent publication was a three-paper series on professional judgment in the *Journal on the Evaluation in Clinical Practice*.

Andrea Muehlebach is associate professor of anthropology at the University of Toronto. She is completing her second book, A Vital Politics: Water Insurgencies in Europe," and is also one of the co-organizers of Distribute 2020 (https://distribute.utoronto.ca/).

Gordon M. Myers is a professor of economics at Simon Fraser University. He was educated at Queen's, Stockholm, and McMaster Universities. He has been an academic visitor at the University of Essex, Bonn University, and the University of Toronto. He has published research articles in top general interest journals in economics and his fields of public economics and urban economics. He was the chair of Economics and served on SFU's Senate and Board of Governors. He recently completed a five-year term as SFU's vice-provost and associate vice-president academic. He is conducting research on university governance and behavioural economics.

Rutu Patel has a BSc in global health, and health and environment. During her undergraduate degree, Rutu worked at the University of Toronto to advance campus sustainability. She hopes to establish a career in public policy to address global health and climate change.

Cindy Peltier is Nishinaabe-kwe with connections to both Wiikwemkoong Unceded Territory and Nipissing First Nation where she lives with her husband, Blair, and son, Colin. Cindy's work in administration includes roles as chair in Indigenous education and associate dean of arts and science at Nipissing University. Her past work as an educator and administrator in First Nations was grounded in strong relationships with communities. Her research in Indigenous health focused on improving health equity through the sharing of Nishinaabe stories, perspectives, and methodologies. She is an investigator on research grants through the Canadian Institutes of Health Research and the Social Sciences and Humanities Research Council. In doing this work, her priority is to share research findings in ways that will be meaningful for Indigenous peoples.

Jennifer Puskar is a special projects officer, Office of the Chief Operating Officer, with a home role as a project manager, Sustainability Office, University of Toronto. Holding a bachelor of environmental studies from the University of Waterloo, her areas of interest include sustainability management, behavioural economics, landscape architecture, human-centred data science, and UX design.

John Robinson is a professor at the Munk School of Global Affairs and Public Policy and the School of the Environment at the University of Toronto and holds graduate appointments in the Department of Geography and Planning and the Daniels School of Architecture, Landscape and Design. He is also an adjunct professor at Copenhagen Business School. At U of T, he is presidential advisor on the Environment, Climate Change and Sustainability. In 2019, he was Utrecht University Visiting Professor on Transdisciplinarity. Dr. Robinson's research focuses on the intersection of climate change mitigation, adaptation, and sustainability; the use of visualization, modelling, and citizen engagement to explore sustainable futures; sustainable buildings and urban design; the role of the university in contributing to sustainability; creating partnerships for sustainability with non-academic partners; the history and philosophy of sustainability; and, generally, the intersection of sustainability, social and technological change, behaviours and practices, and community engagement processes.

Ingrid Leman Stefanovic is an author and consultant in environmental and institutional change management. A professor emeritus and former dean of the Faculty of Environment at Simon Fraser University, Vancouver, Canada, she is also professor emerita, Department of Philosophy, University of Toronto, where she spent much of her career teaching and conducting research on how values and perceptions affect public policy, planning, and environmental decision making. Dr Stefanovic has served as executive co-director of the International Association for Environmental Philosophy and senior scholar at the Center for Humans & Nature, Chicago, and New York. Recent books include *The Natural City: Re-envisioning the Built Environment; The Wonder of Water: Lived Experience, Policy and Practice,* and *Ethical Water Stewardship.*

L.W. Sumner is university professor emeritus in the Department of Philosophy at the University of Toronto. His professional teaching and research have focused on ethical theory, applied ethics (especially bioethics), political philosophy, and philosophy of law. He is the author of six books: *Abortion and Moral Theory* (1981); *The Moral Foundation of*

Rights (1987); *Welfare, Ethics, and Happiness* (1996); *The Hateful and the Obscene: Studies in the Limits of Free Expression* (2004); *Assisted Death: A Study in Ethics and Law* (2011), and *Physician-Assisted Death: What Everyone Needs to Know* (2017). He is a Fellow of the Royal Society of Canada and recipient of the 2009 Molson Prize in Social Sciences and Humanities from the Canada Council for the Arts.

Emma J. Thacker holds a PhD from the School of Social, Political and Global Studies at Keele University, United Kingdom. Her doctoral research focused specifically on academic literacies and contract cheating. Emma is an active member of the Academic Integrity Council of Ontario and holds research interests in higher education policy and academic integrity education. She also serves as assistant secretary of the Governing Council and ombuds officer at the University of Toronto Scarborough, Canada, specializing in governance, policy, and ombuds work. She has held several positions to support institutional quality assurance, academic integrity, and quasi-judicial affairs.

Peter Vuong studied mechanical engineering with a specialization in energy and environment. He serves as a sustainability analyst for Choice Properties Real Estate Investment Trust in Toronto, Canada. In his spare time, he enjoys playing basketball and chess.

Commentary Contributors

Esther Bergman is a consultant with Benchmark Performance Inc. and World Class Productivity Inc. She has supported learning, performance, and change for 20 years, with leading organizations in a variety of industries. Her sharp analysis skills and relevant solutions stem from her ability to marry client business goals with the needs of affected groups.

Nada Conić has a private practice in spiritual counselling and leads retreats at Manresa Jesuit Renewal Centre in Pickering and other places in Canada and the United States. She works mainly with people in recovery from addictions in a religiously pluralist setting. She has been interviewed on Steve Paikin's *TVO Agenda* a few times as a panellist on religious and spiritual topics. Having studied classics and philosophy at the University of Toronto (winning the Governor's General award for best degree at University College in 1981), she went on to study and teach Greek language and literature at U of T and the University of Victoria, BC. She left the academy in 1991 (apart from some sessional and continuing studies teaching at U of T) and eventually pursued an MA in theology at the Toronto School of Theology, Regis College. She has translated from the French a book about Christian de Chergé, the Trappist superior of the Algerian monastery portrayed in the film *Of Gods and Men*. She is also the translator of *Sarajevo Days, Sarajevo Nights* from Serbo-Croatian. Translating the diaries and letters of a woman whose father was Muslim and mother was Jewish, given that her father was a Serb Chetnik during the Second World War, was an ethical decision. She believes that taking a principled stand, finding a spiritual grounding deeper than religious and tribal divisions, and reaching across boundaries to amplify another person's voice and witness were worth family conflict and a certain risk from ultra-nationalists, both then and now.

Anne Koven has spent more than 30 years working in government and business, primarily in environmental and resource management. She is an adjunct professor at the University of Toronto's John H. Daniels Faculty of Architecture, Landscape and Design with an interest in forest policy. She is a registered professional forester (Hon.) She chaired the landmark Class Environmental Assessment by the Ministry of Natural Resources for Timber Management on Crown Lands in Ontario from 1988 to 1994. Dr. Koven served on the Ontario Provincial Forest Policy Committee from 2008 to 2020. She was a trustee and secretary treasurer of the Trees Ontario Foundation and represented the foundation on the Natural Spaces Leadership Alliance. She was the president of the Ontario Forestry Association (which amalgamated with the Trees Ontario Foundation to become Forests Ontario), and she also served as its executive director. She is the founding director of the Mass Timber Institute at the University of Toronto.

Todd Latham is a Canadian media entrepreneur and industry communicator with 30 years' experience in water, environment, and infrastructure. He is president of Actual Media Inc., a niche publishing, events, and design agency that produces ReNew Canada, EnvironmentJournal.ca, and Water Canada. Todd is also an active cleantech investor and a proud IAE alumnus of 2041, an international group committed to the preservation of the Antarctic continent.

B. Alexander Leman is the co-founder of Vitruvian Group, with interests in sectors including management consulting, financial services, insurance, and real estate. Alex is a current or retired member or chair of several corporate and philanthropic boards of directors and advisory boards, and an advisor on governance and performance to family offices and private and public companies.

Sabrina Leman is a licensed architect with LPA Design Studios, based in Southern California. A graduate of the UBC M.Arch. Program, and with over 20 years' experience, Sabrina has focused much of her career in the higher education market segment, including projects in Vancouver, Canada; and Southern California.

Lois Lindsay serves as executive director of Evergreen's Strategic Initiatives team, helping to identify and build innovative new program and partnership opportunities – all in pursuit of Evergreen's mission to help cities flourish. With a dual focus on program design and business development, Lois and her team help ensure that great ideas are elevated, honed, financially supported, and ultimately realized. An 18-year veteran of Evergreen, Lois brings deep institutional memory to her work, as well as a breadth of experience in program design and management, strategic planning, and fundraising. She holds a master's degree in geography as well as a BA from the University of Guelph, and lives in Toronto, in the traditional homelands of the Wendat, Haudenosaunee, and Anishnaabek Confederacies, with her spouse and two children.

Susan McGeachie is head of the BMO Climate Institute, a centre of expertise that bridges climate policy and science with business strategy and finance to unlock solutions for both clients and the bank. She brings to this role over 20 years of experience identifying, evaluating, and managing climate change–related risks and strategic positioning opportunities. Following her years in ESG research and analytics, she held leadership positions in management and engineering consulting firms. Susan is an adjunct professor at the University of Toronto, where she teaches a graduate course in climate finance, and a member of the Canadian Climate Governance Experts panel. In 2021, Susan was named one of 26 Canadian Climate Champions by the Canada Climate Law Initiative and the British High Commission ahead of COP26. In 2014, she was named to the Clean50 and Clean 16 lists of practitioners, which recognize contributions to advancing sustainable capitalism.

David Miller is the managing director of International Diplomacy and global ambassador of Inclusive Climate Action at C40 Cities Climate Leadership Group. He is responsible for supporting mayors in their climate leadership and for building a global movement for socially equitable action to mitigate and adapt to climate change. He served as chair of C40 Cities from 2008 until 2010. Miller was mayor of Toronto from 2003 to 2010. Under his leadership, Toronto became widely admired internationally for its environmental leadership, economic strength, and social integration. He is a leading advocate for the creation of sustainable urban economies, and a strong and forceful champion for the next generation of jobs through sustainability. Miller has held a variety of public and private positions and served as Future of Cities Global Fellow at Polytechnic Institute of New York University from 2011 to 2014. David Miller is a Harvard-trained economist, professionally a lawyer, and author of *Solved: How the World's Great Cities Are Fixing the Climate Crisis*.

Kevin Nilsen is president and CEO of Environmental Careers Organization (ECO) Canada. Kevin started his career in leadership as officer in the Norwegian Army before moving to Canada in 2000. After graduating from the University of Calgary, Kevin worked seven years for ECO Canada, most recently as director of Professional Services. During his absence from ECO Canada, until 2016 when he returned to his present post, Kevin managed large global offshore oil and as projects for Aker-owned companies. The experience in the energy sector gave him exposure to clients and stakeholders in Europe, Asia, and United States while based in Norway and subsequently in Houston, Texas. As a key highlight, Kevin led the development of a cutting-edge Riser Gas Handling tool that ensures a safer and more environmentally friendly drilling process. At ECO Canada, he was responsible for the establishment of the Canadian Centre for Environmental Education. He was also instrumental in the launch of regional networking events across the country, the growing of EP certification, and academic partnerships. In his role as CEO, Kevin's key focus is to ensure that ECO Canada's products and services align well with industry, government, and academic stakeholders.

Christopher A. Ollson is an environmental health scientist, consultant, and adjunct professor at the University of Toronto Scarborough. Over the past 20 years, he has been involved in permitting of several of the most controversial major infrastructure projects in North America.

Indira V. Samarasekera served as president of the University of Alberta and is a director of Magna International, TC Energy, and Stelco. She is an advisor for Bennett Jones and served as director of Scotia Bank. She is an Officer of the Order of Canada and a member of the National Academy of Engineering in the United States.

Stephanie Seymour is an Anishinaabe Kwe from Garden River First Nation who is conducting research for her PhD in forestry at the University of Toronto. Throughout her time in industry and academia, Stephanie promotes a collegial and collaborative relationship between Indigenous people and industries, governments, and organizations. Her knowledge about natural resources and Indigenous people is complemented by her understanding of policies that affect both resources and people, and she is passionate about the inclusion of Indigenous voices in programs and policies for which they are intended. Stephanie's experience is shaped by her formal education and her experiences in her community and her family. As an Indigenous student and scholar, Stephanie hopes to inspire Indigenous youth to bring their voices into the academy and to build bridges between Indigenous and non-Indigenous communities while promoting sustainable development and use of natural resources.

Margaret (Margie) Zeidler is the founder and president of Urbanspace Property Group – a mission-driven developer whose first project, 401 Richmond (created in 1994), contains a vibrant and diverse urban community of artists and cultural entrepreneurs, located in the old garment district of downtown Toronto. Her Robertson Building project (215 Spadina) gave birth to the Centre for Social Innovation (of which she is a co-founder) in 2004. She is also the co-founder of Jane's Walk, Centre for City Ecology, and the Urbanspace Gallery. Margie was awarded the Jane Jacobs Prize in 2003, established to honour Toronto residents who are actively contributing to Toronto's vibrancy, the Order of Ontario, and the Best Friend of the Arts Award from Toronto Untitled Arts Awards. She has also received Lifetime Achievement awards from Sustainable Buildings Canada and the Canadian Urban Institute.

Index

UTP insights

Books in the Series

- Raisa B. Deber, *Treating Health Care: How the System Works and How It Could Work Better*
- Jim Freedman, *A Conviction in Question: The First Trial at the International Criminal Court*
- Christina D. Rosan and Hamil Pearsall, *Growing a Sustainable City? The Question of Urban Agriculture*
- John Joe Schlichtman, Jason Patch, and Marc Lamont Hill, *Gentrifier*
- Robert Chernomas and Ian Hudson, *Economics in the Twenty-First Century: A Critical Perspective*
- Stephen M. Saideman, *Adapting in the Dust: Lessons Learned from Canada's War in Afghanistan*
- Michael R. Marrus, *Lessons of the Holocaust*
- Roland Paris and Taylor Owen (eds.), *The World Won't Wait: Why Canada Needs to Rethink Its International Policies*
- Bessma Momani, *Arab Dawn: Arab Youth and the Demographic Dividend They Will Bring*
- William Watson, *The Inequality Trap: Fighting Capitalism Instead of Poverty*
- Phil Ryan, *After the New Atheist Debate*
- Paul Evans, *Engaging China: Myth, Aspiration, and Strategy in Canadian Policy from Trudeau to Harper*